Who Killed Hazel Drew?

Unraveling Clues to the Tragic Murder of a Pretty Servant Girl

By Ron Hughes

"The death of a beautiful woman is, unquestionably,
the most poetical topic in the world."

Edgar Allen Poe

Hazel Drew

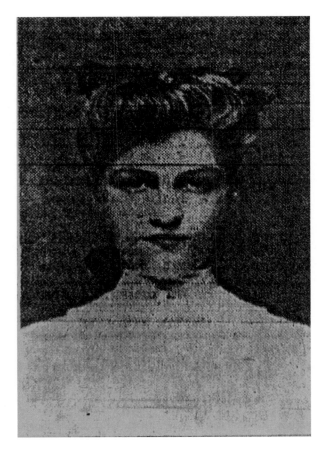

Photo taken from The Troy Press, Troy, NY
July 13, 1908

"My dear fellow," said Sherlock Holmes, as we sat on either side of the fire in his lodgings at Baker-street, "life is infinitely stranger than anything which the mind of man could invent. We would not dare to conceive the things which are merely commonplaces of existence. If we could fly out of that window hand in hand, hover over this great city, gently remove the roofs, and peep in at the queer things which are going on, the strange coincidences, the plannings, the cross-purposes, the wonderful chains of events, working through generations, and leading me to the most *outré* results, it would make all fiction with its conventionalities and foreseen conclusions most stale and unprofitable."

Adventures of Sherlock Holmes: Adventure III- A Case of Identity By A. Conan Doyle

JULY 31, 1908

Rensselaer County Courthouse
Troy, New York

After four long days of testimony Coroner Morris Strope submitted his report. It was the last act and an anticlimactic end to the exhausting investigation. The 119 word document was brief and to the point. It was a statement officially declaring the cause of Hazel Drew's death. It did not convey the warmth of the popular and beautiful 20 year old who died so violently before her life had really begun. It made no mention of the extensive efforts of the investigators who, in three weeks traveled to five states and interviewed hundreds of people but were never able to figure out Hazel's unexplained and mysterious actions during her last days. It did not reveal the motives of friends and family members who did not and would not fully co-operate with the investigators. And it did not betray the secrets that Hazel had been keeping but were known to a select few.

State of New York, Rensselaer County- Inquisition taken at Averill Park, N.Y., July 27, and continued at the Court House in the city of Troy on July 30, 1908, before M.H. Strope, one of the Coroners of said county, on the body of Hazel Irene Drew, which was found in the pond of Coonrad Teal in the town of Sand Lake July 11, 1908. From testimony taken on the above dates I find that the said Hazel Irene Drew came to her death from extravasation of blood in the dura mater

1

caused by a blow on the head from some blunt instrument in some manner unknown.

Dated, Troy, N.Y., July 31, 1908.
M.H. STROPE
Coroner

The detectives would now be re-assigned to other cases and although District Attorney Jarvis O'Brien would officially keep the case open, it would no longer be a priority. The reporters would leave. The media circus that had disrupted the lives of countless people and ruined the reputations and careers of others would go off in search of other fresh stories, all in an effort to sell more papers. Life in the small Town of Sand Lake would return to normal. The quaint village of Averill Park would once again rely on the picturesque lakes to bring in tourists. In time the story would be forgotten, her name would be forgotten, but justice would not be served and a killer would never be caught.

The Town of Sand Lake
Rensselaer County, New York

The Town of Sand Lake is comprised of several hamlets including Sand Lake, West Sand Lake, Averill Park, Taborton, and Glass Lake. It is serenely nestled in the southern and central region of Rensselaer County in upstate New York. Today the town is a quaint suburb of the capital district where many of its nearly eighty-five hundred residents commute to work. Gorgeous homes have been built along the shores of Burden Lake, Crystal Lake, Crooked Lake, Glass Lake, and several other smaller bodies of water.

In 1908 the rural town was home for just over two thousand people. Most of the residents made their living by farming, charcoal production, or working in one of the mills. In the summer however, the biggest source of income was tourism. The refreshing lakes and clean country air enticed hundreds of visitors anxious to escape the sweltering heat of the nearby cities. The town was a paradise resort that offered a respite for the wealthier classes in the crowded, bustling cities of Albany, Schenectady, Troy, and Watervliet. Young lovers dressed in stylish Victorian attire could peacefully ride in the rowboats, oblivious to the world around them. Vacationers of all ages would splash and swim in the crystal clear lakes and couples would go and dine in one of the fine restaurants or browse the quaint shops along Main Street.

Many of the visitors came from the capital city of Albany, fifteen miles to the west and across the Hudson River. Others came from the tough, industrial city of Troy, fifteen miles to the north and west. Still others came from the gritty factory town of Watervliet located north of Albany and adjacent to Troy on the west side of Hudson River. Some came by automobile or by horse carriage, others by rail. Those who took the train arrived at the Averill Park Station where horse drawn taxis were available to take them to their destinations.

Approximately one mile east of Averill Park at the intersection of Routes 43 and 66 is the hamlet of Sand Lake. In 1908 on the southeast corner of the intersection stood Crist Crape's Hotel, a popular gathering place for locals and visitors alike. More than a hotel, restaurant and tavern, Crape's also had a barbershop where men would go to get a shave and a haircut for a reasonable price. It was also one of the first places in town to have a telephone.

Travelers from Averill Park who continued straight through the intersection, passing Crape's Hotel on the right would travel up Taborton Road, a windy mountain lane that became increasingly remote and desolate the further they went. The landscape along the way was the perfect combination of rugged and scenic. The hamlet of Tabortown was about five miles from Crape's Hotel. Although not as popular as Averill Park due to its more distant and remote location, Taborton boasted two large ponds with some of the best fishing in the area. The majority of people who lived in Taborton and on the mountain leading to it were farmers and charcoal burners.

In July 1908 when the summer crowd began to arrive in the peaceful utopian villages, no one could have foreseen the powerful forces that were about to overtake the town. A beautiful young woman would lose her life, Sand Lake, New York would make national and world headlines, a District Attorney would stop at nothing to find the culprit, and disenfranchised media would arrive, fully intending to exploit the woman's death.

Those closest to the young victim had more simple values. They did not seek the publicity that was thrust upon them. They were unable to prevent the intrusion into their private lives. They just wanted to find the killer. They wanted justice but they would be disappointed.

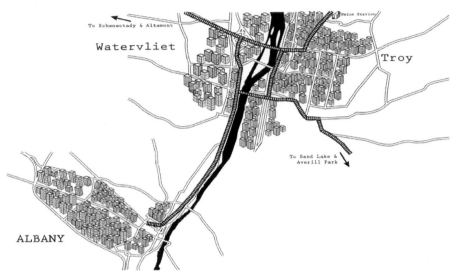

Albany, Watervliet, and Troy, NY. Map by Mikhail Vainblat

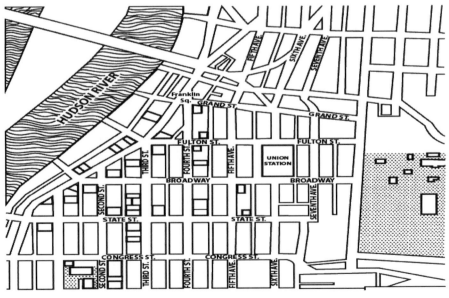

Troy, NY. Map by Mikhail Vainblat

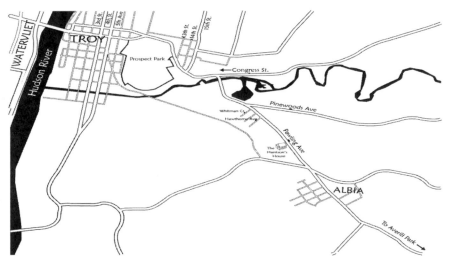

Pawling Avenue, Troy, NY. Map by Mikhail Vainblat

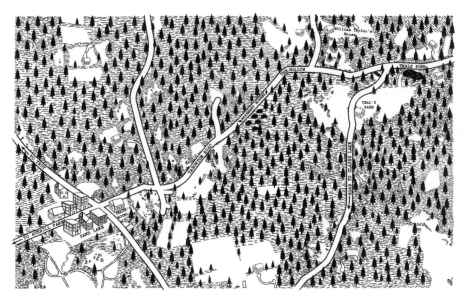

Sand Lake and Taborton Road. Map by Mikhail Vainblat

SATURDAY
JULY 11, 1908

Town of Sand Lake, New York

"Come back! There's a woman's body in the pond!"

The Troy Record July 27, 1908

Conrad Teal, a local farmer and mill operator lived with his family in a farmhouse on Taborton Mountain. His property included a small pond which was located along the the south, or right hand side of Taborton Road as the traveler ascended the mountain from Sand Lake. The pond was about a mile from Crape's Hotel. To get to Teal's farmhouse from Taborton Road, the traveler would take a right turn onto a country lane and go about a quarter of a mile. The newspapers at the time simply called this lane, the road to Glass Lake (today it's Teal Road).

Most of Taborton Road was densely wooded with pine and chestnut trees. A rock strewn creek ran along the south side of the road. Teal used the upper part of the creek to operate his mill and he built a small dam to better control the flow of water. The dam created his pond. From the dam to the opposite east shore was approximately 50 yards. From Taborton Road on the north, over to the south shore of the pond was about 25 yards and down a steep embankment. At the center, Teal's pond was about ten feet deep.

Lorenzo Gruber lived in Averill Park. Like many of his teenaged friends, Gruber worked in one of the local mills. On Friday and Saturday nights in the summer he and several friends would camp in the woods on Conrad Teal's property not far from the pond. It was a regular routine and something the boys looked forward to each weekend.

On Friday night July 10, Gruber and several of his friends including George White and brothers Frank and Edward Sowalsky camped at their usual spot in the woods about 100 feet from the pond. On Saturday morning the boys awoke and, as usual went home to do chores knowing they would meet back at the pond later that night. On that morning, July 11 the Sowalsky brothers left first. From the dam at the southwest end of the pond, they took a path up a small hill through the woods. The path was at one time used by the Teals to get their cows to water. The cowpath led to a dirt farm road that was lined with a stone wall. On the other side of the wall was Teal's cow pasture and farm house. The brothers turned right down the dirt road that led them to the road to Glass Lake.

George White had made plans to see his friend, Gilbert Miller who lived with his parents on a small farm adjacent to Teal's pond. Miller had invited White over for a late breakfast. White left the campsite before Gruber, crossed over the small dam and proceeded along the west shore of the pond, walking towards the embankment that led up to Taborton Road.

Gruber was the last to leave. It was about 9:30 and he could see that his friend had not yet reached the embankment. He slowly made his way through the woods zig-zagging through the pine trees carefully stepping on and over the moss covered rocks. He reached the edge of the pond and was beginning to cross over the dam when he stopped suddenly. Something in the water caught his attention.

Teal's pond as it was in 1908 when Hazel Drew's body was discovered.
Photograph courtesy The Times Union, Albany, NY July 18, 1908

White arrived at the hill leading up to the road. He was just beginning his climb when he was startled by Gruber's panicked shriek, "Come back! There's a woman's body in the pond!"

White turned and scurried back through the high grass along the shoreline. His friend was standing on the dam frantically pointing at the pond. White looked out and saw an object about 15 feet from the south shore. He quietly stared at the form floating peacefully in the water, face down, arms outstretched. He could see it was the body of a woman, her head and shoulders on the surface, the rest submerged and barely visible. The woman was wearing a white shirtwaist. Her hair was held in place by side combs and a hairnet.

White told Gruber he would get help and without another word turned and sprinted back along the west shore of the pond and up the embankment. Gruber was left alone, nervously peering at the lifeless body floating in the water, his mind was racing. White returned a short time later with Gilbert Miller. Standing on the dam, the three teenagers stared indecisively at the body, nervously discussing their options. Miller told the others that he had seen the object in the water the day before but didn't pay much attention to it. Never realizing it was a person's body, he said he thought it was a white bag that someone had tossed haphazardly into the pond.

At some point while still standing on the dam, Miller turned and looked over at the cow path to his right. About 20 feet up the path, partially in the woods, Miller saw a black straw hat with three large plumes. A pair of kid gloves commonly worn by women were lying with the hat. He walked over, picked up the hat and gloves, examined them, then placed them back on the ground where he found them.

The three boys decided that Miller would go down the mountain to Sand Lake and inform the authorities. First though, they would bring the body to shore. Gruber waded into the water, trudging through the mud, trying to maintain his balance on the rocks that lay on the bottom of the pond. He grabbed the woman by the back of her shirt and pulled her lifeless body to shore. She would remain in the water until help arrived.

When Miller departed for town, there was nothing Gruber and White could do except wait. They knew that it was too late to help the poor woman anyway.

In what to the boys must have seemed like a very long time people began to arrive. One of the first was George Alberts, a young man who was at Crape's Hotel and heard about the discovery from Gilbert Miller. Alberts stood near the dam staring intently at the dead body.

Frank Smith a 17 year old farm hand was walking along Taborton Road when he saw the crowd gathering at the water's edge. He went down to investigate. Smith was well known in the area but not very popular. The locals thought he was socially awkward and immature. Most of his neighbors openly referred to him as a halfwit. Smith made his way over to the dam to get a better look at the body that was still face down in the water near the shoreline. While standing near the dam he looked over at the cowpath and he too saw the black straw hat with the large plumes and the kid gloves.

Dr. Elias Boyce, a seventy year old local physician was the first person of authority to arrive. He calmly took charge and asked some boys standing near the dam to pull the body from the water. George Alberts stepped into the pond and carefully rolled the body over so it was face up. Some in the crowd gasped, others looked away from the gruesome sight. It was immediately apparent that the corpse had been in the water for quite some time and was in an advanced state of decomposition. The woman's eyes were open and bulging, her tongue hung loosely from her mouth. The body was severely bloated and a pink ribbon was deeply embedded in the skin around the throat.

Frank Smith, George Alberts and Lorenzo Gruber each grabbed a side of the woman and hauled her lifeless body up onto the dam. Dr. Boyce estimated she had been in the water for about a week. He cut the pink ribbon that was wrapped around her neck and began making mental notes about the clothing and the condition of the body. He was particularly interested in the distorted expression on the woman's face and believed it could be useful in determining the cause of death.

Willis Larkin (standing) in 1903 with his new hearse. It is presumably the same one used to transport Hazel from Teal's pond to the morgue. Photo courtesy of Willis Larkin Jr. Taken from Images of America: Sand Lake by Mary D. French and Robert J. Lilly.

A short time later Willis Larkin the local undertaker arrived. Dr. Boyce had finished his preliminary examination and released the body to the mortician. The body was placed on a stretcher, covered with a blanket, and carried to Larkin's horse-drawn hearse that was waiting on the road. Larkin drove the hearse slowly down the mountain. He went past Crape's Hotel, through the hamlet of Sand Lake and on another mile to Averill Park. Willis Larkin operated the Larkin Brothers Funeral Home which also served as the local morgue. The body was carried to the basement and prepared for the autopsy they knew would be done later that afternoon.

With his work completed at the pond, Dr. Boyce went to Averill Park and notified the Justice of the Peace, Ebenezer Martin of the situation. Boyce informed Martin that, in his opinion, the death was suspicious and an official investigation would need to be conducted. Martin relayed the message to Rensselaer County Coroner Morris Strope who in turn notified Rensselaer County District Attorney Jarvis O'Brien.

(II)

Jarvis P. O'Brien was born in Fort Edward, New York in 1866. He and his two brothers spent most of their adult lives in public service. His brother John served in the New York State Legislature and later became a judge in Plattsburgh, New York. His brother Edward was the Commissioner of Emigration in New York City, and also served as President of the Dock Board. Edward was later appointed US Minister to Uruguay and Paraguay. The day before the body was discovered in Conrad Teal's pond, Edward narrowly escaped death in an ambush in Paraguay where others were killed.

Jarvis spent his entire political career serving in the judicial system in Rensselaer County. Like his brothers, he rose to prominence in the Republican Party. Unlike his brothers however, Jarvis served in Troy, New York a city with strong Democratic Party traditions and influence.

In the mid 1890s O'Brien was appointed Assistant-District Attorney of Rensselaer County, by then District Attorney W.O. Howard. He was a successful prosecutor who quickly earned the reputation as a tough but fair attorney. In December 1899, following Howard's reelection in November, O'Brien was re-appointed Assistant-District Attorney.

In addition to prosecuting criminals, as a loyal Republican, O'Brien was also expected to give speeches and attend rallies promoting his party and its candidates. In October, 1900 O'Brien gave rousing speeches at Republican rallies in West Sand Lake supporting among others, Governor Theodore Roosevelt, a frequent visitor to Averill Park.

In November 1902 O'Brien's boss, W.O. Howard ran for and won the election for state judge. At the same time O'Brien won the election for District Attorney of Rensselaer County. Because Howard's position began immediately, O'Brien served as acting District Attorney in November and December.

On December 28, 1902 even before he was sworn in as District Attorney on his own right, the Troy papers reported that Jarvis O'Brien on his own accord, dismissed 380 members of the Grand Jury. Nothing so drastic had ever happened in the Rensselaer County judicial system before and O'Brien's critics were quick to attack. O'Brien quickly justified his action. Because the 380 names did not appear on the Commission's list, and fearing fraud and corruption, O'Brien took the moral high ground and eliminated the Grand Jurors.

On January 1, 1903 O'Brien was officially sworn in as the District Attorney for Rensselaer County. He appointed Chester Wager to be Assistant-District Attorney.

O'Brien had a very successful year prosecuting criminals. His name frequently appeared in the local newspapers, a necessity for politicians hoping to climb the political ladder and advance their careers. O'Brien however was happy with his position. He did not have lofty political ambitions. He liked being a lawyer. In addition to his responsibilities as District Attorney, O'Brien also worked as a consulting lawyer for the Boston and Maine Railroad. Today that would be considered a conflict of interest, but in 1903 it was a perfectly acceptable practice. Being a lawyer is what O'Brien loved, he was good at it and he felt it was where he belonged.

He was shocked later that year when Republican Party leaders asked him to run for Mayor of Troy against the Democratic incumbent, Joseph Hogan. The party wanted to capitalize on O'Brien's publicity and his reputation for toughness and honesty. It was not however, a job that O'Brien wanted. The Mayor's term only lasted two years, as opposed to three for District Attorney. It would mean a pay cut and more aggravation but more importantly, O'Brien didn't think he would make a good mayor. He tried to reason with Party leaders but they would not be swayed. Being loyal to the party O'Brien accepted the nomination.

The Democrats used his reticence against him. They asked voters why they should elect someone who didn't want the job. Because he would be taking a cut in pay, his Democratic opponents argued that the Republicans were getting rid of O'Brien by "promoting him upstairs". In November, the voters elected Joseph Hogan for another term. O'Brien must have been relieved. He could now give his full attention to the job he preferred.

During the 1904 political campaigns, O'Brien once again attended rallies and gave speeches in support of fellow Republicans. On October 19 he and former New York Governor Frank Black gave enthusiastic speeches at Warger's Hotel in Averill Park. The rally had a very high turnout and the crowd was exuberant. So many people were present that the hall couldn't accommodate everyone and cheering crowds gathered in the streets. O'Brien was a popular figure in Averill Park just as he was in most parts of Rensselaer County.

A week later on October 25, O'Brien returned to his hometown of Fort Edward to attend a rally at the Bradley Opera House. It was not recorded how many people were present but the opera house could seat up to one thousand people. O'Brien along with Judge Lewis Griffith and Senator Edward Brackett gave speeches and continued to motivate crowds in support of Republican Party candidates seeking election or reelection at all levels of government.

In the first week of November 1905 at the height of his popularity, O'Brien was reelected for a second three year term as District

Attorney. On November 26 a horrific train accident involving the Boston and Maine Railroad occurred near Lincoln, Massachusetts. Shortly after one train pulled out of the Baker Bridge Station it was rear ended at high velocity by an express train bound for Montreal. Several cars on the leading train burst into flame killing seventeen people and seriously injuring thirty more. Some died on impact, other's burned to death as frantic bystanders, desperate to get to them, were driven back by the intense heat. As a lawyer for the railroad, it was O'Brien's job to defend the Boston and Maine Company. When such highly emotional accidents occur, lawyers defending large corporate interests are not viewed with any compassion. O'Brien was no exception. His reputation suffered from the fall out of the accident and the legal proceedings that followed.

O'Brien was sworn in for his second term on January 1, 1906. On the same day, the city of Troy welcomed a new Mayor, Republican Elias Mann. Mann defeated incumbent Joseph Hogan and another Republican challenger Thomas Hislop. Hislop served as Treasurer for the city of Troy from 1900 to 1905. Thomas Hislop at the time of the election employed a domestic servant named Hazel Drew.

(III)

On July 11, after District Attorney O'Brien talked to Coroner Strope, he called County Detective Duncan Kaye and Dr. Harry O. Fairweather and told them that they were needed in the Town of Sand Lake to investigate the death of a woman. The three met at the courthouse in Troy and left in O'Brien's automobile for the fifteen mile trip to the Larkin Brother's Funeral Home.

When they arrived in Averill Park, they were met by Coroner Strope, Dr. Boyce, and Dr. Elmer Reichard who, like Dr. Boyce was from Averill Park. As District Attorney, Jarvis O'Brien was officially in charge of the investigation. Coroner Strope was to oversee the autopsy which would be conducted by Doctors Fairweather, Reichard and Boyce. They were to determine if the woman died as the result of an accident or if she was the victim of homicide or suicide.

When the coroner and three doctors began their task in the Larkin Brothers basement, O'Brien and Kaye drove to the pond to examine the scene and to interview any people who might still be gathered there. Their first priority was to identify the victim and then to learn what they could about her. O'Brien and Kaye left Averill Park and drove the mile to Sand Lake. They continued straight at the intersection, passing Crape's Hotel on the right. They proceeded up the mountain noting the dense woods and how secluded the area was. They passed a road on the left that the locals simply referred to as the New Road. They continued past a clump of raspberry bushes followed by a grove of chestnut trees. They came to a bend in the road known as the Hollow. Just past the Hollow a road turned off to the left. The two men continued another quarter of a mile and passed the road on the right that led to Teal's farm and to Glass Lake. In all, they had traveled about a mile from Crape's Hotel when they arrived at the pond. There were several people still milling about including Gilbert Miller, George Alberts, and Frank Smith.

O'Brien and Kaye stepped out of the car, climbed down the embankment, identified themselves to those still gathered there and began asking questions. Gilbert Miller recounted his story of how George White informed him of the discovery of the body and how, when he went over to the dam he saw the hat and gloves on the cowpath. He told the investigators about his trek to Sand Lake to alert the authorities and how he had seen the object floating in the pond the day before but did not know at that time it was a person. Miller told O'Brien and Kaye that he did not recognize the victim and was unaware of anybody in the area who might be missing.

George Alberts told O'Brien and Kaye that he was one of the people who helped take the body out of the water. Like Miller, he did not recognize the victim. He told the investigators that he saw Dr. Boyce cut the pink ribbon which he said was wrapped around the victim's neck and was deeply imbedded in her skin.

Frank Smith told O'Brien and Kaye of his arrival at the pond and how he assisted in taking the body out of the water. He told O'Brien and Kaye that he looked closely at the hat with the black plumes and the gloves on the cow path. Like the others he said he did not recognize the victim. Because of his somewhat immature behavior and the general way he conducted himself, O'Brien and Kaye quickly understood why the locals looked down on Frank Smith.

Kaye and O'Brien examined the cowpath where the hat and gloves had been found. The ground did not appear to be disturbed. They did not see any footprints or heel marks. No branches appeared to be broken and there was no sign of blood. There was nothing to indicate that a struggle had taken place there.

Based on the evidence they had gathered so far, O'Brien and Kaye agreed that the most likely scenario was that the woman went to the pond alone. At some point she took off her hat and gloves and set them down on the ground. She walked over to the water, possibly to the dam and either fell in or more likely, for reasons they had yet to determine, jumped in and intentionally took her own life. There did not appear to be any indication of foul play at the scene.

O'Brien and Kaye left to see if they could locate other witnesses. They stopped at homes and farms near the pond and along the mountain road. They spoke to farmers and homeowners with the hope that someone would be able to provide information as to who the victim might be or provide information on what may have happened to her. They had no luck until they stopped at Crape's Hotel at the base of the mountain.

Crape's Hotel. Photo courtesy of Lawrence Herzog. Taken from Images of America: Sand Lake by Mary D. French and Robert J. Lilly.

The proprietor of Crape's Hotel, Chris Crape told the investigators that late on the night of the Fourth of July he was sitting on the porch of his establishment. He said that an automobile with two men and two women sped past at a high rate of speed. They came from the direction of Averill Park, probably from Albany. It is not recorded why Crape thought the car came from Albany but it was credible enough for detectives to begin the investigation there. The car drove up Taborton Road with its lights off. Crape said the car returned a short time later with the two men but with only one of the women. Instead of taking the road back to Albany, the car turned right and headed in the direction of Troy with its lights still off.

(IV)

While Jarvis O'Brien and Duncan Kaye were at the pond and interviewing local residents, the doctors were preparing for the autopsy in the Larkin Brothers basement. As they placed the body on the morgue table, decomposition was so advanced that the scalp and hair slipped off the victim's head.

The doctor's noted that the victim's clothes were in good condition. They were neither torn nor displaced. The doctors carefully removed them and set them aside. The Northern Budget newspaper on July 12 described the clothing.

> She wore an overskirt of black material of good quality, a black silk underskirt, a waist of white material, gauze underwear, patent leather ties of La France make, with the case number 71,066 in them, and her hat, a black straw, high crowned, which was found about twenty feet from the edge of the pond, has on it three large black plumes. In her hat was found her gloves, black kids, and in the hat a stick pin with an initial letter, which may help in identification.

Attached to her shirtwaist the woman wore a gold-plated society pin. Written on the top was the Latin inscription *Concordia Salvus*. The pin contained the emblems of four countries of the United Kingdom, divided by two white crossbars; England, represented by a rose, Scotland by a thistle, Ireland by a shamrock and Canada by a beaver. A crown surmounted the image. Engraved on the back were the initials, H.I.D. which the doctors knew could be useful in identifying the victim.

The hat found on the cow path was fashionable and in good condition, showing no sign of distress. The stick pin attached to the front-center bore the initial H. No purse, handbag, or other accessories were found.

The woman's body was extremely bloated, her face and head were badly decomposed. The lower extremities and the limbs were in a slightly better condition. The hands and feet were in, what the doctors called, a parboiled condition and were not cramped (The Troy Press, July 28,1908). The cooler water below the surface had kept the lower parts of the body in a better state of preservation. The woman had gold fillings in her teeth.

According to the July 12 Northern Budget, "The deceased was between 30 and 35 years of age, of medium height, well formed, blonde complexion, light hair and was neatly...dressed." The victim, as it turned out, was actually much younger.

The doctors began by examining the woman's face and head. They found a large contusion on the upper occipital region, on the back of the head near the top. The wound was brutal and obvious. Newspaper accounts differ as to the exact description of the wound which was reported anywhere between the size of a silver dollar to five inches in diameter. Because it was neither sharp nor precise, the doctors determined it was caused by a blunt object. However, the skull was not fractured. A clot had formed between the skull and the covering of the brain. The doctors all agreed that the wound was severe enough to cause the woman's death.

Doctor Boyce pointed out the distressed look on the woman's face. He told the doctors how he cut the pink ribbon from the woman's neck and he voiced his opinion that strangulation could have contributed to her death. He believed that the ribbon came from the victim's corset and that her assailant could have used it either before or after the fatal blow to the head to assure the woman was dead.

Coroner Strope and the two other doctors were skeptical. They thought it was more likely that the ribbon became imbedded in the woman's throat due to her body bloating after being in the water for a week. To them, there was no medical evidence to support the theory that the woman had been strangled. They appeased Dr. Boyce, telling him that the body was too badly decomposed to know one way or another but Dr. Boyce was undeterred.

The doctors proceeded to cut into the victim to examine her organs. They discovered that, although the woman had been in the pond for quite some time, neither her lungs nor her stomach contained any water. This meant that the woman did not drown. If she had, water would have been present in her lungs. She did not strike her head after jumping, falling, or being pushed into the pond because even if unconscious but still alive, water would have been ingested. The doctors were now convinced that the woman died from the blow to her head and her body was placed in the water after she was dead. Death was instantaneous or nearly so. The doctors all agreed that the woman could not have walked or stumbled from the cowpath to the pond after receiving such a vicious blow.

The doctors then examined the contents of the woman's digestive tract. They found a small amount of partially digested food in her system. Dr. Fairweather recorded the findings.

The doctors went on to examine the victim's reproductive organs. As noted in the July 28, 1908 Troy Press, "There was a slight rupture in the female organs. (Dr. Reichard) could not tell if it was a fresh rupture," but, as verified by all four doctors, the victim was not pregnant. Doctor Reichard stated for the record that the victim showed no sign of ever having been sexually active but Doctor Boyce strongly disagreed. Dr. Fairweather and Coroner Strope examined the victim, noted the rupture but again determined that decomposition was too far advanced to be able to know for sure how or when the rupture occurred. The victim may or may not have been sexually active, the doctors were unable to make a definitive determination. Even if they decided that the woman had been sexually active, it was impossible to know if it was consensual or if she was the victim of sexual assault. Nor could they determine how long before death sexual activity had occurred, if at all.

When O'Brien and Kaye returned to the Larkin Brothers they were still under the assumption that the woman had committed suicide but were curious about the mysterious automobile that Chris Crape said drove by his inn on the Fourth of July. They had not learned the name of the victim and no one in the area reported or knew of anyone who was missing. They were now anxious to hear what Coroner Strope and the medical staff had found.

Although Doctor Boyce disagreed with Doctors Reichard and Fairweather on several important matters, Coroner Strope was satisfied with the overall findings. He told the District Attorney that the woman was definitely the victim of homicide, and that sometime after death her body was placed in the water.

The victim was still unidentified but Willis Larkin agreed to handle the burial arrangements. Due to the condition of the body, unless someone came forward to claim the victim soon, he said she would be buried in a pauper's grave on Monday July 13.

Duncan Kaye collected the victim's clothing and along with Jarvis O'Brien and Harry Fairweather drove back to Troy. He knew he would be returning to Averill Park the next day with several other detectives but he had no way of knowing the extensive investigation that would consume him for the next three weeks.

(V)

With no identification, detectives had to make certain assumptions based on the victim's clothing and evidence collected at the pond. It was obvious to them that the woman had fashion sense and cared about her appearance. Her clothes were stylish and hand tailored. She appeared to have money, but did not appear to be part of the upper class.

The woman was not wearing a wedding ring. Except for the society and hat pins, she was not wearing any jewelry. She did not have a purse and no money was found. As a result, robbery was considered a possible motive for the murder.

The hat and gloves were found on the cowpath on the side of the pond opposite the main road. There were two possible ways to get there. The easiest and most logical was from Taborton Road, down the embankment, through the high grass along the west shore of the pond and over the dam. The other was from the road that led to Glass Lake across Conrad Teal's cow field and down the path.

The hat and gloves were found in the woods in a remote corner of the pond. What the woman was doing there was a mystery. It was obvious that she cared about her appearance. She was wearing a long black skirt and shoes with heels so it is unlikely that she would have voluntarily gone to that part of the pond. At the same time it is unlikely that the woman's assailant would have forcibly taken her there. The woman would have logically been struggling as he brought her through the rugged terrain. There was no sign of a struggle. If the assailant had a knife or some other weapon to control the woman, it is unlikely that he would have used a blunt object to kill her. The logical assumption of why the killer would take the victim to the isolated spot would be to sexually assault her. The doctors could not determine if such an assault had occurred but the victim's clothes were not torn and her underclothing was intact and in place.

The victim could have been killed elsewhere and her body brought to the pond. But if so, why would the killer bring the accessories to the pond and leave them on the path where they would more easily be discovered? If the woman was killed on the road near the pond did the assailant then carry the woman to the water then go back and place her hat and gloves in the woods twenty feet short of the pond? If the killer made an effort to place the body in the water, why not the hat and gloves too? Did he want them to be found? If so, why?

Did the killer simply not think the details through? If not, it indicates the killing was spontaneous. The fact that the killer used blunt force to kill the woman supports this. Did the killer intend to destroy the evidence by putting the items in the water with the body but for some reason forgot or became distracted and left them there? If so it indicates the killer was nervous, spooked, or in a hurry.

Teal's pond is located near the top of Taborton Mountain in a very isolated part of Rensselaer County. The remoteness of the pond and the placement of the hat and gloves on the far side indicates that the killer was familiar with the area.

SUNDAY
JULY 12, 1908

Troy, New York

"Mr. (Gilbert) Miller summoned help and, after the body was secured, word was sent to Coroner Strope at Poestenkill, who caused the remains to be taken to the undertaking room of Larkin Brothers, at Averill Park, where they now lie awaiting identification."

The Northern Budget July 12, 1908

O n Sunday morning, July 12 The Northern Budget newspaper broke the story. The paper was widely circulated throughout Albany, Schenectady and Troy and was the only local paper printed on Sundays. The article described the discovery of the woman's body in the secluded area around Teal's pond. It provided a basic description of the victim and went into specific details on her clothing and the society pin with the engraved initials on the back. Readers learned that the woman died from a head injury and her hat and gloves were placed near the water to give the appearance of suicide. To Dr. Boyce's dismay, the article stated that there was no evidence of sexual assault. It went on to say that the clothing was being held at the District Attorney's office in Troy while the body was being prepared for burial and awaiting identification in Averill Park. With the release of the story Jarvis O'Brien and Duncan Kaye hoped that someone would come forward to identify the victim or to provide more information on what might have happened.

Duncan Kaye was in charge of the investigators. John Murnane and William Powers, working for the District Attorney's office would assist. The three investigators spent that Sunday on and around Taborton Mountain. They interviewed shopkeepers and waiters in the village of Averill Park, farmers and mill operators in Sand Lake, and vacationing beach goers around the lakes. Nobody could provide any information useful in identifying the victim. Neither the local residents nor the summer vacationers reported anybody unaccounted for. Remembering Chris Crape's story and the lack of physical evidence around the pond, Detective Kaye became increasingly convinced that the murder must have occurred at some other location, perhaps in Albany and the body was dumped in Teal's pond. Kaye realized however, that the seclusion of the pond did imply that the killer had knowledge of the area.

That evening a man who appeared to be about 50 years old, thin with a weather beaten face, strong features and a thick black moustache showed up at the Larkin Brothers Funeral Home. He introduced himself as John Drew and said he lived with his family on Fourth Street in Troy. He read about the body that was found in Teal's pond and had reason to believe that it may be his twenty year old daughter, Hazel. Mr. Drew was brought downstairs to the morgue for the excruciating task of viewing the body to determine if it was his child. Due to the advanced state of decomposition however, Drew was unable to know for sure if the lifeless figure lying on the table was his daughter. He knew that Hazel had gold fillings in her front teeth and one look into the mouth revealed his greatest fear; the woman was in fact his daughter.

MONDAY
JULY 13, 1908

Troy, New York

"While the identity of the young woman is thus completely made known, the mystery surrounding her death remains unsolved and the district attorney's office seems to have no substantial ground to work upon."

The Troy Record July 13, 1908

O n Monday morning John Drew was summoned to Jarvis O'Brien's office in the courthouse on Congress Street in Troy. The District Attorney needed to be certain that the clothing and jewelry worn by the victim did indeed belong to his daughter, Hazel. He also wanted information about Hazel's lifestyle, a list of her friends, and the men she associated with. Detective Kaye was also present.

Drew arrived with his wife Julia, his daughter-in-law Eva, and the woman who made Hazel's clothing, Mrs. John Schumaker. The group was escorted to the District Attorney's office. After brief introductions, Detective Kaye excused himself and returned a few minutes later with the clothing and accessories.

John quietly examined the articles of clothing. He stared down at the waist, the black skirt, and the underclothing. He gently picked up the hat with the three black plumes, turned it then set it back down. He picked up the society pin, stared at it for a moment then placed it back on the table. He turned to Detective Kaye and apologized. He said he just didn't know if the items belonged to his daughter, though he admitted that the initial H on the hat pin and the society pin with H.I.D. engraved on the back were likely Hazel's. Drew came across as a man with dignity but did not appear to know much about his daughter or at least her belongings.

Julia Drew's behavior was peculiar under the circumstances. Although everyone grieves differently, Mrs. Drew did not express the emotions typical of a mother who had just lost her child. She remained aloof and seemed inconvenienced. She glanced at the clothing from across the room, never going near enough to take a close look. Without any apparent effort or emphasis, she merely stated that the clothes looked like Hazel's.

Eva Drew was married to Hazel's older brother, Joseph. She was 22 years old and was closer to Hazel than either of the parents were. Joseph and Eva lived on Seventh Avenue in Troy. Mrs. Schumaker, Hazel's dressmaker, lived on Thirteenth Street. Hazel called on Mrs. Schumaker whenever she wanted a new piece of clothing made, which was often.

John and Julia Drew. Photo courtesy of The Evening World, July 16, 1908

Together the two women walked to the table and carefully examined each item. Eva picked up the hat pin. She studied it then carefully
placed it back on the table. She picked up the society pin, focusing on
each detail. She turned it over and stared at the initials engraved on
the back. She closed her eyes; the reality had sunk in.

Mrs. Schumaker intently examined the waist and skirt. She
pulled a piece of white material and some lace trim from her handbag and held them against the waist. She picked up the black skirt and
examined the hem line. She recognized her work. She turned to Eva
and pointed at a seam. Eva whispered and nodded. Mrs. Schumaker
placed the skirt back on the table.

Mrs. Schumaker turned to the investigators. She told them she
made the skirt for Hazel a few months earlier, in March. She made
an identical one for Eva at that time. Eva nodded in agreement. Mrs.
Schumaker said she made the shirtwaist that Hazel was wearing just

ten days earlier, on Friday night July 3. She said Hazel showed up at her house unexpectedly with material and lace that she had just purchased at the Boston Store in Troy. She realized it was short notice but pleaded with Mrs. Schumaker to make the waist immediately. She wanted it to wear the next day. Hazel told Mrs. Schumaker she was planning to go to Lake George for the Fourth of July weekend. The resort village is 60 miles north of Albany. The dressmaker showed the investigators that the waist Hazel was wearing when she died was made from the same material and lace that she brought to the house that evening.

Eva confirmed that the society pin on the table belonged to Hazel. It was given to her now deceased sister-in-law by a former employer, Mrs. John Tupper. Hazel cherished the piece and wore it on special occasions.

Eva said the last time she saw her sister-in-law was on the morning of July Fourth. Hazel showed up at her house with her aunt, Minnie Taylor, Julia's sister. She asked if she could leave her suitcase for a few hours, that she would return later that afternoon to retrieve it. Eva of course agreed. Hazel's brother, Joseph was home at the time but he did not come out to greet his sister or his aunt. Eva was not home when Hazel and Minnie returned later that afternoon to get the suitcase.

(II)

For the rest of the morning Jarvis O'Brien and Duncan Kaye attempted to gather from the family as much information as they could about Hazel. Although Eva answered questions openly and honestly, the investigators grew increasingly frustrated by how little Hazel's parents seemed to know or were possibly withholding about their daughter. Mrs. Drew told them that Hazel was born on June 3, 1888, that her daughter just celebrated her 19th birthday. Perhaps it was due to the stress or maybe it was a simple oversight, but Hazel had just celebrated her 20th birthday, a milestone that most mothers would be aware of.

Detective Kaye asked Mrs. Drew if she knew if Hazel had any reason to be out in Sand Lake. She said that Hazel had many friends in that area and that she visited them frequently. It was quite possible that Hazel went out to the country to visit those friends. But when asked, Mrs. Drew was unable to produce even a single name of any of Hazel's friends who lived out there.

Mrs. Drew told the investigators that Hazel had spent a month in Averill Park the previous summer but did not know the name of the family she stayed with. Eva interjected to say that Hazel stayed with a family named Bly who lived somewhere up Taborton Road. Neither Mrs. Drew nor Eva believed Hazel had plans to go back to the Bly's.

Mrs. Drew had not been helpful in providing the names of Hazel's friends in Sand Lake so O'Brien asked for the names of Hazel's friends or the people she associated with in Troy. Neither parent could produce the name of any of Hazel's friends. When asked, they did not know if Hazel was dating anyone, nor did they know of anyone who would want to hurt their daughter or even worse who would have wanted her dead.

Mrs. Drew said that at the time of her death, Hazel was living and working as a domestic servant for a family named Cary who lived on Whitman Court in Troy. The last time she saw her daughter was on July 2. They spoke briefly and Julia loaned Hazel $2.00. On Monday evening July 6, Hazel's trunk which contained most of her possessions, arrived unexpectedly at their house on Fourth Street. She didn't know why the trunk was sent but made no effort to contact Hazel or the Carys.

John and Julia Drew leaving the Rensselaer County Courthouse by trolley, July 12, 1908. Photo courtesy of The Thrice-A-Week World, July 17, 1908

After a long and tedious morning, O'Brien felt he had obtained all of the information he was going to get from John and Julia Drew. When they left he told them he would keep them updated as the investigation progressed. The Drews left the courthouse but stopped outside to pose for a picture for a newspaper. They boarded a trolley for home but had to make one stop along the way. Hazel had a $500 life insurance policy that Julia wanted to cash in.

(III)

Hazel Irene Drew was the second of John and Julia's five surviving children. She was born in Poestenkill near Sand Lake and educated in the Poestenkill schools. She had two brothers. Joseph was twenty two and William, who the family called Willie, was eight. Hazel also had two sisters. Carrie was fifteen and Emma was eleven.

Hazel left Poestenkill in 1902 at the age of fourteen for the economic opportunities in Troy. Her first job was as a domestic servant for Thomas Hislop on Third Street. Hislop was married to Nellie and the couple had a twelve year old daughter, Mabel and a ten year old son, Thomas Jr. Thomas Hislop, was the Treasurer for the city of Troy. At the time that Hazel worked for him Hislop was embroiled in a controversial and fierce legal battle that nearly led to his incarceration. Hazel left the Hislops in 1906 and began working as a governess for John Tupper's family. Tupper had been a candidate for Mayor of Troy in 1897, but lost to incumbent Francis Malloy. Thomas Hislop and John Tupper were both prominent members of the Republican Party and officers in the New York State National Guard. That is the known connection between the two families. The reason for Hazel's change of employer has never been published.

John Tupper, a successful coal merchant, lived with his wife and family on Fulton Street in Troy. Hazel and Mrs. Tupper had a very close relationship. In the summer of 1907, the Tuppers traveled to Canada. It was there that Mrs. Tupper purchased the United Kingdom society pin with the *Concordia Salvus* inscription. She had Hazel's initials engraved on the back and presented it to her when they returned. Hazel adored the pin and was wearing it when she died.

In the winter of 1907-08 Hazel was stricken with some illness. She left the Tupper's, she believed temporarily, to recuperate. However, Hazel's condition kept her away for so long that the Tuppers were not willing to wait and despite their close relationship, Mrs. Tupper was forced to terminate Hazel's employment. Mrs. Tupper did give Hazel the name of a friend who was looking for a governess. When Hazel recovered she collected her belongings from the Tuppers and began working for the Cary family on Whitman Court.

Edward Cary was a professor of Geodesy and Surveying at Rensselaer Polytechnic Institute (RPI) in Troy. He lived with his wife Mary and their 11 year old daughter Helen. The house was on a dead end street in an upper middle class neighborhood on the outskirts of Troy. Hazel began working for the family in February 1908. Mrs. Cary spoke very highly of Hazel. She was impressed with her work habits and her character. She said Hazel was a beautiful young woman who was bright, caring, friendly and a delight to be around. Hazel attended church regularly and always behaved properly. Mrs. Cary said Hazel made friends easily, always honored her curfew, and gave her no reason to question her behavior. For the five months Hazel worked for them, Mrs. Cary claimed that Hazel did not have a steady boyfriend and no men called for her. Hazel's employment with the Carys came to a sudden and unexpected end on the morning of July 6.

The City of Troy, New York. Map by Mikhail Vainblat

(IV)

Later that afternoon, Detective Kaye picked up Julia Drew's sister, Minnie Taylor who lived and worked for George B. Harrison, a wealthy Troy merchant. The Harrisons lived in a large Victorian mansion on Pawling Avenue about three quarters of a mile south of where the Cary's lived on Whitman Court. Kaye brought Minnie to the courthouse so he and Jarvis O'Brien could interview her.

Minnie told the investigators that she and Hazel spent a lot of time together despite their difference in age. Hazel had just celebrated her twentieth birthday and Minnie was 39 years old. Minnie claimed that she and Hazel went out several times a week and sometimes on the weekends. The relationship between Hazel and her aunt was a source of wonder to the investigators. Hazel, by all accounts was stunningly beautiful, outgoing, vibrant, and dignified. According to the July 24, 1908 Greenwood Times (Greenwood, NY), Minnie Taylor was,

> ...the confidante and frequent companion of Hazel Drew. She is 33 (read 39) years old, of medium height, has blond hair and blue eyes. The lines of her face are severe, her manner reserved to the point of austerity. When she speaks she employs short sentences and her mode of address is sharp and direct. Rensselaer County authorities find it difficult to understand why the young and pretty governess should have chose her as a companion.

O'Brien and Kaye immediately sensed that Minnie was reluctant to tell everything she knew. Her responses were guarded and she chose her words very carefully. They were able, however to obtain some useful information. When questioned about the area around Teal's pond, Minnie stunned the investigators when she told them that her brother, William Taylor owned a farm less than a half mile from the pond, information that Julia apparently felt was not important enough to mention.

Investigators asked Minnie if she thought Hazel could have been at, or on her way to her uncle's farm. Minnie said she didn't know but told them that Hazel had spent several weeks at her uncle's farm the previous winter, recovering from an illness, another fact Julia neglected to mention. This was the illness Hazel was recuperating from when the Tuppers replaced her.

The interview then centered around the July 4 weekend. Much of what was learned about Hazel's last weekend alive came from Minnie Taylor and verified by other witnesses.

(V)

In May Hazel spent Memorial Day weekend in New York City. On the Monday she returned, she asked and was granted permission by Mrs. Cary to have the Fourth of July weekend off so she could go to Lake George. On Friday morning, July 3 one of Hazel's closest friends, Carrie Weaver met her at the Cary's house. The two young women spent the morning packing, laughing, and talking about Hazel's trip. After Carrie left, Mrs. Cary paid Hazel's her $4.50 weekly wage.

Minnie Taylor covering her face as she leaves the Rensselaer County Courthouse, July 13, 1908. Photo courtesy of The Evening World, July 16, 1908

That afternoon Hazel went to the Boston Store in Troy to purchase white fabric and lace. She then went to Mrs. Schumaker's house and asked the seamstress to make a shirtwaist for her. Mrs. Schumaker said that Hazel was very excited about going to Lake George for the weekend. She didn't say who she was going with or if she was planning to meet anybody there. Hazel waited until 11:00 that night for Mrs. Schumaker to finish then took the late trolley back to the Cary's house.

Hazel woke up early the next morning and left the house before the Cary's awoke. She boarded the trolley at the corner of Whitman Court and Pawling Avenue and rode to the Harrison's mansion to meet her aunt.

Because both women had packed fairly lightly, Hazel and Minnie consolidated their clothing. When Hazel opened her light brown suit-case, Minnie saw that Hazel had packed, among other things, a night-gown, underwear, a kimono, some toiletry items, a locket and a black handbag. She also saw "several new shirtwaists" (The Evening World, July 15, 1908). Minnie placed her own clothes in the suitcase, closed the lid and latched it. The two women left the Harrison's house and boarded the trolley for Union Station in Troy.

Troy, N. Y   Union Station

Union Station was a busy terminal with trains coming and going to New York, Montreal, Boston, Buffalo and all points in between. Rebuilt in 1903, the designers of the modern station spared no expense. A giant compass was built in the marble floor in the center of the station. A huge green terracotta clock with two mythological figures on each side served as a focal point and hung over the steps that brought passengers under the tracks to the train platform. Waiting passengers could get a shoeshine or buy magazines or newspapers at the newsstand.

The lobby in Union Station, Troy NY. The ticket counter is at left and the steps going down to the trains are at the right. Photo taken from from Postcard History Series:Troy in Vintage Postcards by Brian and Becky Nielsen

At some point during the morning the plans changed. Minnie told the investigators that she and Hazel had intended to go to Lake George together but then decided against it.

"Hazel was with me...on the Fourth," said Miss Taylor today.
"She had intended to take a trip to Lake George and wanted

me to go with her but I didn't want to go there on that day
because the trains are so crowded on holidays." (The Rome
Daily Sentinel, July 17, 1908)

Minnie suggested instead that they remain in Troy and watch
the Fourth of July parade. After it was over they could go to Rensselaer
Park to enjoy the rides and attractions. That evening, she suggested,
they could go to Schenectady to spend the night with relatives. Minnie
told the investigators that it was her idea not to go to Lake George and
it was she who suggested the new itinerary and that Hazel was totally
receptive to it.

A patriotic celebration in Troy in 1908, probably the Fourth of July. Hazel and
Minnie reportedly watched the parade. Photo taken from from Postcard History
Series: Troy in Vintage Postcards by Brian and Becky Nielsen

Not wanting to carry the suitcase, Hazel and Minnie went to Hazel's brother's house on Seventh Avenue. They left the suitcase with Eva and left to watch the parade. When it was over, the two women took a trolley to Rensselaer Park in North Troy. Rensselaer Park was an amusement park with rides, attractions, and a fairground. They spent much of the afternoon there and left, Minnie said, around 5:00. They took a trolley to retrieve their suitcase then went back to Union Station. Hazel and Minnie purchased tickets then boarded a train for Schenectady. They went to Pearl Street to spend the night with Anna Weinmann and her family and Etta Becker. Sisters Anna and Etta were Hazel's cousins and Minnie's nieces. Hazel and Minnie spent the entire next day at Anna's house. The cousins would later tell investigators that Hazel's mood was cheerful. She did not appear to be preoccupied or distressed. Neither Hazel nor Minnie left the house and nobody called on them.

Rensselaer Park, North Troy, NY. Hazel and Minnie reportedly spent the Fourth of July here.

A Hot Air Balloon rises over Rensselaer Park, July 4, 1908. Hazel and Minnie may be somewhere in the crowd.

Around 9:00 Sunday night Hazel and Minnie took the train back to Union Station. They boarded the Beman Park trolley that took them through Troy and up Pawling Avenue. The conductor, Roy Beauchamp knew both women. He said Hazel got off at Whitman Court. Carrying her suitcase, she walked the short distance to the Cary's house arriving around 10:30. Minnie stayed on the trolley and got off at the Harrison's house. The Fourth of July weekend had come to an end but for Hazel events were just beginning.

Pawling Avenue, Troy New York. Whitman Court is to the right, behind the parked car. Hazel would have departed the trolley at this spot on the night of July 5, 1908. Photo taken from from Postcard History Series:Troy in Vintage Postcards by Brian and Becky Nielsen

(VI)

The next morning around 9:30 Mrs. Cary was in the backyard when Hazel came outside. Mrs. Cary had a list of chores and asked Hazel if she would do some laundry. In a rare show of defiance, Hazel refused. She told Mrs. Cary that she was going to leave. A stunned Mrs. Cary said nothing and Hazel turned and went back into the house. Mrs. Cary's account of the incident was printed in the July 17, 1908 Thrice-A-World (New York) newspaper.

> "I was nonplussed when she told me after breakfast on the morning of July 6 that she was going to leave us. There had been no trouble nor even slight unpleasantness. I did not question Hazel and she departed without giving any explanation of her leave-taking."

Hazel came out a short time later carrying her suitcase and a brown purse. She thanked Mrs.Cary then casually strolled down the street. Mrs. Cary would never see Hazel again. Later that afternoon a man from the Westcott Express Company arrived at the house with an order to pick up Hazel's belongings which she had packed in her trunk. The trunk was then delivered to Hazel's parents house on Fourth Street.

Hazel walked to the corner of Whitman Court and Pawling Avenue. She took the trolley to the Harrison's house, arriving shortly before 10:00. She went there to return Minnie's clothes. When Hazel opened the suitcase Minnie saw the same robe, kimono, and most of the other items that Hazel had packed for the intended trip to Lake George.

Minnie didn't ask Hazel why she wasn't at work and Hazel apparently didn't volunteer the information. She closed her suitcase and told Minnie she was going across the river to Watervliet to visit friends. Minnie watched as Hazel boarded the trolley heading back down Pawling Avenue. She told investigators that Hazel,

> ...had with her a dress suit case, a soft brown hand bag, and wore nose glasses. (Troy Record, July 13, 1908)

According to the The Troy Press on July 13, 1908, Minnie added that Hazel's initials were engraved on the suitcase near the handle.

Hazel's movements were accounted for up until the time she left Minnie Taylor around 10:00 on Monday morning but the investigators wanted to know why she went to Watervliet. They wondered what was there that was so important for Hazel to abruptly quit her job, take her suitcase and leave without providing any explanation to anyone.

A trolley makes its way up Pawling Avenue. Whitman Court, where Hazel worked is approximately half a mile behind the trolley and the Harrison mansion where Minnie worked is approximately a quarter of a mile ahead of the trolley. Photo taken from from Postcard History Series: Troy in Vintage Postcards by Brian and Becky Nielsen

Investigators learned that Hazel had three friends who lived in Watervliet, Mrs. Thomas Moran who lived on 25th Street, Mrs. John Rowe who lived on 16th Street and Mrs. E.V. Huntley who lived on 3rd Street. Hazel met the three women the previous summer when they all stayed with the Bly family in Taborton. The four became very good friends and met occasionally throughout the year but none of the three friends were expecting Hazel and none of them had seen her in over a month.

(VII)

The last weekend of Hazel's life apparently did not go as she had planned. For several weeks she had been looking forward to going to Lake George. On July 3, both Carrie Weaver and Mrs. Schumaker said that Hazel was very excited about the upcoming weekend. Hazel even had a new shirtwaist made for the occasion. But as investigators delved more deeply into the case, there were some details that didn't make sense.

If the trip was planned a month in advance, why did Hazel wait until the very last day to have the new waist made? It could have been because she didn't have enough money and was waiting to get paid. Just the day before she had to borrow two dollars from her mother with whom her relationship is questionable. But if she couldn't afford the clothes, how would she be able to afford the weekend away? With a month to prepare, Hazel did not appear to be financially ready for her vacation.

On July 4 Hazel went to the Harrison mansion to meet her aunt. None of the people that the detectives questioned were aware that Hazel planned to travel with Minnie Taylor. Outside of the fact that Hazel was planning to go to Lake George, no one seemed to know any of the details about her trip, not her friends, not her family, not her employer. They didn't know who, if anybody she was traveling with. They didn't know where she intended to stay and they didn't know if she was planning to meet anybody, male or female, when she arrived.

When Hazel died, she was wearing the brand new shirtwaist that Mrs. Schumaker had made for her. She was also wearing the special brooch that her former employer, Mrs. Tupper had given her. She was found in a wooded area in a remote part of Rensselaer County. The investigating officers had not determined how she got there or why was she dressed in her newest clothes. She wasn't going to the Bly's to see her friends, they were all in Watervliet. The Bly's were not expecting Hazel and it is unlikely she would be inquiring about staying with them as her funds appeared to be limited.

If Hazel went out to Sand Lake voluntarily, it is more likely that she was going to see her uncle. The investigators had not yet questioned William Taylor but Hazel apparently felt comfortable enough to go to his farm when she was ill the previous winter. But why would she dress in her finest clothes and wear her favorite society pin and a fashionable hat just to see her uncle?

Hazel's actions on July 6 would confound investigators throughout the case. Her mood on July 4 and 5 was positive. She gave no indication that she was unhappy or that she planned to leave her place of employment. Mrs. Cary was surprised by Hazel's sudden and abrupt departure. As far as she was concerned Hazel was an excellent worker, she seemed happy and gave no indication that she was planning to leave. When Hazel returned Minnie's clothes she did not tell her aunt that she had quit her job. She said she was going to Watervliet to visit friends, yet investigators were never able to find who she visited or if she went there at all.

The initial belief that Hazel was brought to Teal's pond in an automobile, possibly from Albany was based on Chris Crape's story of the mysterious car he saw drive by his hotel. However, Crape told investigators the incident happened late on the night of July 4. Because Hazel was in Schenectady that night, she couldn't have been in the car that Crape claimed to have seen. Investigators would have to determine how Hazel ended up in the country and if she was alive when she got there.

The Thomas Hislop Affair

Thomas Hislop was elected Treasurer for the city of Troy in November 1899 and was sworn in on January 1, 1900. A Republican, Hislop had the reputation for honesty and integrity. In 1902 he hired Hazel Drew to work as a domestic servant for his family. She held that position until 1906 when she left to work for the Tuppers.

In 1904 Hislop appointed Frank Carrington to be Deputy City Treasurer. Although Hislop was officially in charge of the city's finances, Carrington was given considerable leeway and much responsibility. Hislop placed a great deal of trust in his deputy treasurer.

In 1905 Hislop ran against Joseph Hogan for Mayor of Troy. In addition to Hislop, the Republicans also put Elias Mann on the ballot. The press was not kind to Hislop, referring to him as "the disgruntled city treasurer". They gave much more praise to Elias Mann who defeated Hogan to become the first Republican Mayor of Troy in thirty years. Hislop continued in his capacity as City Treasurer.

In the 1906 election for City Treasurer, Hislop was challenged by Arthur Smith. The Democrat accused the City Treasurer of misappropriation of funds, an accusation that Hislop dismissed as ludicrous.

In a surprise upset, due in large part to the negative press he received, Hislop lost the election. The new Treasurer was sworn in on January 1, 1907. It didn't take long for Smith to prove that his campaign accusations were not at all ludicrous, pointing out that $10,000 of Troy's money was unaccounted for. Although Smith accused Hislop of stealing the funds, the ensuing investigation by Jarvis O'Brien revealed that Frank Carrington was responsible for the theft. Thomas Hislop would not be charged but Carrington's actions destroyed Hislop's political career.

O'Brien charged Carrington on three counts of forgery, one count of grand larceny and one count of felonious misappropriation of public funds for his own use. However, as a sympathetic gesture and an example of the "good old boy" machine political system of the era, O'Brien arranged for his friend and political ally former judge Lewis Griffith to be one of Carrington's attorneys. Griffith would be paid through public funds arranged by O'Brien. At the same time, O'Brien would prosecute Carrington.

Carrington's lawyers argued that their client could not get a fair trial in Rensselaer County and asked for a change of venue. A judge would have to decide the matter. On December 7, 1907 Carrington's lawyers presented their arguments in Kingston, New York. Jarvis O'Brien made his counter arguments to the judge, W.O. Howard, former District Attorney of Rensselaer County and O'Brien's old boss. Howard sided with O'Brien and refused the change of venue.

Carrington went on trial and on May 20, 1908 was convicted on all counts. He was sent to the Clinton Correctional Facility in Dannemora, New York. Thomas Hislop was sued by the city of Troy for $10,000. The prosecution argued that as Treasurer, Hislop was ultimately responsible for the money and because it was stolen under his watch, he would be held accountable.

TUESDAY
JULY 14, 1908

Sand Lake, New York

"Her beauty was marked, and even among the host of pretty girls of Troy Hazel Drew was distinctive."

The Evening World July 14, 1908

Duncan Kaye knew that July 14 was going to be a busy day. New leads were developing rapidly and more manpower would be needed. Jarvis O'Brien used his influence with the Troy Police Department to procure two detectives who were placed under Kaye's supervision. Louis Unser and John Lawrenson began that Tuesday. For reasons never explained, but most likely to avoid competition among jurisdictions, Kaye split the four investigators into two teams. John Lawrenson was paired with John Murnane and Louis Unser with William Powers. Lawrenson and Murnane would conduct the investigation and follow up leads in Troy. Unser and Powers would concentrate in Sand Lake and Averill Park.

The investigators were still trying to determine where Hazel went after she left her aunt at 10:00 on the morning of July 6. Either Hazel lied to Minnie about going to Watervliet or something happened to prevent her from going there. Lawrenson and Unser interviewed the

51

conductors and passengers on the Pawling Avenue trolleys and they interviewed people at Union Station to see if anyone remembered seeing Hazel. Because Hazel was an extraordinarily pretty young woman the investigators were confident that someone would remember seeing her. They wouldn't be as fortunate as they hoped.

Meanwhile Louis Unser and William Powers went to Sand Lake. Their task was to find anyone who may have seen Hazel, figure out how she travelled out to the country, and if she had company. They started at the Averill Park train station and worked from there. They talked to shopkeepers, waiters, and people on the streets. Because Hazel was originally from that area and had returned on several occasions, the likelihood of finding someone who saw Hazel, they believed, was very strong.

(II)

Hazel's funeral was held that Tuesday. Although the family owned a plot in the Mount Ida Cemetery in Troy, they decided to bury Hazel in her native Poestenkill instead. The service at the Larkin Brothers Funeral Home was conducted by the Reverend George P. Perry from the First Baptist Church in Troy. The graveside service at Barbersville Cemetery in Poestenkill was conducted by Reverend J.H.E. Rickard of the Methodist Church on Third and State Street in Troy, the church that Hazel attended.

Having many friends and admirers, Hazel was a very popular young woman. Her extraordinary beauty and warm disposition did not escape the notice of young men, although at the time of her death it was believed she did not have a steady boyfriend. Surprisingly, very few people attended her funeral. The low turnout was both a shock and a disappointment. It could have been due to the heavy rain that fell but the newspapers reported that only 8 to 10 people, mostly family were present. Hazel's uncle, William Taylor attended the funeral but did not go to the burial service at the cemetery.

Following the graveside service, Kaye and Powers drove up Taborton Road to interview Taylor. They passed through the Hollow and took the left turn onto the road that led to Taylor's farm.

William Taylor had lived on his farm for 18 years. He was 52 years old, tall and powerfully built but his body showed the inevitable signs of wear that comes from a life of labor. Taylor was a sullen man. He spoke slowly and deliberately. His neighbors thought he was odd and they avoided him. Prone to bouts of depression, Taylor attempted suicide by cutting his wrists following the death of his wife the previous winter. He was detached from the rest of his family and except for his farm, he did not seem to have any interests.

When young Hazel left Poestenkill to work for Thomas Hislop in 1902, John Drew and his family lived on the farm with Taylor. Drew and Taylor were partners but they could not get along. About two years before Hazel's death the two men had such a major feud that John moved his family to Troy. Only John's oldest son, Joseph and his wife Eva remained with Taylor. They continued to work with their uncle until the spring of 1908 when they too had a falling out. Joseph and Eva moved to Troy where Joseph found work as a baker. On April 1, Taylor took in two new boarders, Frank Richmond and his wife, to help him work the farm.

Taylor told the detectives that he did not know that Hazel was in the vicinity and she had not been to his farm in several months. He had not seen his niece and he was not expecting her. He didn't know if she was coming to see him or anybody else. The last time he claimed to have seen her was the previous winter when she showed up at his house unexpectedly. Hazel claimed she was ill and for about three weeks Eva took care of her. Taylor did not ask about her illness and did not assist in her care. He merely allowed his niece to stay at his farm until she felt well enough to leave.

Hazel did not leave her room for more than a week. Eva brought her meals and tended to her needs. After Hazel regained her strength she did go out occasionally, usually with Eva. She spent most of her time reading books and writing letters and postcards. Except for neighbors, no one called on or visited Hazel while she was at the farm, not even her parents.

Taylor told the investigators that on Wednesday morning July 8, his boarder, Frank Richmond asked him if Hazel was at the farm. To Taylor, it seemed like an unusual question. He told Richmond he hadn't seen his niece and the matter was dropped.

On July 11 Taylor said he learned that a woman's body had been pulled out of Conrad Teal's pond, just up the road from his farm. Even though he was told three days earlier that Hazel might be in the area and he had not heard from her, Taylor had no interest in going to the pond or learning who the victim might be.

That same evening, which was the night before John Drew identified Hazel's body, Frank Smith's father, stopped in to see his neighbor, William Taylor. Smith told him that his son had helped pull a woman's body from the pond and had reason to believe the victim may be Taylor's niece, Hazel. Still the uncle did nothing. He did not notify his family of the possibility that Hazel may have died and he did not go to the Larkin Brother's to see if he could identify the victim. He simply did not want to get involved.

Family squabbles aside, William Taylor's actions were beyond the realm of normal and the investigators could not rule out the possibility that he may have had something to do with his niece's death.

Through the combined efforts of the investigators working in and around Taborton Mountain on July 14, a story was slowly beginning to unfold. The detectives learned about a witness who knew Hazel and claimed to have seen her walking up Taborton Mountain the night of July 7.

Frank Smith, William Taylor, and Minnie Taylor. Taken from the Times Union, July 17, 1908

(III)

Tuesday Evening July 7

7:30 pm

Rudy Gundrum was a 35 year old charcoal burner who lived on the mountain near the village of Taborton. He had invited two friends who lived in Albany to come and spend a few days fishing in the country. Gundrum prepared his horse and wagon and left his house at 6:00, leaving plenty of time to be in Averill Park to meet his friends' 8:00 train. Shortly after 7:00 as he was approaching the summit of Taborton Mountain. He saw Frank Smith walking along the road and offered him a ride. The young man accepted and climbed aboard.

Rudy Gundrum in 1935. Photo from Images of America: Sand Lake Revisited by Mary D. French and Andrew St. J. Mace

Just after Smith joined Gundrum, they passed a rig coming from the opposite direction. The two men recognized the couple in the wagon, Henry Ryemiller and his wife who lived near Taborton. The four people exchanged greetings as they passed and continued towards their respective destinations.

Smith and Gundrum traveled down the mountain at a slow pace. They drove by Teal's pond, the road that led to Glass Lake and then the road that led to Taylor's farm. When they reached the Hollow around 7:30 Gundrum saw a very attractive, well dressed young blond woman casually making her way up the road. Gundrum told investigators,

> "We had just passed Taylor's road...which turns off from the main road when I saw a girl with light hair carrying a black hat trimmed with black feathers in her hand. She said 'Hello Frank' and he answered hello and then said to me 'That's John Drew's oldest girl.'" Neither Smith nor I got out of the wagon and the girl went on up the road. (The Jamestown Evening Journal, July 15, 1908)

Smith and Gundrum continued down the mountain. Within a couple of minutes of passing the young woman, another wagon approached. Once again, Smith and Gundrum recognized the occupants. William and Elizabeth Hoffey were neighbors who lived further up Taborton Road. Once again the four people exchanged greetings and continued on their separate ways without stopping.

When Smith and Gundrum arrived in Averill Park they stopped at Harris' Saloon to have a few drinks. Gundrum eventually left to meet his friends but Smith remained. At 8:00 the train arrived and Gundrum brought his friends up the mountain to Taborton. They arrived at Gundrum's home at 10:00. They did not encounter anybody on the mountain road the entire way home.

8:15-10:00 pm

Frank Richmond and his wife had been living on William Taylor's farm for three months. Before going there, friends warned them not to move out to the country. As quoted in the Troy Record on July 14, 1908, Richmond "...remarked that when he first took up farm work on the mountain, having lived in Troy, he was told that it was a tough place near Teal's pond." Richmond and his wife ignored the warnings. From the time he moved in with Taylor on April 1, Richmond claimed he never saw or met Hazel.

On the night of July 7, Richmond's brother, Harry came in from Troy. He took the train that arrived in Averill Park at 9:00 pm. Around 8:15 Frank and his wife hitched their horse to a wagon and left Taylor's farm. Taylor was sitting alone on his porch quietly smoking his pipe when they left. The couple went down the road and turned right onto Taborton Road. They passed through the Hollow about 45 minutes after Smith and Gundrum saw Hazel. The Richmonds continued down the mountain. They did not see or pass anyone along the way.

The train station in Averill Park, NY. Frank Smith was asking about Hazel here the night she was last seen alive. Photo taken from Images of America: Sand Lake by Mary D. French and Robert J. Lilly.

The Richmonds arrived at the station just before 9:00. They went inside and sat down on a bench. While they waited they heard a noise and turned to see Frank Smith peering at them through a window. He entered the station, approached the couple and said, "I see you have company up at the house." (Troy Times July 14, 1908)

Richmond had no idea what Smith was talking about and asked him to explain. Embellishing his encounter Smith said, "I met John Drew's daughter on the road and she wanted to know if Will was home." (The Troy Times, July 28, 1908)

The Richmonds were confused. Taylor had not said anything about Hazel visiting the farm. He was alone when they left and they didn't pass anyone on their way to town. They couldn't understand how and when Hazel would have arrived at the farm. Smith, they thought, must be mistaken.

When the train pulled into the station, Harry Richmond stepped off and greeted his brother. Frank, his wife and Harry all climbed onto the rig and left for Taborton Road. It was 10 o'clock when they arrived back at the farm. When they went inside, Frank looked around but Hazel was not there. Taylor's bedroom door was open but he was in bed. Richmond would speak to his employer about Hazel the following day.

11:00 pm

George Shriner, the Postmaster at the Averill Park Post Office and his good friend and ex-supervisor Mr. Carman were sitting on a bench outside the post office around 11:00 pm. They were relaxing, taking in the cool night air when their serenity was suddenly interrupted by the sound of running feet and heavy breathing. They looked up and saw an exhausted and breathless Frank Smith running towards them, coming from the direction of Sand Lake. He ran directly to Wright's Pharmacy and pulled hard on the door, desperately trying to get inside. The two elderly gentlemen knew the teenager. They called over to him, asking if everything was alright. Smith told them that he needed to get something inside, that it was really important. When they told him that the pharmacy had been closed for hours and Smith realized that he wouldn't be able to get what he was after, he turned and without another word sprinted back towards Crape's Hotel and the Taborton Road.

(IV)

Frank Smith had reportedly seen Hazel walking up Taborton Road at 7:30. At 9:00 he inquired about Hazel's whereabouts at the Averill Park train station and two hours later he was seen frantically trying to get into the pharmacy. The day the body was discovered in Teal's pond, Smith's father told William Taylor that his son believed the woman he helped pull out of the pond was Hazel Drew. This was before John Drew identified the victim as his daughter. Jarvis O'Brien and Duncan Kaye talked to Frank Smith the day the body was discovered and he had not mentioned any of this to them. O'Brien and Kaye knew they had to re-interview Frank Smith immediately.

Smith worked on Phillip Brown's farm near the top of Taborton Mountain. The two officials drove to the farm and met with the teenager. They remembered Smith telling them about pulling the body out of the pond and seeing the hat and gloves on the cowpath.

Wright's Pharmacy, Averill Park, NY. Frank Smith was seen desperately trying to get into the pharmacy the night Hazel was last seen alive. From Images of America: Sand Lake, by Mary D. French and Robert J. Lilly

Smith was familiar with Hazel. He said the first time he met her was about a year and a half earlier at Taylor's farm. He saw her again when she was staying with Taylor in January. He went over one night to play cards and at one point Hazel and Eva visited the Smith's farm. They stayed for a few hours listening to the phonograph.

The last time Smith said he saw Hazel was on Tuesday July 7 around 7:30 in the evening. He looked at his watch when he left work at Brown's. It was eleven minutes after seven. He accepted a ride down the mountain from Rudy Gundrum. He confirmed that they passed Henry Ryemiller and his wife riding in the opposite direction.

Smith told the investigators that he and Gundrum continued down the mountain. Just past the road that leads to his father's house and Taylor's farm, at the bend in the road called the Hollow they saw Hazel leisurely walking towards them. She was wearing a white waist, black skirt, and carrying her unusual hat, the one with three large feathers. She was alone and didn't appear to be in a hurry.

Smith said Gundrum slowed the horse as they approached the pretty twenty year old. Hazel smiled and pleasantly said, "Hello Frank". Smith nodded and replied, "Hazel". Gundrum didn't stop. After they went a short distance Smith said he turned and watched Hazel continue through the Hollow. She had not yet reached the turn to her uncle's farm when he lost sight of her. He turned back around and told Gundrum that the girl was John Drew's oldest daughter.

The two continued and a short time later passed William and Elizabeth Hoffey coming up the mountain. Smith and Gundrum continued on to Sand Lake.

Jarvis O'Brien was furious. He demanded to know why Smith did not mention any of this when they met at the pond three days earlier. Smith nervously replied that he did not realize at the time that it was Hazel's body that he helped pull out of the water. He said he did not make the connection between seeing Hazel on the road and pulling the decomposed corpse out of the pond until later, after O'Brien and Kaye had driven away. O'Brien did not believe him.

Whereas it is true that Hazel's body was so badly decomposed and disfigured that her own father didn't recognize her, Smith said he noticed Hazel's hat when he saw her walking up the road. He examined the same hat on the cowpath four days later. The hat was unique and not easy to forget with three large plumes and the letter H pin stuck prominently in the front. Even if he did not recognize Hazel, O'Brien believed that he should have remembered the hat.

Smith confessed that he had been thinking about Hazel since he saw her walking up the mountain. He told the investigators that Hazel was the prettiest girl he knew. He liked Hazel and wanted to call on her. Throughout the week he visited neighbors, including Libbie Sowalsky and asked if they had seen Hazel but no one had. It is unclear, however why Smith never went to Taylor's farm if he was so interested in calling on Hazel and thought it was where she was staying.

O'Brien wanted Smith to explain the conversation he had with Frank Richmond at the Averill Park train station. Smith said that when he and Gundrum arrived in the town, they stopped at Harris' Saloon. They had a couple of beers and Gundrum left to meet some friends. Smith remained at the saloon, drinking and talking to the bartender, Mr. Harris.

Just before 9:00 Smith, for reasons never published, went to the train station and ran into the Richmonds. Knowing that they stayed at Taylor's farm and remembering that he saw Hazel on the road earlier, Smith inquired if she was at the farm. Richmond told him he didn't think she was. That's when Smith decided he would ask his neighbors if they had seen her.

O'Brien demanded an explanation for Smith's mysterious run to the pharmacy at 11:00 that Tuesday night. Smith explained that after leaving the train station he walked to Crape's hotel and continued drinking whiskey and beer. He met some men from New York who challenged him to a series of bets. They first wagered that he could not run around a tree 75 times in one minute. Smith said he lost that bet but they agreed to let him win his money back by running to Averill Park and back in 15 minutes. But to prove that he went all the way, he would have to return with a postcard from Wright's Pharmacy. An inebriated Smith took the bet. He claimed that Chris Crape timed him and, even without the postcard, he lost the bet by one minute.

O'Brien didn't trust Smith and was very skeptical of his answers. The more the boy talked, the more the District Attorney was convinced that Smith was somehow involved with Hazel's death. The following exchange was printed in the July 14 Troy Press.

> The district attorney came out flatly and asked Smith: "Frank, didn't you hit Hazel on the head and throw her body into the pond? Tell the truth now."
>
> With a shudder the youth replied: "No, sir, I didn't. Why I wouldn't do anything like that to a dog."

(V)

By the end of the day on Tuesday the investigators had a better idea of Hazel's movements. She was now believed to have been alive as late as 7:30 on Tuesday evening July 7, but they still needed to find out where Hazel spent Monday night and figure out specifically when and where she died.

Hazel's destination was another mystery still confounding the investigation. If Frank Smith was telling the truth when he said he turned and watched Hazel walk up the mountain, she had not yet reached the turn to her uncle's farm. Was she intending to go to Taylor's farm? If so, why? Why would Hazel abruptly quit her job, deceive her aunt about going to Watervliet, spend the night in some unknown location then show up unexpectedly at her uncle's farm, this time without Eva being there? Why would she visit her uncle who she hadn't seen in five months and apparently had only a lukewarm relationship with at best.

Could Hazel's destination have been the Bly's house where she vacationed the previous summer and where she met her Watervliet friends? The Bly's lived several miles from Sand Lake. Hazel was walking up the lonely mountain road, wearing nice clothes, and heeled boots. Smith and Gundrum claimed they saw Hazel in the Hollow around 7:30. It was beginning to get dark and she would still have had a long way to travel. Did she encounter a murderous stranger on the road?

When Smith and Gundrum saw Hazel walking through the Hollow they both noticed the hat she was carrying but neither recalled seeing a handbag or suitcase. Minnie Taylor said that when Hazel left the Harrison's house on Monday morning she was carrying both. What happened to them? It was approaching dusk when Hazel was going up the mountain, walking away from the train station. If she was intending to spend the night with someone on the mountain, why didn't she bring a change of clothes?

Detective Kaye and the other investigators needed to verify the accuracy of the witnesses' statements. They had to be sure that Taylor was being truthful and that Hazel never went to his farm on July 7. They couldn't rule out the possibility that Hazel did go to Taylor's farm and the eccentric uncle for some reason murdered his niece. They had to look into the possibility that, after seeing Hazel, Frank Smith returned up the mountain to meet Hazel who then rejected the socially awkward teen and was killed as a result. They had to look into the possibility that Smith and Gundrum together assaulted Hazel along the isolated stretch of road.

In the opinion of the investigators, the witnesses were unreliable which meant anything they said was suspect. Every detail of their statements would have to be verified. Because so much of the mystery revolved around Hazel's intended destination, the focus was placed on finding her suitcase. It did not make sense that Hazel was in such a remote area at that time of the night if she was not intending to stay there. Investigators had to be sure that Hazel really was without her suitcase and that Smith and Gundrum simply did not notice the luggage. The area around the pond was searched but not the pond itself. The first first order of business on July 15 would be to open the gates of the dam to drain the water. The investigators would have to see what clues lay undiscovered on the bottom of Conrad Teal's pond.

WEDNESDAY
JULY 15, 1908

Conrad Teal's pond

"Some suspicion this afternoon points to the uncle of the dead girl, William Taylor, as being connected with the crime. The authorities are at least convinced that he knows more of the case than he has told, and he was questioned at length this afternoon."

The Morning Call (Paterson, NJ) July 15, 1908

"While District Attorney O'Brien does not commit himself directly, he regards as peculiar the actions of (Frank) Smith."

The Times Union (Albany, NY) July 15, 1908

By mid-morning on Wednesday, the gates of Teal's dam were opened and the water flowed freely down the mountain. Louis Unser and William Powers were on hand, ready to trudge through the mud to look for Hazel's suitcase, purse or any other evidence including a possible murder weapon. The pond was expected to be completely drained by noon but as 12:00 approached it was apparent that more time would be needed.

Newsmen were on hand hoping the detectives would uncover some piece of new evidence they could use to entice their readers.

However, boredom set in as they waited for the water level to recede. Some reporters stood by, patiently waiting; others walked along the shore of the pond. Two New York reporters, Louis Howe and John Kelly wandered over to the cowpath. They were examining the ground where Hazel's hat and gloves were found when something shiny attracted their attention. Howe reached down and picked up a pair of woman's eyeglasses. He brought them over to the detectives standing nearby at the dam. Detective Kaye knew immediately the glasses matched Minnie Taylor's description of the ones Hazel was wearing.

The discovery of the glasses convinced the detectives that Hazel had not struggled with her attacker on the cowpath. The loose fitting nose glasses would have logically fallen off in the early stages of an assault. The neatly stacked hat and gloves, with the glasses lying nearby was not consistent with a crime scene where a violent struggle took place. It was more likely that the glasses were tossed on the ground, landing near the other items. The detectives reasoned that if Hazel tried to defend herself from an attacker in the woods, her possessions would be scattered. There would be no reason for her killer to neatly consolidate her accessories before fleeing. This left two possibilities. Either Hazel walked into the woods voluntarily, maybe to meet someone or was escorted by someone she knew and trusted, or she was murdered somewhere else and her hat, gloves and glasses were placed in the woods to conceal them. The detectives didn't think it was likely that Hazel went into the woods voluntarily. So by deductive reasoning, they believed that Hazel was killed in some other location and not in the woods by Teal's pond.

Following the discovery of Hazel's glasses, Powers and Unser began an extensive search of the woods. They started at the dam and continued around the south side of the pond, the side opposite Taborton Road. The water level continued to recede and the detectives were extending their search when they came across a white handkerchief lying on the ground. The letter "P" was embroidered in the fabric. Hoping it may be an important clue, they turned it over to Detective Kaye.

By 2:00 the pond was completely drained. To the disappointment of the investigators and the reporters, there was no suitcase or any other evidence lying in the mud. Smith and Gundrum's claim that Hazel wasn't carrying a purse or suitcase was at least partially verified.

Detective Kaye carefully examined the handkerchief with the embroidered letter P. He determined that it was too old, too worn and had been lying exposed to the elements for too long to have had any relevance to the case.

While Unser and Powers continued their investigation in Sand Lake, Detective Kaye returned to Troy to brief Jarvis O'Brien. The District Attorney was in his office talking to reporters when the detective arrived. O'Brien was in the process of debunking some of the medical rumors. Apparently Dr. Boyce had been spouting his belief to the press that Hazel had been strangled by her corset string, a theory the doctor was single handedly perpetuating. Dr. Boyce presented his belief to reporters that Hazel was out walking along on the lonely road when she was dragged into the woods, sexually assaulted, then struck over the head. To assure that she was dead, the killer strangled her with her corset string then dumped the body into the water.

O'Brien and Kaye had interviewed several people including George Alberts regarding their opinion on the ribbon. The following was printed in the July 14, 1908 Troy Record.

> The statement that when the body of the girl was found a corset string was tied about the neck and had to be cut off was disputed this morning by George Alberts, who was one of those who helped remove the body from the water. He

stated to Detective Kaye that it was nothing more than an ordinary silk cord that any woman might wear as an article of dress. Alberts said that being in the water the twine shrunk, causing it to be imbedded in the flesh. He said that he took particular notice of the ends of the cord and they did not contain the brass tips used on corset strings. Detective Kaye also had doubts as to the use of the corset string.

Wanting to see for themselves, the reporters asked the District Attorney if they could examine the ribbon. O'Brien, realizing the importance of keeping the press accurately informed and not wanting to alienate the reporters, allowed it. Kaye left to retrieve the clothing. When he returned he began to spread the items out. When he picked up one of Hazel's gloves, a nickel fell out and loudly bounced on the table.

(II)

The discovery of the nickel in Hazel's glove raised important questions. Investigators wondered what Hazel was doing with the five cent piece and where it came from. Was the nickel all the money Hazel had? Why was it in her glove? Where was her purse? Was the nickel all the change she had left from some larger amount?

Minnie Taylor told investigators that when Hazel left the Harrison's she boarded the trolley intending to go to Watervliet. If Hazel did go to Watervliet, she would have transferred to another trolley that would take her across the Hudson River. If she didn't go to Watervliet, as investigators were beginning to believe, and if she didn't get off anywhere else, Hazel would have continued to Union Station. If her trip out to the country began at Union Station, she would have taken a trolley back up Pawling Avenue to the Albia train station which was about a mile past the Harrison house. This would have cost five cents. From Albia Station Hazel would have transferred to the Troy and New England Railroad that would have taken her out to the Averill Park station, costing fifteen cents more. If Hazel had a quarter when she started at Union Station, five cents would be the amount she had left.

Hazel may have begun her trip to Averill Park with her last twenty five cents but once she arrived she would not have enough money to return. She could have been going to her uncle's to borrow money or she could have been planning to meet somebody in Averill Park and assumed she would not need return fare.

(III)

As unlikable and untrustworthy as Frank Smith was his stories were slowly being confirmed. He claimed that after he and Rudy Gundrum saw Hazel in the Hollow they went to Harris' Saloon in Averill Park. Harris, the proprietor, was tending bar that night and verified that Smith and Gundrum arrived together. Gundrum left to meet his friends coming in on the train but Smith remained and had a few more drinks.

At approximately 9:00 Smith was at the train station telling Frank Richmond about his encounter with Hazel in the Hollow. The exchange was witnessed by Richmond's wife.

Around 11:00 George Shriner and Mr. Carman witnessed Smith's frantic run to Wright's Pharmacy which he claimed was part of a bet. Chris Crape confirmed that Smith had been drinking in his bar and did partake in several bets with out of town guests. Crape said that he timed Smith's run and watched as he left the tavern, sprinting towards Averill Park. He also verified that Smith lost the bet by one minute.

As difficult as it must have been, Jarvis O'Brien came to the conclusion that Frank Smith, one of his prime suspects, could not have murdered Hazel Drew. His actions were all accounted for, his alibis all checked out. He simply did not have the time or the opportunity to go back up the mountain, locate Hazel, who would not be waiting on the road all that time, murder her, dump her body in the pond then leave the hat and gloves on the far side. Based on the times that Frank Smith was seen, he could not have been involved with Hazel's death. Detectives were forced to eliminate him as a suspect and had to rethink the possibilities.

Hazel was in a precarious situation but didn't appear to know it. She was all alone on a desolate road with the sun going down and not enough money to return home. Although the idea of a random attack at first seemed improbable it was never ruled out. Dr. Boyce among others insisted that the remoteness of the area was conducive to such a danger. Frank Richmond had been warned by friends in Troy that the area was dangerous. Hazel however, did not display any signs of anxiety or distress as she passed along the road. If Hazel felt that she was in any danger she would have sought assistance from Smith and Gundrum, both of whom stated that Hazel appeared pleasant and unconcerned. Investigators began to question if Hazel, naively walking along the isolated country lane, after passing Smith and Gundrum crossed paths with some dangerous person who attacked and ended her life. After investigators spoke to Bertha Neustiel, the random attack theory was given more attention.

Bertha Neustiel lived with her brother on the road to Glass Lake not far from Teal's farm. She told detectives that a couple of years earlier, while walking along the road near Teal's pond, she was accosted by two men. She said she frantically fought them off, was somehow able to escape and returned home safely. She never reported the incident.

If Bertha Neustiel was telling the truth, and there is no reason to believe she wasn't, it means there was at least one predator who had been active in the same area that Hazel's body was found. Investigators could not rule out the possibility that the vulnerable young woman was simply in the wrong place at the wrong time.

In other developments, detectives were investigating a rumor that Hazel frequently visited Averill Park with an unidentified man, possibly an insurance or real estate agent and would dine in some of the finer restaurants. They learned that she and her companion may have been in Averill Park on July 6. They were also investigating a rumor that Hazel and her aunt, Minnie Taylor were in Averill Park on June 21 riding in a carriage with two unidentified men.

(IV)

On this fourth day of the investigation, Jarvis O'Brien was beginning to publicly voice his frustration at the lack of cooperation he was receiving from Hazel's friends and family. He told reporters that investigators had talked to dozens of Hazel's friends and people she associated with. They were unanimous in vouching for Hazel's moral character but not one of them knew where she spent the night of July 6. As far as her friends knew, Hazel was not dating anyone at the time of her death. She was not the type of girl who would spend the night with a boyfriend and she most definitely would not go home with someone she just met.

Besides vouching for her character, Hazel's friends provided no other useful information.

District Attorney O'Brien deplored the fact that the friends of the girl are so reticent about disclosing facts which might

> lead to clearing up many perplexing questions. He attri-
> butes to the silence of those who knew her much of the mys-
> tery surrounding the disappearance of the handbag and
> suitcase... (Troy Times, July 15, 1908)

O'Brien was unable to determine if the friends didn't know any more than what they were sharing or if they were cleverly withholding information. They did not go to the authorities on their own but rather waited for the detectives to locate them and most of them were reluctant to provide the names of any of Hazel's other friends.

Hazel's friends frustrated the investigators but Minnie Taylor infuriated them. She steadfastly refused to cooperate with the investigation or provide the names of any of Hazel's male friends.

> (Minnie Taylor) has refused to tell who Hazel's male friends
> are, saying they had nothing to do with the crime. (Evening
> World, July 15, 1908)

The press reported that Minnie confirmed to O'Brien that she and Hazel did go on the carriage ride in Averill Park on June 21 but she would not reveal the names of the men who accompanied them. She stated that Hazel's friends had nothing to do with the murder and she would not destroy the reputations of innocent people.

The following exchange took place at the Harrison residence between Minnie and a reporter for the Evening World newspaper. It is consistent with how Minnie cooperated with the investigation.

> "Were you Hazel's chum?" was asked.
> "Yes, she fancied me more than others. She wanted my company."
> "You and she took auto and carriage rides?"
> "None of your business, Mister," snapped the woman. I
> refuse to tell you or anyone else our private affairs. None of our
> friends had anything to do with the murder. I won't drag innocent

persons into this. I don't know how she died and can't explain why she went to Teal's Pond." (Evening World, July 15, 1908)

After Hazel left the Cary's, she had her trunk delivered to her parent's house. On July 15 the newspapers reported that Detective Kaye examined the contents. The trunk contained Hazel's clothes and some personal items. The most significant discovery in the trunk however, was a bundle of letters and postcards that Hazel had saved. Detectives sorted through over one hundred pieces of correspondence in the hopes of obtaining some insight into Hazel's personal life. They also hoped to learn more names and addresses of Hazel's friends, including some that Minnie and others would not reveal. One writer in particular deserves attention.

The C.E.S. Letters

A bundle of six letters and postcards found in Hazel's trunk were signed with the initials C.E.S. The unknown writer cared a great deal for Hazel, "the flaxen haired girl" and in one instance scolds her for "being a flirt".

The C.E.S. letters were sent from Boston and New York. Published in the July 14 Evening World, one of the letters read:

> Your merry smile and twinkling eyes torture me. Your face haunts me. Why can't I be contented again? You have stolen my liberty. Please don't forget a promise to write. When I reach Albany again, I will meet you at the tavern. I must see you soon or I'll die of starvation.

Not allowing reporters to read the letters, Jarvis O'Brien revealed that Hazel met the mysterious C.E.S. in New York no later than June 13.

(V)

The discovery of the nickel in Hazel's glove was one of the most important clues the detectives had yet encountered. It provided evidence that whatever Hazel's intentions may have been, she did not intend to stay the night in Sand Lake. It also excludes robbery as a motive for her murder.

Along with her suitcase, Hazel was also carrying her purse when she left her aunt on July 6. Minnie described the brown purse as oblong shaped about six inches in length and with straps. Hazel's whereabouts were unknown from the time she left her aunt at 10:00 Monday morning until 7:30 Tuesday evening when she met Smith and Gundrum on Taborton Road. She was not carrying her suitcase or her purse at that time.

It is logical to assume that Hazel's suitcase and handbag were at the place she spent the night of July 6. When she was walking along Taborton Road she was carrying a nickel in her glove. The importance might not be so much that she was carrying money, but where she was carrying it. Or, to look at it another way, why wasn't she carrying her purse?

Hazel may have spent that Monday night in the Sand Lake area, possibly somewhere on Taborton Mountain. She could have merely been out for a short stroll when she was seen by Smith and Gundrum. That would explain why she wasn't carrying her handbag. But if she was only out for a walk, then why would she be carrying money? The area where she was walking was remote and desolate. If she was just out getting some fresh air she wouldn't need any money and would have left the nickel at the place she was staying. It is unlikely that she decided to go out for a walk and just in case bring some money with her. So rather than bring her purse, she decided instead to bring her gloves so she could carry her money in them. Why bring her gloves but not her handbag?

Perhaps Hazel wasn't just out for a walk, but rather went someplace where she did need to bring money, maybe to get a bite to eat or to buy something in the village. So again, if she needed money, why not bring her purse? Because she was seen in the Hollow walking away from Averill Park as the sun was going down, it makes sense that she was returning from town, not on her way there. A nickel, then would be the change that was leftover from some greater amount. It is much more likely a women as conscious of fashion and style as Hazel was would have been carrying her money in a purse, not in her glove.

So regardless of Hazel's purpose or destination when seen by Smith and Gundrum, she wasn't carrying her purse and was left to carry change in her glove as an alternative. Her purse then was inaccessible and probably located at the place she was staying. That place was not in the Sand Lake area. If it were, she would have had access to it.

It can be assumed that Hazel had gone to Sand Lake but was not intending to spend the night. If she was, she most certainly would have access to her purse and her suitcase. If Hazel had a place to stay like she had with the Blys the previous summer, someone would have come forward and her possessions would have been turned over to the authorities during the investigation. No one did, and they were not. So building off the clue of the nickel found in the glove, it is unlikely that Hazel was in Sand Lake very long and she was not planning to stay.

The nickel found in the glove also indicates that robbery was not a motive for her attack. If she was walking up the lonely road and came upon someone who killed her and stole the purse, a nickel would not be in the glove, it would be in the purse. She was carrying the nickel in her glove because she did not have her purse with her.

If Hazel was in Sand Lake temporarily then she had to have been staying somewhere else. The question was where? Keeping Unser and Powers back in Sand Lake, Kaye and the other detectives now shifted the focus of the investigation to Albany and Troy. Detectives checked all of the hotels and other boarding places where Hazel may have spent the night of July 6. No Hazel Drew was registered in any of them.

Detective Kaye logically assumed that Hazel went to Union Station on July 6 after she left her aunt. She placed an order with the Westcott Express Company at 1:15 for her trunk to be picked up at the Cary's house. The Westcott Company's office was located at Union Station. She may have also made (or planned to make) a trolley connection to Watervliet.

Kaye went to the baggage room at Union Station and talked to the parcel clerk, Adelbert Atwood. Atwood said there were a number of unclaimed bags and remembered one in particular that had been there for about a week. He excused himself and went to a back room to retrieve the light brown suitcase. He returned and handed the piece to Detective Kaye. Kaye took a close look and saw the initials H.I.D. engraved near the handle. He immediately realized the importance of his find. Hazel's suitcase was checked at Union Station at 1:49 pm, on Tuesday July 7.

THURSDAY
JULY 16, 1908

The District Attorney's Office
Troy New York

"That Hazel Drew's mother believes the murdered girl never intended to stay overnight at Sand Lake when she made her fatal trip, and that the authorities are likely to seek for a secret admirer of the young woman were the latest developments this afternoon in the mystery."

The Evening Telegram (New York) July 16, 1908

The items in Hazel's suitcase were the same items that Minnie Taylor had previously described. Lying on top was the pretty, softly hand-printed Japanese kimono. The stylish garment was consistent with Hazel's extraordinary fashion taste. Beneath the kimono was a bathrobe with a pink sash. Other items included a comb, toothbrush, washcloth, handkerchief, underwear and a nightgown. At the bottom of the suitcase was a purse made of black Russian leather with silver metal trimmings. A heart shaped gold plated locket with imitation diamonds running diagonally across the front was on the bottom. The locket was on a gold chain but did not contain a picture or photograph. The only item that Minnie claimed she saw in the suitcase on the Fourth of July but was not in the suitcase now was Hazel's shirtwaist.

> It is stated that a shirt waist, which was in the much sought for and now found dress suit case when Miss Taylor, Hazel's aunt, last saw it in the latter's possession, has disappeared. It was not found in the case when the latter was recovered in the parcel room at the Union station yesterday afternoon. What has become of it? Did she leave it at the place she stopped at a week ago Monday night, or did she leave it at some friend's house before she was last seen on the streets in this city a week ago Tuesday afternoon? (The Troy Record, July 16, 1908)

Lying beneath the clothing, Detective Kaye found a small personal advertisement that had been printed in the Troy Record. Dated October 23, 1907 it read:

> "Edward LaVoie has departed for Chattanooga, Tenn. where he will remain for the winter."

Written in Hazel's handwriting on the bottom of the ad was the date: October 6, 1907.

Detective Kaye brought the suitcase to Mrs. Cary to have her identify the contents. She recognized all of the items. The washcloth and comb, she claimed, belonged to her but were kept in Hazel's room.

The discovery of the suitcase was now the most important lead in the case and provided opportunities from which to base the direction of the investigation. The detectives were able to make several assumptions based on the items found in the suitcase but they were also puzzled by what wasn't there. For example, where was Hazel's brown purse? Mrs. Drew insisted that Hazel had two handbags. The black one that was in the suitcase and a newer brown one that Hazel preferred and that Minnie said Hazel was carrying when she left the Harrison's on July 6. If it wasn't with the suitcase and she didn't have it in Sand Lake, where was it?

No money was found in the suitcase or the black purse. The investigators had gathered enough information to roughly approximate how much money Hazel should have had. They knew that Mrs. Cary paid Hazel $4.50 (approximately $113 in today's currency) on July 3. In addition Mrs. Drew loaned Hazel $2.00 (approximately $50 today) on July 2. Thus Hazel had at least $6.50 (approximately $163).

However, Hazel paid Mrs. Schumaker $3.00 ($75) for the new waist leaving her $3.50. On July 4, she and Minnie went by trolley to see the parade in Troy. They took another to Rensselaer Park. Hazel would have paid the 50 cents (approximately $12.50) admission into the park, possibly bought something to eat and maybe paid for rides or attractions. They left the park at 5:00 and paid the fare back to Joseph and Eva's house to pick up their suitcase. The two women then paid for train fare to Schenectady. They remained at Anna Weinmann's house the following day, and paid the train fare back to Troy at 9:00 on Sunday night.

The detectives had no way of knowing exactly how much money Hazel had left because it would have to be based on the exact amount she started with and her unknown purchases. She may have had only the five cents they found in her glove. Any amount above that, they reasoned, would probably be found in her still missing purse.

For a person with so little funds, Hazel did not appear to be concerned. She had no job, little or no money, and didn't appear to have any prospects. However, she did have a suitcase with clothes packed for an overnight excursion and plans she did not reveal to anyone.

Hazel's claim ticket for her suitcase had not been located. When bags were checked at Union Station a ticket was placed around the handle. The end of the ticket contained the ticket number and was ripped off and given to the customer. Hazel's suitcase had the ticket attached to the handle but Hazel's copy, the part that had been ripped off was not found. It is likely that it was in her purse.

Investigators went back to Union Station to question Adelbert Atwood about the person who checked the suitcase. Among other things, they wanted to know if a woman or a man left the luggage and if the person was alone at the time. Atwood was home sick but the investigators wouldn't wait. They went directly to his house on Seventh Avenue to interview him. Atwood said he remembered when the suitcase was received but, when shown Hazel's photograph, couldn't say if the person who left the bag was her. He remembered a blond woman checked the suitcase but he couldn't recall if she was alone or if she had a companion.

The investigators looked into Edward Lavoie, the person mentioned in the personnel ad. On the one hand they were excited that they had the name of a person that Hazel must have known well enough to carry his personal ad and who might be able to provide more information into her life. On the other hand, because the article was dated October 1907, investigators feared the clue wouldn't bear much relevance to the case.

(II)

John Murnane and Jack Lawrenson were interviewing people in Troy who may have seen Hazel on July 6 or 7. Carrying Hazel's photograph, they went store to store asking employees and customers if they had seen the girl. They knew it was a long shot but a necessary step in the investigation.

When they went into Kerin's grocery store on Congress Street they spoke to a young employee named Lawrence Eagan. Eagan looked at the photograph and said he thought he remembered seeing the girl on Monday July 6 but didn't know her name. He thought it was around noon and he didn't think she was carrying a suitcase. He said she was so pretty that he pointed her out to Anna O'Donnell, another employee in the store.

O'Donnell was shown the photograph and said that it did resemble the girl that Eagan pointed out. She told the detectives that she was with a customer when Eagan called her over, pointed to the woman and said, "Ain't she a daisy?" O'Donnell agreed that the woman was very pretty and went back to the customer. She said she hadn't thought of the incident since. She thought it may have been Monday July 6 and she didn't remember what time it was.

Later that day Murnane and Lawrenson interviewed Thomas Carey who lived on Third Street. He said he definitely saw Hazel Drew in Troy. He couldn't remember if it was on Monday July 6 or Tuesday July 7 but did know that it was between 11:00 and noon. She was walking up Congress Street between Fourth and Fifth Streets. He thought she was carrying a suitcase. Carey said he knew Hazel and was positive it was her. Before he moved to his home on Third Street he lived near the Drew's. There was no doubt in his mind that it was Hazel.

Congress Street, Troy, NY in 1913. Kerin's Store, located between Fourth and Fifth Streets is seen on the left. Photo taken from Images of America: Troy, by Don Rittner

The investigation still had a long way to go but investigators could now begin to plot some definite places and times that Hazel was seen. They knew that on July 6 she left the Harrison's on Pawling Avenue at 10:00. She was carrying her suitcase at that time. She was at the Westcott Express Company at Union Station at 1:15 placing an order for her trunk to be picked up at the Cary's. According to the Eagan and O'Donnell sightings she may have been on Congress Street between those times. From 1:15 on Monday until 1:49 on Tuesday afternoon when she checked her suitcase at Union Station her whereabouts were unknown. She disappeared again until 7:30 when she was seen by Frank Smith and Rudy Gundrum on Taborton Road. Investigators were still trying to find out where Hazel spent Monday night and what she was doing the five and half hours on Tuesday after checking her bag and before walking up Taborton Mountain.

(III)

On Tuesday, July 14 a postcard was delivered to the Cary's house on Whitman Court. Sent from Ohio, it was addressed to Hazel. The Carys forwarded it to John and Julia Drew who then turned it over to the investigators.

The card was sent by Carrie Weaver, Hazel's friend who visited her at the Cary's on July 3. It was postmarked Sunday July 12, from New Carlisle and read:

Hazel,

Have been out riding. Having a lovely time and wish you were along.

With love,
Carrie

Investigators wanted to know more about Carrie Weaver and her relationship with Hazel. They went back to Whitman Court and spoke to Mrs. Cary. They learned that Carrie was one of Hazel's closest friends. She worked as a domestic servant for Professor Arthur Greene who lived on Hawthorne Avenue, two streets up from the Cary's. Mrs. Cary told the detectives that Carrie was on vacation in Ohio. She didn't know when she left but confirmed Carrie's visit with Hazel on July 3.

Hazel and Carrie would get together several times a week. They would take walks or just sit and chat in Hazel's room. They were both very religious girls and they joked about attending the other's church. Hazel went to the Methodist Church on the corner of Third and State Streets and Carrie went to the Methodist Church on Pawling Avenue. Neither would leave their respective church because they liked their pastors.

Mrs. Cary told the detectives that Hazel loved to travel. In the five months that Hazel worked for them she had gone on four vacations. In April she went to Providence, Rhode Island for one trip and to Boston on another. She spent two days in Providence and three days in Boston. In May she twice went to New York City spending two days each time. Her second visit was over Memorial Day weekend and Carrie went with her.

When Hazel went to Providence she stayed with a friend named Mina Jones. Mina and her husband, Frank had once lived in Troy. She was a dressmaker and before she moved Mina made many of Hazel's clothes.

Mrs. Cary said that each time Hazel returned from her trips she was very enthusiastic and spoke of the wonderful things she had seen and the exciting adventures she had been on. It occurred to Mrs. Cary that she never asked Hazel where she stayed and except for the one trip to New York, Mrs. Cary didn't know who, if anyone had accompanied her.

Detectives were immediately dispatched to Ohio and to Rhode Island. They were very interested in Hazel's vacations and wanted information that only Carrie Weaver and Mina Jones could provide. They wanted to know if Hazel traveled with anyone else or if anyone called on her.

Mrs. Cary again vouched for Hazel's character. She said in the five months Hazel was with them, she never had any men call on her and was certain that Hazel wasn't dating anyone. She rarely went out at night and the few times she did go to dances or parties she always returned in time to meet her 11:00 curfew. She would spend most nights reading books in the family library. Except for her trips out of town, Hazel never spent a single night away from the Cary's. She never gave them any reason to doubt her morals, her integrity, or her decisions. She was pleasant and personable. She seemed to be the perfect young woman.

Hazel's brother Joseph spoke to reporters about his sister. He reminded them that he and his wife were staying at William Taylor's house the previous winter when Hazel arrived ill and needed a place to stay. Like his uncle he did not inquire about the nature of Hazel's illness and did not call a physician. The last time he saw his sister was when she left Taylor's farm in early February.

Like everyone else, Joseph defended his sister's honor. He said Hazel was an extremely pretty girl and had many admirers but didn't think she was serious with anyone at the time of her death. When asked, he told the investigators that Frank Smith stopped by his uncle's farm a few times when Hazel was there. One night they all played cards. He believed Smith was one of many who had feelings for his sister but was convinced that nothing in Hazel's past would have been a motive for her murder.

(IV)

By Thursday the Hazel Drew tragedy had become a national story. Headlines as far away as California, New Mexico, Idaho, and Wyoming were keeping readers informed on the latest developments. Reporters across the northeast were descending on Troy and the quiet villages of Sand Lake and Averill Park. Most of the reporters were reputable, writing unbiased pieces about the latest developments. Others were sensationalizing the facts and making accusations against key figures involved in the case. Jarvis O'Brien would spend the next two weeks defending his actions and differentiating between the accurate facts written in the papers and the yellow journalism printed to sell copies and create scapegoats.

The Evening World was a popular New York City newspaper with a large circulation. Their investigative reporters interviewed people directly involved in the case and wrote sensational stories very often designed to create controversy.

The July 16 edition of the Evening World took aim at the doctors who conducted the autopsy. Specifically the paper focused on the inconclusive findings and differing opinions of the three doctors and Coroner Strope.

> Hazel Drew, like 'Billy' Brown may have gone to her doom because her sweetheart, like Chester Gillette found her a burden. The advanced decomposition of her body and the delicacy and lack of thoroughness of country doctors who sought only the cause of death has centralized public opinion here to almost demand that a sworn report of the autopsy be made to Mr. O'Brien, specifying what, if any examination was conducted other than learning how she died.

> Opinions not in harmony have been expressed by Drs. Boyce, Fairweather, and Strope as to the girl's condition and the cause of death.

Grace "Billy" Brown was murdered on July 11, 1906 two years to the day from when Hazel's body was discovered in Teal's pond. She was killed by Chester Gillette because she was pregnant with his illegitimate child and he was not ready or willing to be a father. Gillette took Billy Brown to the Adirondack Mountains in upstate New York. While out on a lake in a small boat, he beat her to death with a tennis racket. He attempted to flee the scene and make it appear that Brown died in a boating accident. He was later convicted and executed for the murder. Although the Evening World was making insinuations that Hazel was in the same condition that Billy Brown was, the doctors were unanimous in their conclusion that Hazel was not pregnant.

There were, however two main points of contention among the autopsy doctors that the Evening World exploited. The first was that, in addition to the blow to the head which the doctors agreed was the cause of death, they disagreed on the role that strangulation played in the murder. The second was the disagreement regarding Hazel's virginity and the possibility that she may have been sexually assaulted prior to death.

From the beginning Dr. Boyce's opinion differed from that of the other doctors because he believed that strangulation from her corset string contributed to Hazel's death. Drs. Reichard and Fairweather as well as Coroner Strope were certain that the ribbon had not come from Hazel's corset but was a stylish accessory worn by women at that time. They believed it became embedded in Hazel's throat when the body bloated due to its being in the water for several days.

The doctors noted a tear in the "female organ" but due to advanced decomposition were unable to determine its cause. Dr. Boyce believed there was sufficient evidence to show that Hazel had lost her virginity which he maintained could have happened as the result of an attack at the time of her death. Dr. Fairweather did not disagree. In an interview with the Evening World he stated,

> "While the body's condition was not conducive to an infallible decision as to her physical condition, I believe a motive for her death such as accompanied 'Billy' Brown's murder is lacking. However, it is likely the girl was slain after an assault. Further than this I cannot say." (Evening World, July 16, 1908)

The Evening World insinuated that the doctors were incompetent and performed an incomplete autopsy. Out of modesty or respect for the victim they avoided focusing on Hazel's reproductive organs. They criticized the doctors for concentrating primarily on the cause of death and argued that a more thorough examination may have provided a more clear motive for the murder.

Dr. Fairweather defended the competency of the doctors and the autopsy. In the same interview with the Evening World he stated,

> "The autopsy was performed by Drs. Boyce and Reichard. I noted observations. The process was thorough, every organ being examined."

(V)

Investigators and reporters were anxious to get more information about Edward LaVoie. Specifically they were interested in what his relationship with Hazel may have been. Hazel's suitcase was packed for an overnight stay and LaVoie's personnel ad was found in that suitcase. Investigators reasoned that Hazel would not be in possession of the ad unless she was planning to see LaVoie. They needed to find out if he had returned from Tennessee and if he had plans to meet Hazel. If they could locate him he might be able to provide much needed information.

An Evening World reporter located and interviewed LaVoie's uncle, Edward Rice who lived on Second Street in Troy. He learned that shortly after arriving in the south LaVoie enlisted in the army and was currently stationed in Tennessee. Rice also admitted that LaVoie and Hazel had once dated.

> "Yes, Eddie and Hazel were sweethearts...Last fall he went south. Hazel would ask me where he was. When she got a letter she would read it to me and cry. But Eddie is an adventurous lad, and not sentimental. He wouldn't love any girl long." (Evening World, July 16, 1908)

Rice then stated, "He's been up north somewhere lately, I don't know where, exactly."

This last statement piqued the investigators' interest. They would check with the army to see if LaVoie had been on leave the week of July 6 and if he had been in the north. If so it may explain Hazel's mysterious actions and why she was in possession of his ad. Investigators would also check to see if LaVoie had been to New York, Boston or Providence in the spring. Knowing that Carrie Weaver accompanied Hazel on her second trip to New York, and Hazel had stayed with Mina Jones in Providence, their interviews became all the more important.

(VI)

July 16 offered many new opportunities for the investigation. Despite the fact that none of Hazel's friends or family members claimed to have known where she went, her movements have been narrowed down. Hazel was in Troy on Monday and Tuesday July 6 and 7 but where she spent Monday night and the crucial hours on Tuesday afternoon had yet to be learned.

Hazel's vacations and especially the people she traveled with and stayed with were important elements in the tragedy. Discussions with Carrie Weaver and Mina Jones would provide new avenues in the investigation. Hazel's relationship with Edward Lavoie will be examined and a closer look into the controversial and now exposed autopsy will bring new light to the investigation.

Hazel's suitcase was checked at the baggage room of Union Station on the afternoon of July 7. Could it be possible that someone other than Hazel checked the bag, perhaps even her killer? Adelbert Atwood, the employee on duty was not certain that the person who checked the bag was Hazel. He could not identify the woman when shown Hazel's photograph. He did believe, however that the woman did have blond hair.

The logical assumption is that it was Hazel who checked the bag and not some other blond woman for the simple fact that there would be no reason for anyone else to leave it in the baggage room.

The press emphasized that a shirtwaist was missing from Hazel's suitcase. Minnie Taylor claimed that when Hazel opened the suitcase on the morning of July 4 before the two women spent the weekend together, she saw, among other things, a shirtwaist. After the suitcase was discovered at Union Station and the contents revealed, the shirtwaist was not among the packed items. Reporters speculated that the waist would be found in the place that Hazel spent the night of July 6.

The newspapers had created a story where there was none. The so-called missing shirtwaist was never missing. It was in the possession of the investigators since July 13, the day they searched Hazel's trunk. The Troy Record on July 17, 1908 explained.

> ...the shirtwaist...missing from the suitcase...has been discovered. It was in the trunk Hazel sent to her home from her last place of employment...

The question investigators had not figured out though, was why did Hazel transfer the waist to the trunk? Or, to put it another way, why didn't she keep it with her in her suitcase?

The fact that Hazel packed a separate suitcase is an essential point. Sometime, either on Sunday July 5 or Monday July 6 Hazel decided to quit her employment with the Carys. She packed most of her belongings in her trunk and the rest she placed in her suitcase. But, why did she pack a suitcase? If she was dissatisfied with the Cary's, she would simply pack everything in the trunk, go to her parents house and begin looking for new employment. Why the separate suitcase?

It must be assumed that Hazel had plans to meet someone with whom she intended to spend the night, but only the night. She did not pack clothes or other items necessary for an extended stay, she only had the clothes she was wearing. Someone of Hazel's attention to appearance, would have packed more if her intention was to stay somewhere longer than one night.

The clothing in the suitcase indicates that Hazel was prepared for a romantic encounter. Specifically the Japanese kimono was not an item of clothing that women would wear informally especially since she had a traditional bath robe packed.

The problem arises from statements made by everyone of Hazel's friends, family, and employers. They were unanimous in vouching for her character. Two of the autopsy doctors substantiate these beliefs. Hazel did not have a steady boyfriend that anyone knew about and no men ever called on her at the Cary's. Except for occasional walks with her friends, including Carrie Weaver, she did not typically go out at night or on weekends. She spent most nights inside quietly reading. She was never known to lie or be deceitful. But, as unlikely as it may have seemed, Hazel had packed all the necessities for a short romantic escape.

The evidence suggests that Hazel must have been dating someone but she either kept it from the people closest to her or they concealed the relationship from the authorities. On July 6 she must have planned to go away with this person. She did not inform her family that she left the Cary's, not even Minnie Taylor. Instead she most likely lied to her aunt about visiting friends in Watervliet which gave her the time and the opportunity to get away.

But why would Hazel leave her suitcase at Union Station? She could have been there to catch a train or to meet someone arriving from out of town. Either way, there is no reasonable explanation for why she checked her bag.

Based on the assumed amount of cash that Hazel had, it is not likely that she had the means to travel very far. The fact that she had to borrow $2.00 from her mother to help pay for a new shirtwaist is evidence of Hazel's low cash flow at the time. Hazel simply did not have enough money to travel very far without someone else paying for her ticket and her expenses. So why didn't he? If this was the scenario then Hazel would have either boarded a train with her companion or she would have taken her suitcase with her either when he arrived or when plans did not work out.

An examination of the train schedule around 1:49 on Tuesday July 7 shows that a train from New York was due at Union Station. Remembering that Hazel had twice traveled to New York it is possible she had a love interest there and could have been planning to meet him at the station.

The theory has potential until other factors are figured in. For example, if Hazel was planning to meet this person on Tuesday afternoon, why so much activity on Monday? Why would she mysteriously quit her job, presumably lie to her aunt and vanish on Monday if she wasn't planning to meet this person until Tuesday?

If Hazel met this mysterious person on Monday as planned, spent the night with him and then saw him off at the station on Tuesday, why would she check her suitcase? Her romantic night was over and it was time for her to do whatever it was she had planned to do next. And what was that? She had no job, no references, and a family that didn't appear to get along. In addition, whatever they may have been, when were these plans made, and how were they communicated? Hazel's movements July 3-5 have been accounted for. Her behavior and attitude were normal. She did not appear preoccupied or upset. She did not reveal to Mrs. Schumaker, Carrie Weaver, Minnie Taylor or her cousins in Schenectady her intention to quit her job or meet someone at the train station. Hazel returned to the Cary's around 10:30 on Sunday night. Her strange actions didn't begin until the next morning. At what point would all of these plans have come together? What triggered her mysterious behavior?

The central question to solving the murder revolves around why Hazel was in Sand Lake at 7:30 Tuesday night and why she didn't have her packed suitcase with her. Once the contents of Hazel's suitcase were revealed, her parents were convinced that Hazel did not intend to spend the night in Sand Lake. On July 16, Julia Drew spoke to The Evening Telegram reporters.

> "There, that settles it. Hazel never intended to stay at her uncle's overnight for that was one of the things she was always fussy about. Wherever she went she always took her nightgown with her unless she was sure she would be back home to sleep. She would even take it when she went to her sister's overnight. Hazel would never have left the nightgown behind unless she expected to call for her bag again before bedtime."

Hazel brought her suitcase with her to Schenectady on July 4. She had it with her in Troy yet she didn't bring it to Sand Lake.

And how did she get to Taborton Road? Every motorman on the trains running from Troy to Averill Park was questioned. Remembering that Hazel's beauty was far above average, it is likely that someone should have noticed her. Nobody did or at least nobody said they did. Assuming that Hazel did take the train, she would most likely have gotten off at the Averill Park Station like she had on her previous visits. She then would have traveled approximately two miles in Cuban heeled shoes, gone through the villages of Averill Park and Sand Lake, and then walked up a mountain. Yet she was not seen or recognized by anyone along the way even though she was well known in the area and had spent time there the previous winter and summer.

The past several times Hazel went to her uncle's farm, she took the train to Averill Park and then took the livery taxi from the village up the mountain. The drivers were all questioned, most of them knew Hazel. None of them gave her a ride up the mountain that Tuesday night.

The evidence suggests that Hazel did not take the train to the country so it must be assumed she was driven there. But why then was she walking up the mountain? And if she was driven to Averill Park the only explanation for why she left her suitcase at Union Station was because she planned to return. Therefore, it must be concluded that, however Hazel traveled to Sand Lake, by train, automobile or carriage, she did not intend to stay the night.

Could Hazel have quit her job and on her way to visit friends in Watervliet have met someone who swayed her to go with him? The July 16 Oswego Daily Times speculated on the scenario.

> If Hazel had been a different kind of girl it might be presumed that after she left her aunt and took the car for Troy she met a man and, changing her mind decided to spend Monday and Tuesday in his company. If so this would explain how Hazel got to the pond without being seen...She was driven there.

The individual pieces of the story do not support the theory. Hazel had an overnight bag packed. Her intention already was to spend the night somewhere. Why would this man have driven Hazel all the way out to Sand Lake to kill her?

The Hazel sightings in Troy help to pinpoint where Hazel was. Although all evidence can be useful, the sightings have limited value. This is especially true of Lawrence Eagan and Anna O'Donnell who were working at Kerin's store on Congress Street and claimed to have seen Hazel on Monday morning. However, they both stated that they only thought the woman may have been Hazel, they couldn't be sure. Because they did not know her personally there is room for doubt.

Neither one was sure what time they saw the woman. Eagan guessed she passed the store around noon. O'Donnell admitted that she was not certain of the day she saw the woman pass by the store.

Hazel left her aunt at 10:00. She may have gone to Troy and was seen by Eagan and O'Donnell around noon. She may even have gone to Watervliet and had come back when they saw her. Hazel was at the Westcott Express Company at 1:15 which does fit into the possible time that Hazel was seen by Eagan and O'Donnell.

Thomas Carey's statement is more reliable. He knew Hazel and saw her between 11:00 and noon not far from Kerin's store on Congress Street. The problem was he couldn't recall if it was on Monday or Tuesday but he thought she was carrying her suitcase at that time.

If the sightings are to be believed, where was Hazel going and what was she up to? If she had innocently stayed with a friend on Monday night, why hadn't that friend come forward?

Carrie Weaver provided insight into Hazel's life. Just two years older than Hazel, the girls were apparently very close. Carrie sent the postcard from Ohio the day after Hazel's body was discovered, the day the story was first released in the Northern Budget newspaper, and more than a week after the two girls last talked. It arrived at the Cary's the day Hazel was buried. The message was simple, the tone was jovial. There was no suggestion of concern in the note. If Hazel had confided any pending trouble to her friend before she left there is no indication of it in the writing.

Because the postcard was sent to the Cary residence it shows that Hazel had not informed her friend of her intention to quit her job. Nothing in the note hinted of such a decision. If Hazel had known she was going to terminate her employment with the Cary's on July 6, it is probable she would have confided that to her good friend on July 3, the last time the two spoke.

If Hazel was contemplating leaving the Cary's, her friend would have either held off sending the card to the Cary's house, or more likely would have asked Hazel in the postcard if her situation had changed. Carrie did not know that Hazel was quitting because as of July 3, Hazel did not know she was quitting.

To obtain more information about Carrie's trip to New York with Hazel, investigators were sent to New Carlisle. For now though Hazel's vacations need to be examined.

Hazel earned $4.50 per week working for the Cary's. That was a decent wage at that time for a domestic but still not a lot of money. Hazel had a fondness for clothes. She loved to dress in the latest fashion and a large part of her wardrobe was hand tailored. She had her own personal dressmakers, first Mina Jones and more recently Mrs. Schumaker. How could a person, making as little money as Hazel did, with a penchant for spending her money on nice clothes and fine accessories afford to take four vacations in two months? Why, if she was merely interested in traveling and seeing new and exciting places, would she travel to the same city twice in a month? What was the lure to New York City? Was there a specific reason she traveled to the places she did?

The Evening World was very critical of the autopsy and of the doctors who performed it. They did, however raise some important questions and held the doctors accountable for their findings. In particular, attention must be paid to the corset string controversy. Dr. Boyce alone claimed that the string he cut from Hazel's neck had come from her corset.

A solution to this controversy is important. If Dr. Boyce was correct and the string did come from the corset, it has great implications. It means that, at some point during the attack, Hazel must have been at least partially undressed. That would be the only way the attacker would have access to Hazel's underclothing. If this in fact was the case, the motive for the murder had a sexual component. Most likely Hazel would have been murdered either in the process of, or immediately after a sexual assault.

If, however Dr. Boyce was incorrect as the other doctors believed, and the only evidence of violence was the wound on the back of Hazel's head, the motive would not be sexual. Instead the killer most likely would have acted out of anger, jealousy or rage.

The conclusion is debatable but more than likely Dr. Boyce was in error. Corset strings had brass fittings at the ends to permit easier lacing. The ribbon cut from Hazel's neck did not have such fittings. Also, corset strings were typically round with a smaller diameter. The ribbon around Hazel's throat was flat and approximately one quarter of an inch in width.

No evidence is available to show if the corset itself was examined or if a string was missing but it must be assumed that the authorities would have done so. Three doctors, a coroner, a district attorney, and several detectives were involved and only one of them, Dr. Boyce was convinced the ribbon came from the corset. It is more likely that the ribbon was just a fashionable accessory that Hazel wore around her neck.

The area where Hazel's hat, gloves and glasses were found showed no sign that a struggle had taken place there. Surely Hazel would have defended herself if she could have. If a sexual assault had taken place in some other location, followed by Hazel's murder what reason would the perpetrator have to relocate the body to Teal's pond?

Hazel's clothing was not torn, in disarray or stained. Her underwear was intact and in place. She had combs in the sides of her hair that were not disturbed. There is no physical evidence to support the theory that Hazel was involved in any kind of struggle, and only inconclusive evidence to suggest that she was the victim of a sexual attack.

Questions about the tear in Hazel's reproductive organ are also inconclusive. Due to the modesty of the era and an appropriate regard for the victim's privacy, no other details were printed. However, the doctors all agreed that Hazel was not pregnant at the time of her death. They did not come to a unanimous decision however on Hazel's sexual past. Decomposition made it impossible to be certain of Hazel's sexual experience. Even if they determined that she was sexually active, specific information concerning the when and how of the potential sexual activity was not possible to know. They could not be certain if Hazel ever had sexual intercourse and even if she had, doctors could not determine if it occurred at the time of death or if it was consensual.

Doctor Boyce and Doctor Fairweather held to their opinion that Hazel had probably been the victim of a sexual attack. She was murdered shortly after the assault in an effort by the attacker to conceal his identity. The body was then placed in the pond which intentionally or not, destroyed evidence and made motive difficult to ascertain.

The personal ad naming Edward LaVoie and the Evening World interview with Edward Rice indicates that Hazel was in a relationship within a year of her death. It appears that Hazel continued to have strong feelings for LaVoie and was serious about the relationship. LaVoie, however seemed to have taken a more casual approach. If Hazel was intending to share a romantic evening with some unknown person on the night of July 6 and packed her suitcase in anticipation, why would she include LaVoie's newspaper clipping unless she was planning to see him? Could the soldier have been in the area and made promises to the smitten ex-girlfriend?

Investigators were sent to Chattanooga, Tennessee to talk to LaVoie. They were most interested in finding out if he had recently been in the north and when the last time it was that he was in contact with Hazel Drew.

FRIDAY
JULY 17, 1908

Hawthorne Avenue, Troy New York

"Mrs. Drew said the girl possessed a brown leather bag, which was shirred at the top and which, she says, Hazel preferred to carry rather than the black hand bag which was found in the suitcase. The brown bag is missing."

Auburn Democrat-Argus (Auburn, NY) July 17, 1908

While detectives and reporters were enroute to New Carlisle, Ohio Jarvis O'Brien and Duncan Kaye went to Hawthorne Avenue to speak with Carrie Weaver's employers, Professor and Mrs. Arthur Greene. They learned that the Greenes moved from Ohio to Troy in the summer of 1907. Professor Greene was the head of the Mechanical Engineering Department at RPI and Mrs. Greene had been a school teacher in Ohio. They knew Carrie from back home and after they settled in Troy they asked if she would come and work for them. Carrie arrived early in 1908. Professor Greene met Professor Cary at the college and the two families became friends. Carrie was introduced to Hazel and likewise the two girls became close friends.

Mrs. Greene spoke very highly of both girls. As a former teacher, she felt she was a good judge of moral character and had no doubt as to the honesty and integrity of both Carrie and Hazel. For that reason, she felt comfortable allowing Carrie to accompany Hazel on a trip to New York City on Memorial weekend. She even made arrangements for the girls to stay at the YWCA. (The Troy Daily Press, July 17, 1908)

Mrs. Greene knew that Hazel was an experienced traveler because she had sent Carrie postcards from New York, Boston and Providence. She said Hazel and Carrie left for New York on Friday May 29 and were supposed to return on Sunday evening but something happened and they didn't get back until the following Monday morning.

Around noon on July 6, Professor and Mrs. Greene brought Carrie to Union Station. She had plans to visit her family and a former employer in Ohio and was not expected back until August 1. A few days after the discovery of Hazel's body, as the murder was becoming a national story, Carrie sent a letter to Mrs. Greene and enclosed an article about the case that she took from a Springfield, Ohio newspaper. She wrote, "Is this the Hazel that I know so well?" (Troy Record July 17, 1908)

(II)

Investigators located Carrie outside Dayton, Ohio. They wanted to know about her relationship with Hazel. As quoted in the Albany Times Union on July 18 Carrie told them,

> "From the time we met we began to chum together. She was an exceedingly fine girl, good habits, honest, and of nice appearance. She was a blonde. The Carys always seemed to think much of her as did everyone in the neighborhood."

The investigators questioned Carrie about the trip to New York. Carrie told them that she and Hazel didn't take the train, but instead went by ship down the Hudson River. After they arrived, Hazel lost her purse which contained all of her money, $6.00. Carrie said she paid their expenses for the weekend. The two went to the theatre and enjoyed riding the elevated trains. She said they traveled alone and did not meet anybody. They had a wonderful time and expected to take the day liner back to Troy on Sunday. When they arrived at the dock however, they learned that the ship did not depart until night. They waited and later that evening boarded the ship for their return ride home. They arrived early the following morning. While on their return trip, Hazel told Carrie she was going to go to Lake George for the Fourth of July.

The last time Carrie saw Hazel was on July 3rd at the Cary's house. They were in Hazel's room laughing and joking and talking about Lake George. Carrie had the impression that Hazel was going with some of her girl friends. She said she was certain that Hazel did not have a boy-friend; she was Hazel's confidente and would have known if she did.

Carrie said that when she left Troy on July 6 for her trip to Ohio, Hazel promised to meet her at Union Station to say goodbye but never showed. Carrie was disappointed but understood that something must have come up. She was sure her friend would have been there if she could.

When asked if she had any knowledge of why Hazel may have been out in Sand Lake she replied, as quoted in the Times Union on July 17:

> "The papers say that Hazel was supposed to be on her way toward the home of an uncle when she met her death. Why she was out where she was I cannot say...If she had an uncle there I never knew it but she never talked to me of any of her folks."

Jarvis O'Brien heard from the detectives he sent to Providence. He learned that Mina Jones and her husband had moved to Waterville, Maine. The detectives were on their way. In the meantime, Mina had written a letter to the Troy Record asking them to send her articles on Hazel's case.

(III)

Reporters from the Evening World located Edward LaVoie's sister who lived on Second and Jackson Street in Troy. She confirmed that her brother was in the army but she didn't know where he was stationed or if he'd been back north since he enlisted.

Detectives located LaVoie in Chattanooga, Tennessee. The following excerpt was published in the Evening World on July 17, 1908.

> I had been told, he said, that she had disappeared on July 5 but I did not believe that the poor girl had been murdered. I do not think that she had an enemy on earth and there is no cause I can think of for the murder. The last time I was there was a year ago when I went on a pleasure trip to Troy. I have heard from her a number of times since then but of late our correspondence has been irregular.

> Asked if she may have committed suicide because of not hearing from him he replied in the negative saying the affair was not that serious. He said Miss Drew's character was beyond reproach.

The article stated that LaVoie had an excellent record. He did not drink and was considered a model soldier.

(IV)

In September 1901, seven years before Hazel's death, when Jarvis O'Brien was still Assistant District Attorney, the body of a young woman was discovered floating in the Hudson River just south of Troy. The victim was Mamie Killian. Details of her death are eerily similar to those of Hazel Drew. Both victims were young working class woman from Troy. Both were considered extraordinarily pretty and both had many admirers. Both women were very social and extremely popular. Both murders were staged to give the appearance of suicide but autopsy results determined that both women were dead before they were placed in bodies of water.

While Jarvis O'Brien and the Rensselaer County officials were investigating the Hazel Drew murder, their counterparts in Albany were working on a missing person's case. On April 29, fifteen year old Mary Lewis left her house and was walking to school. She never arrived. Later that week she was seen in Schenectady. Her family had no relatives who lived there and as far as they knew, Mary did not have any friends in that city. At 5:00 am on Sunday May 3, Mary bought a ticket at Union Station in Troy for New York City. She was alone at the time.

Mary Lewis was a happy and content young lady. She had a loving relationship with her family. She did not have a boyfriend and although she did have friends, they were not the type to persuade her to run away. There is no known motive for her actions or her disappearance.

Mary Lewis was very attractive. She was five feet tall and slender. She had blue eyes and blond hair.

(V)

Jarvis O'Brien was keeping his mind and his options open. His detectives were working overtime, running down leads and checking on stories but the investigation was not progressing as quickly as the media demanded. Pressure was building. O'Brien was spending valuable time briefing reporters, debunking rumors and clarifying misunderstood evidence.

Something was missing. He knew it but he couldn't figure out what it was so he asked his investigators to go back to the beginning and rethink and reevaluate old theories. He posed the possibility of suicide again and shared it with reporters. He reminded them that Hazel was out of money. She was unemployed and had no man in her life that loved her. She could have been distraught and gone back to the place she was born and found herself on the bank of Teal's pond. She took off her glasses, hat and gloves, walked over to the dam, jumped head first into the water, smashing her head on a rock causing instantaneous death.

He also shared with the reporters the possibility that Hazel may have been struck by a car. The road between Troy and Averill Park was macadam and used by automobiles. Hazel could have been struck while walking along the road. The driver, not wanting to accept responsibility and having knowledge of the area, drove her lifeless body up Taborton Road and dumped her remains in Teal's pond.

When a reporter asked O'Brien to comment on a rumor that detectives were concentrating on livery stables in the area, he shared an anonymous letter that he had received. It said that Hazel met a man at the depot in Troy and the two took a carriage ride to Averill Park. He said that the man was alone when he returned the wagon after midnight. O'Brien told the reporters that all of the livery stables in and around Troy were being investigated.

O'Brien answered positively when a reporter asked if he believed Minnie Taylor knew more than she was saying. He added that he thought the aunt knew where Hazel spent the night of July 6 but was withholding that information. He added that he had no legal way to force her to talk but was planning to hold a Coroner's Inquest where she would be put under oath and compelled to answer his questions thoroughly and truthfully. When asked when the inquest would be held he said as soon as all the witnesses had been interviewed and the letters that were discovered in Hazel's trunk could be more thoroughly investigated.

The letters and postcards discovered in Hazel's trunk covered a period of two to three years. Some were written by young friends, others by people more refined. The detectives were trying to identify and locate each of the writers. Their progress was slow because most of the letters were signed only with initials.

(VI)

Carrie Weaver provided greater insight into the relationships and events in Hazel's life than anyone else. Their talks together and their trip to New York provided clues to Hazel's life and some of her secrets. Without realizing it, Carrie revealed more information than she knew.

The fact that Hazel never mentioned her uncle or "any of her folks" to Carrie suggests a family rift much greater than previously believed. By using the word "folks," more than just William Taylor, it must assumed that Carrie did not know about Hazel's parents or possibly her brother Joseph. The first time detectives interviewed Julia Drew they were struck by her lack of emotion regarding the death of Hazel. John Drew knew very little about his daughter's habits or activities. Joseph had not seen his sister since February when she left her uncle's farm after staying there for three weeks. Hazel went to her brother's house on the Fourth of July to drop off her suitcase and, although he was home, he never bothered to greet his sister.

Hazel seemed to have had a closer relationship with Minnie than with her other relatives with the possible exception of her sister-in-law, Eva. It is not known from Carrie's statement if Hazel ever mentioned these two more favored relatives.

Carrie stated that Hazel never mentioned William Taylor's name to her. This is a significant omission. When Hazel was so ill the previous winter that she needed a place to recover, she did not go to her parent's house, she went to William Taylor's. She never told her parents she was there, they found out later. The implication is that Hazel had at least a comfortable relationship with her uncle.

There are two possible reasons why she never mentioned Taylor's name to her good friend or her three week hiatus at the farm. One is that Hazel was not as close to her uncle as it seemed. When she stayed there it was Eva who cared for her, not William. She apparently did not want to go to her parents. Aunt Minnie was staying at the Harrison's so she couldn't go with her. Her only solution was to go to Taylor's farm to be with her sister-in-law. So she didn't go to the farm to see her uncle, she went to see Eva. When Hazel left in early February, according to Taylor she never went back.

If it is true that Hazel and William Taylor were not close, then what was Hazel doing on Taborton Mountain on July 7? Eva was not at the farm this time so it doesn't seem likely that she was paying a visit to her uncle.

The second possible reason Hazel never mentioned her uncle to Carrie is that she did not want her friend to know about her life or her connections in Sand Lake. Carrie's statement, "Why she was out where she was I cannot say" implies that Carrie had no knowledge of Hazel's other life in Sand Lake. Besides spending the three weeks with her uncle that Carrie didn't know about, Hazel also spent a month out in the country the previous summer when she stayed with the Bly's. If Carrie was aware that Hazel spent the previous summer there, why wouldn't she assume it's what she was doing there his time? The most likely reason was that Hazel had a secret. The secret was so intense that she kept it even from her closest friend.

That Hazel and Carrie were good friends cannot be doubted. Their trip to New York on Memorial Day weekend reveals the depth of their friendship. The girls had won the trust of their employers. Their reputations were solid and both the Cary's and the Greene's felt comfortable allowing Hazel and Carrie to travel together to the metropolis. Mrs. Greene made it clear that she approved of the trip, and was responsible for making the accommodations for the girls at the YWCA in New York.

When the investigators interviewed Carrie she gave a slightly different version of their accommodations as quoted in the July 18, 1908 Times Union.

> "Hazel and I went by way of the River on Memorial Day. We had intended to stay at the Margaret Louise home but it being full we stayed at a private boarding home recommended by the people at the home."

It appears at first that the girls were being deceptive. Mrs. Greene was very clear that the accommodations she made were at the YWCA but Carrie told investigators they intended to stay at the Margaret Louise Home. As it turns out however, the Margaret Louise Home was a boarding establishment for women and was associated with the YWCA.

The Boston Cooking School Magazine in March 1905 describes the Margaret Louise Home.

> The Margaret Louise Home in New York City caters to self supporting women, is to all intent and purposes a woman's inn.

It is not known where Carrie and Hazel stayed that weekend but they found a place somewhere in the city. They stayed Friday and Saturday night and it appears they had a fun weekend. Carrie said they did not meet anyone and returned on the Sunday night boat.

Because Hazel lost her purse containing $6.00 right after they arrived, Carrie had to pay for everything. It is amazing that Carrie could afford to pay all of the expenses for both women. Carrie did not make as much money as Hazel. Even if it was possible, the room and the boat ride home were not prepaid. So Carrie had enough money with her to pay for two nights in a private boarding home, all the meals for two people, train rides, theatre tickets and a return boat trip up the Hudson River from New York to Troy.

The fact that Hazel reportedly had $6.00 on Memorial weekend and so much less than that on the Fourth of July is also noteworthy. In April and May Hazel had been to Boston, Providence and New York twice. The Memorial weekend trip was the last of these excursions and Hazel somehow had $6.00 for that trip. But five weeks later Hazel was so broke on the Fourth of July weekend that she was forced to borrow $2.00 from her mother, whom she did not seem to have a close relationship with.

Hazel's low funds and her visit to Mrs. Schumaker on July 3 give question to her July 4 plans. Hazel told Carrie on their way home from New York that she was going to spend the Fourth of July in Lake George. When she arrived in Troy she asked Mrs. Cary if she could have that weekend off. She had five weeks to prepare. Yet the day before the planned excursion Hazel was borrowing money and waiting until 11:00 at night for Mrs. Schumaker to finish making the shirtwaist. With five weeks to prepare, Hazel did not appear to be ready for the trip.

Based on their conversation on July 3, Carrie was under the impression that Hazel was going to go to Lake George with some girl-friends. If she was correct, that never happened. Could Carrie have been misinformed? Was there a reasonable explanation for why the plans changed? Or was Hazel intentionally deceiving her friend?

Hazel spent the weekend with her Aunt Minnie and never went to Lake George. When looked at in it's entirety the whole weekend was either poorly planned or something more complicated was happening.

Carrie never saw her friend again after July 3. She was steadfast in her belief that Hazel did not have a man in her life and was not going to Lake George to meet a male companion. Hazel would have told her if she was.

Carrie left for Ohio at noon on July 6. Although Hazel had promised to meet her, she didn't. Hazel had mysteriously quit her job two hours earlier and her whereabouts were not known. Hazel's situation appeared to be spiraling out of control. She had made several drastic decisions and was apparently too busy and too preoccupied to say goodbye to her friend.

On July 17 the case was nearly a week old and Jarvis O'Brien was feeling the pressure. He was frustrated because so many promising leads had gone nowhere. He was trying to distract the media by reintroducing old theories that he knew were not plausible.

He knew that Hazel was dead before her body was placed in the water. There was no possible way the doctors would support or the media would believe the suicide theory. Still, he reintroduced the theory to buy more time.

Likewise O'Brien hoped that by introducing the theory that Hazel may have been struck by a car, it would distract the reporters long enough for his detectives to discover some piece of evidence that would lead to a miraculous breakthrough. He knew though that once the reporters remembered Hazel's injuries and the condition of her clothing, the hit and run theory would be rejected.

By taking advantage of their insatiable desire for new facts and information O'Brien skillfully teased the reporters with morsels of evidence. The mysterious livery had become their priority, the name Mina Jones, and hundreds of letters and correspondence found in Hazel's trunk gave the press something to write about while O'Brien and his men continued to search for that one witness or clue that had eluded them and would lead to their big break.

> Officers Fail to Get New Evidence
> Detective Unser and District Attorney's Officer Powers, accompanied by William M. Clemens, a New York criminologist, were out this morning on the case, and they interviewed the family of John Smith, who resides near the scene of the murder. No new evidence was secured. (The Troy Times, July 17, 1908)

Jarvis O'Brien had no way to know it but things would soon go from bad to worse.

SATURDAY
JULY 18, 1908

Waterville, Maine

"The great Teal pond mystery-who murdered Hazel Drew, good looking vivacious governess-is further than ever from a solution. Clew after clew, which promised in turn to reveal the identity of the murdered, have proved fruitless. The gloomy briar-bordered pond near Averill Park, a suburb, holds its secret grimley."

Albuquerque Citizen July 18, 1908

On July 18 the Troy Record printed a letter from Carrie Weaver to Jarvis O'Brien summarizing her relationship with Hazel and her discussion with detectives in Ohio.

"It is a remarkable coincidence," stated Miss Weaver, "that Miss Drew should disappear immediately after my leaving for a visit with Friends and relatives in Ohio, but I am at sea as to the cause of her Disappearance. We were chums and I was much of the time in her company. As far as I know Hazel did not associate with any men, and I think if she had I would have known it. On Decoration day we both made a trip to New York city to take in the sights, but there were no companions with us. We just went down to spend the day and came back together. I left for Ohio on Monday, July 6, about noon, and arrived in Springfield Tuesday morning at 11:40 going to the residence of Mr. Wallace and have just come to

Dayton to-day, where I expect to stay until Monday. The last time I saw Hazel Drew alive was on the Friday before the Fourth, when I went over to her room and we laughed and joked as usual. While talking to her she told me that she was going to Lake George, where she would spend the Fourth. I am sure she did not have any male companions to go with or she would have told me, but from that time on, according to the papers, she disappeared as if the earth had swallowed her up until her dead body was found. All the rest is a mystery to me."

"Some time before Hazel had been on a visit with friends in Boston and Providence and she had sent me some very pretty postal cards, so when I came back to Ohio I sent her one containing a view of Springfield. I also sent several others to friends in Troy. I am almost broken-hearted over the affair, as she was my bosom friend. But if there is anything in my power to help solve the mystery I would not be one bit backward in aiding the authorities. I intend to return to Troy about the first of August. I did not know Frank Smith or Rudolph Gunderman, who claim to have seen her."

On the same day the letter was published, O'Brien heard back from his detectives in Waterville, Maine. He learned that Mina Jones and her husband, Frank had known Hazel for thirteen years. As did everyone else, Mina and her husband both spoke very highly of Hazel. She said Hazel came alone and no one called on her the entire time she was in Providence. Mina said that Hazel asked her to mail a postcard. She could not recall the person's name but remembered he worked for the Sturtevant Company in Hyde Park, Massachusetts.

During the visit, Hazel and Mina discussed relationships. Hazel revealed to her friend that she could get married anytime she wanted. The Northern Budget on July 19, 1908 printed Mina's account.

Mrs. Jones said that Hazel often made reference to a friend who worked in a dentist's office in Troy, but never mentioned his name. She said that one day she asked the girl: "Who is your fellow?" and Miss Drew replied that she could get married any time she decided, as there was a fellow in a dentist's office in Troy anxious to marry her.

Hazel would not reveal the man's name. Anytime Mina started asking for details, Hazel would change the subject but she did say that he was "young and good looking" and that she met him at her church in Troy, at Christmas time two years earlier. (New York Tribune, July 19, 1908)

Hazel confided to Mina that she had been having problems with a strange man who had assaulted her on two separate occasions. She was able to get away both times, once by hitting him with an umbrella. She did not know the man but described him as either Armenian or Italian and said he still followed her.

Armed with this new knowledge, O'Brien and Kaye asked Hazel's parents to meet them at the Cary's house. John Drew arrived alone. When asked about Hazel's relationships, Mrs. Cary repeated that to her knowledge, Hazel had not had a steady boyfriend. Mr. Drew spoke up and said that two years earlier, Hazel had been engaged. He couldn't recall the man's name but remembered he had distinguished features, a prominent nose and a receding hairline. He said the man had married one of Hazel's friends instead and the couple lived in South Troy. To his knowledge, John did not believe Hazel had had a steady boyfriend since.

The investigators then asked about Hazel's dentist. Mrs. Cary could not recall his name but knew his office was on Third Street. She said that several weeks earlier, after they had finished supper, Hazel asked if she could go to her dentist. Mrs. Cary thought it was a strange time and did not allow her to go. Hazel stayed home and never asked again.

O'Brien and Kaye drove to Fourth Street to ask Julia Drew about Hazel's relationships. Mrs. Drew provided the following account as reported in the July 18, 1908 Troy Record.

> "Hazel to my knowledge, has not had a beau for more than a year," said Mrs. Drew. "I asked her recently, Haven't you got a fellow yet Hazel? And she replied, 'No, I don't care for one. If I got one some other girl would cut me out.' Hazel then referred to her last love affair with a man who stopped calling on her when she became ill with the grip a year ago last spring, and married another girl."

The Troy Daily Press on July 18, 1908 provided some more detail.

> The only other person she ever heard Hazel speak of who proposed marriage was a young man whose name she thought was Wolf.

> He told Hazel that in three years he wanted her to be his wife. According to Mrs. Drew, her daughter did not care for the young man, and said she would never marry him.

The investigators then asked about Hazel's dentist. Mrs. Drew said that Hazel had work done on her teeth a number of times but she did not remember his name.

(II)

Based on Mrs. Cary's recollection that Hazel's dentist had an office on Third Street, The Troy Daily Press announced on July 18, 1908 that,

> All the dentists on that thoroughfare were seen this morning. None of them had any recollection of doing any work

for the girl. Those who had book accounts quickly showed them to the newspaper men. Others where a cash business only is done said the girl might have been to their places, but they had no special remembrance of her.

Perhaps the newspaper men were a hurry to meet their deadlines because there was a dentist on Third Street that did know Hazel. His name was Edward Knauff. Investigators spoke to him on July 18.

Dr. Knauff told the investigators that about two months earlier, on a Thursday night Hazel stopped by his office. She was with a friend who the dentist did not know. Hazel asked if she could make an evening appointment. Dr. Knauff told her that he did not work evenings. She thanked him and left. He didn't know if she went to another dentist or if she never had another opportunity to schedule an appointment but she never returned.

On July 6, Dr. Knauff was in Kerin's store when Lawrence Eagan pointed out the attractive blond woman to Anna O'Donnell.

> Dr. Knauff was in the grocery store on Congress Street on Monday afternoon, July 6, when Lawrence Eagan, a young man employed in the store, was said to have seen Hazel Drew passing. The dentist said today that the girl was not Hazel Drew. "I was in the store a few minutes before 6 o'clock making some purchases when I heard one of the employees say, 'Ain't she a daisy?' referring to a girl who was passing. I glanced at the girl who was blonde, wore glasses and had on a white dress. A few minutes later the same girl boarded an Albia car on which I was going home, and I am positive she was not Hazel Drew." (Troy Record, July 18, 1908)

The detectives went back to Kerin's and re-interviewed Eagan. He said he could not be sure the woman he saw walk by the store was Hazel Drew but based on the photograph he was shown, he thought it was. He also admitted that he was not certain what the time was that he saw her.

(III)

Detectives working in Troy located a woman who claimed to have seen Hazel on the Fourth of July in the city.

> ...District Attorney's Officer Murnane and Detective Lawrenson learned yesterday from a young woman who was well acquainted with Hazel that the latter was on Fulton Street about 4 o'clock in the afternoon of the Fourth and with the company of a woman. The young lady yesterday told the officers she did not speak to Hazel because she was not near enough to be recognized had she spoken. Miss Taylor denies this story, but the officers are not inclined to dismiss it altogether. (The Troy Times, July 17, 1908)

Because they knew that Hazel had been at Union Station on at least three different occasions in the days before her disappearance, the detectives working in Troy returned with the hopes of finding someone who may have seen her there. They were in luck. That Saturday O'Brien announced to the press that he had interviewed a friend of Hazel who had seen her at the depot on July 6.

Mrs. Mary Robinson lived on Bedford Street in Troy not far from where John and Julia lived. She was at Union Station between 11:20 and 11:30 when she saw Hazel. The following exchange between the women was printed in the July 18, 1908 Evening World:

> "Hello Hazel! Where are you going?"
> "Oh just down the river," replied the girl whom she knew well.
> "How far down?"
> "I'm going to New York if I meet..."

At that moment an announcement was made for a train's departure. Hazel excused herself and quickly walked to the ticket counter. Mary did not hear the destination of the departing train but she watched Hazel purchase her ticket then walk down the subway steps to a waiting train. According to the Times Union on July 18, 1908, "(Mary Robinson) said (Hazel) had her suitcase with her and acted as if she was expecting someone." The Troy Times on the same day wrote that Mary Robinson saw Hazel carrying her black gloves.

Union Station, Troy, NY. Hazel abruptly excused herself from her conversation with Mary Robinson to purchase a ticket at the window, left. She then went down the steps on the right to the waiting trains, presumably to go to Albany. Photo taken from Images of America: Troy, by Don Rittner

(IV)

Jarvis O'Brien was working in his office when a man named Peter Cipperley knocked on his door. Cipperley told the District Attorney that on the afternoon of July 7 Hazel was on the train going to Averill Park and she was not alone.

Peter Cipperley was a farmer who lived outside Averill Park at Snyder's Lake. He told the District Attorney that on July 7 he boarded the 3 o'clock train at Albia Station on Pawling Avenue. There was nobody else on the train and he took the second seat. A couple boarded the train right after him and sat in the seat in front of him.

Albia Station. Travelers from Troy would pick up the Troy and New England Rail here to take them to Averill Park. Peter Cipperly saw a couple board the train at this station. The woman, he claimed matched the description of Hazel. Photo from The Troy & New England Railway Co. 1895-1925 by Charles Viens and Sanford Young

As the train pulled out of the station, Cipperley said the girl took out a piece of paper and pointed to something. The young man seemed very interested in what she was saying and showing him. Cipperly said the man was very attentive to the young lady.

Because the woman sat directly in front of him, Cipperly admitted that he did not have a great angle to see her face. The woman had blond hair that she wore in a pompadour style. She was not wearing a hat although she may have been carrying one. Cipperley could not recall what she was wearing.

A train car of the Troy and New England Railway that ran between Albia Station in Troy and Averill Park. Peter Cipperley claimed a woman matching Hazel's description boarded a similar train with a male companion on July 18. Photo taken from A Visit to Old Troy in Pictures and Prose, compiled and edited by H. Irving Moore.

The man with her was tall, slim, and very well dressed. He had a long, thin face, long nose and brown hair with a receding hairline.

O'Brien showed Cipperley Hazel's photograph. He said the woman in the photo looked similar to the woman on the train but not exactly the same. O'Brien noted that the photo was several years old and Hazel's appearance had changed.

(V)

While the investigation continued in Troy, Duncan Kaye, Louis Unser and William Powers made an important discovery in Sand Lake. They recalled that Frank Smith and Rudy Gundrum claimed that on the night they saw Hazel, they first passed Henry Ryemiller and his wife coming up Taborton Mountain. On July 18 Detective Kaye met with the Ryemillers.

Henry Ryemiller told the detective that he and his wife were returning from Troy on the night of July 7. They drove by Crape's Hotel, heading up the mountain to their home in Taborton. Just after they passed the road they called the New Road, they saw Henry Rollman and his wife coming down the mountain. The Ryemillers continued up the mountain, passed some raspberry bushes, and went through the Hollow. They continued past the road to Taylor's farm and eventually went by Teal's pond. A short time later, they passed Smith and Gundrum. They didn't see anybody else on the road. Detective Kaye was curious why they hadn't seen Hazel who was walking up the mountain when Smith and Gundrum passed her in the Hollow. The Ryemillers, after passing the Rollmans should have passed Hazel before the Hollow. Perhaps Henry Rollman and his wife could clear up the confusion.

Later that day William Powers went to the Rollman's house. They lived on the road that led to Glass Lake not far from Conrad Teal's farm. Henry Rollman said that on the night of July 7 he and his wife drove down Taborton Mountain to the village of Averill Park. They went past Taylor's road and about two hundred yards after the Hollow, approached the raspberry bushes. The Troy Record on July 18, 1908 described the encounter that followed.

> On Tuesday night, July 7, (the Rollmans) took the Taborton Road and when at a point about a quarter of a mile west of where Smith and Gundrum saw Hazel they met a girl. Mrs. Rollman glanced at her and incidentally remarked to Mr. Rollman, "Isn't she pretty?" The latter looked closer at the girl and replied that she was. Mrs. Rollman noticed that the girl was well dressed and she noticed her hat particularly. It was large with plumes on it.

> The Rollmans continued on, and the girl remained where they first saw her. She was standing near the side of the road picking raspberries. Mrs. Rollman looked around after they had driven a considerable distance and the girl was still there at the berry bushes. Mrs. Rollman then said to her husband, "My, but that girl is having a good time with those berries."

Henry Rollman commented to his wife, "...she's a fool to be alone on this road. It's a bad place." (The Troy Daily Press, July 18, 1908)

The Rollmans continued towards the village. After the so-called New Road they passed the Ryemillers. Just before reaching Crape's they passed William Hoffey and his wife, Elizabeth. The two couple spoke briefly and the Rollmans continued on to town.

Later that night after they returned home,

> ...the wife said to her husband: "Did you notice her hat?' and he answered, "No, was it a Merry Widow?" The woman replied that it was a black hat with large black plumes, such as she desired to have. (Troy Daily Press, July 18, 1908)

(VI)

The relationship between Hazel and Mina Jones is ambiguous. Either Hazel was closer to Mina than to anybody else and felt comfortable confiding her deepest, most personal secrets or Mina was nothing more than a sounding board for Hazel's fabrications and mistruths. If this was the case then it doesn't appear that Hazel had much respect for Mina which makes her trip to Providence all the more suspect.

Perhaps the opposite was true and Mina was Hazel's closest friend and confidante. Whereas every one of Hazel's friends and relatives in and around Troy stated that Hazel had no steady male companionship for at least a year, Hazel told Mina that she was contemplating an engagement.

What was the truth? Did Hazel's friends and relatives all lie to the authorities to cover-up Hazel's relationships and affairs? Did Mina lie to the authorities about a non-existent proposal? Did Hazel lie to Mina about a serious relationship that never existed? Was Hazel being truthful to Mina but kept secrets from everyone else? Unless Mina made up stories about Hazel's relationship with a dentist, why was Hazel being so secretive? Did this secrecy have anything to do with Minnie Taylor's reluctance to cooperate with the investigation?

Hazel's telling Mina that she was twice attacked is also unusual. Not one of Hazel's close friends or relatives had ever heard and never knew about the assaults. If true, why would Hazel confide this information only to Mina but nobody else? If not, what would be her motive for making up stories about being harassed?

Who was the mysterious man that Hazel asked Mina to mail a postcard to in Hyde Park, Massachusetts? What was the relationship between he and Hazel? Is there a reason that Hazel had her friend mail the postcard and not do it herself?

Hazel's previous engagement confirms the emotional detachment with her parents, neither of whom could recall the name of their daughter's former fiancé. If what her parents said was true, that the engagement ended and Hazel's fiancé married one of her friends instead, it might explain Hazel's recent detachment to men and the reason for her reluctance to enter into relationships. The hurt associated with such a separation is powerful and scars run deep. The embarrassment she must have felt by being passed over and replaced by one of her friends may have been her motivation for either avoiding serious relationships completely, or for keeping a relationship she may have been in private.

Mary Robinson's encounter with Hazel at Union Station provides yet another fixed time in plotting Hazel's movements. It also reveals that Hazel was very active at Union Station. She was seen there as early as 11:20 or 11:30 on July 6, about an hour and a half after she left her aunt.

The timing creates another problem, however. If Hazel boarded a train at 11:30 as Mary Robinson said she did, where could she have gone and been back at Union Station in time to place her order at the Westcott Company at 1:15?

Upon closer inspection, the only train departing Union Station at that time was the 11:30 local to Albany. Albany is "down the river" from Troy, the words Hazel used when Mary Robinson asked where she was going. Hazel added that she may be going as far as New York but that would depend on something that Hazel never finished saying when she left Mary Robinson to purchase her ticket.

If Hazel did catch the 11:30 local, she would have arrived in Albany around 12:00. If she planned to go to New York, she would have barely had enough time to purchase a ticket and catch the train to New

York which left at 12:05. And if going to New York was her intention, why didn't she buy a ticket to New York at Union Station? The evidence shows she didn't because she was back at Union Station before 1:15. With a ticket already purchased to New York, it doesn't make sense for Hazel to have returned to Troy from Albany on the first available train. She did have her suitcase with her which suggests she was prepared to spend the night somewhere. But there would not be enough time in Albany for her to meet whoever it was that she started to tell Mary Robinson about before departing for New York.

If Hazel missed the train to New York or did not meet the person she may have been intending to go to New York with, she could have returned to Troy on the 12:30 train. She would have sufficient time to go to the Westcott Company and place the 1:15 order.

It appears that Hazel's plans had gone awry. If she had planned to go to New York, why didn't she place the order with the Westcott Company before she left for Albany? She had sufficient time. Could Hazel have planned to meet somebody at the Albany station, knowing full well that she would be returning to Troy, with or without that person? Why then did she bring her suitcase? Where did Hazel disappear to after 1:15? To play out the scenario, Hazel traveled to Albany at 11:30 only to return to Troy on the next available train, then disappeared altogether until the next day. Could Hazel have returned to Troy on the 12:30 train with a companion she met in Albany?

If Peter Cipperly was correct and Hazel was on the 3:00 train going to Averill Park, more of the mystery would be cleared up. It would explain how Hazel arrived in the country and that she had a male traveling companion. It may also provide a description of her killer, or at least a person of interest. Between the Albia Station on Pawling Avenue where Peter Cipperley boarded the train and Averill

Park, there were twenty eight stops. Peter Cipperley got off at Snyders Lake, the eighth stop. Hazel and her companion could have gotten off at any one of the next twenty but in all likelihood would have ridden all the way to Averill Park, the end of the line.

However there are so many problems with Cipperly's story that virtually none of it is useful. The train would have arrived in Averill Park at 4:30. Hazel wasn't seen until 7:30. That leaves three full hours for Hazel and her companion to be in the small town. Someone would have seen her there. She and her companion would have gone somewhere. They would have had to walk or been picked up by someone they knew because none of the taxi drivers saw Hazel. She was known in the area, yet no one reported seeing her in the village. If she and her companion did get off at an earlier stop, how did they get to Taborton Road and where did her companion go?

The conductors on the trains were interviewed. According to the Watertown Review on July 18, 1908,

> Conductors on all the trolley cars running to Averill Park have been closely questioned and not one has been found who remembers seeing Hazel on his car. It would have been next to impossible for the girl to have ridden on a trolley and not to have been recognized.

Peter Cipperley stated that there were just the three passengers on the train. The train conductor would most like remember seeing the beautiful woman.

The Rollman's sighting of Hazel on Taborton Road confirmed Smith and Gundrum's story but it also created more mystery. When the Rollmans drove down the mountain, they were ahead of Smith and Gundrum. They passed Hazel standing by the side of the road apparently picking and eating raspberries. Hazel did not appear to be in a hurry to get to her unknown destination and didn't appear to be in any danger.

The Rollmans continued down the mountain and passed the Ryemillers. The Ryemillers came up the mountain, passed the raspberry bushes, traveled through the Hollow and later passed Smith and Gundrum on the other side of Teal's pond. They didn't see Hazel on the road. Smith and Gundrum went down the mountain and crossed paths with Hazel in the Hollow.

Henry Rollman and his wife were approximately 10 minutes in front of Smith and Gundrum. The Ryemillers should have seen Hazel somewhere between the berry bushes and the Hollow, about five minutes after the Rollmans saw her. They did not. About five minutes after Smith and Gundrum passed the Ryemillers they saw Hazel in the Hollow. Why didn't the Ryemillers see her anywhere on the road? Where did she go? Smith and Gundrum and the Rollmans all said they passed William and Elizabeth Hoffey coming up the mountain. Perhaps they could shed some light on Hazel's movements.

When Hazel's autopsy was performed, Dr. Fairweather recorded the contents of Hazel's digestive tract. He said there was a little bit of undigested food. The following was printed in the July 18, 1908 Troy Daily Press.

> Dr. Harry O. Fairweather, who performed the autopsy on the body, said this afternoon that no berries were found in the stomach. If she had been killed that night, they naturally would have been there.

Either Hazel was not eating raspberries when the Rollmans passed her or she died after the berries digested. Based on the condition of the body, Hazel had been in Teal's pond for a very long time, in all likelihood her body was placed there that night. If so, the raspberries could not have digested and Hazel was only pretending to eat them when the Rollmans passed her. But why?

SUNDAY
JULY 19, 1908

"Hazel Drew's slayer, who struck down the pretty girl and then threw her body into the waters of lonesome Teal's Pond it is believed, has been brought nearer to the electric chair by a grilling cross-examination of her aunt by District Attorney O'Brien here to-day. The woman, Minnie Taylor, fought hard against the 'third degree' but finally told the names of the two young men who had accompanied her and the dead girl on many drives shortly before the murder."

The Washington Herald, July 19, 1908

In an attempt to discover what Hazel might have been doing in Sand Lake, John Murnane looked into the possibility that she went there to secure employment. Hazel had enjoyed the previous summer out in the country and Murnane thought that Hazel, now unemployed and low on funds might have gone back to find work. She was seen in the area dressed in her newest and finest clothes. It was reasonable, he assumed that she could have gone back for a job interview.

Assuming that Peter Cipperley had been correct and it was Hazel that he saw riding the train on July 7, she and her companion were intently looking at a piece of paper. The following advertisement was printed in the July 6, 1908 Troy Record:

> Wanted-Girl for general housework to go to Sandlake for summer; references required. Box 21 Record.

Could Hazel have seen the advertisement, pointed it out to her companion on the train, and the couple was going to Sand Lake to secure employment?

There are two problems with this theory. The first is that references were required. Hazel had not asked for a reference from Mrs. Cary before leaving and due to her abrupt departure there was little chance she could count on one. The second problem is that no address was listed in the advertisement, only a Box number. Hazel would have no way of knowing where to go to be interviewed. Hazel's actions as seen in their entirety do not support the theory that she went to Sand Lake to seek employment.

(II)

The July 19 papers reported that Jarvis O'Brien had finally obtained from Minne Taylor, the names of the two men that she and Hazel had gone riding with in Averill Park. O'Brien, Kaye, and Murnane put extensive pressure on the aunt, causing her to become extremely agitated. After revealing their names to the officers, Minnie pleaded with them to keep her friends' identities private and to not drag innocent people into the affair. O'Brien informed the Evening World reporters that his men were on their way to question the two men and arrests were expected.

Jarvis O'Brien apparently kept his promise to Minnie. The names of the two men were never printed in any newspaper. The assumption is they were questioned but what they had to say must not have had any relevance to the murder. O'Brien and his men had encountered yet another dead end, another encouraging lead that went nowhere.

MONDAY
JULY 20, 1908

Troy, NY

"Much has been said about the character of Miss Drew, and one might con-ceive her a Dr. Jekyll and Mr. Hyde girl, but is impossible to believe she wore the mask of goodness at home and cast it aside elsewhere. The proof thus far is that she was a good girl, a church attendant and home early at nights. There is nothing to show she ever had any liaisons. Her trips outside the city can all be explained on the theory of innocent amusement.

The Troy Press, July 20, 1908

For several days Jarvis O'Brien and his detectives had been read-ing the letters that Hazel had stored in her trunk. Those letters provided the names of friends that Hazel had been close to. The detectives had been busy interviewing those friends. Some of the let-ters were reprinted in the July 20 papers and O'Brien discussed the results of the interviews.

Most of the letters were signed with initials. O'Brien was partic-ularly interested in a man from Dedham, Massachusetts who worked at the Sturtevant Blower Works Company and signed his correspon-dence W.C.H. Remembering that Hazel asked Mina Jones to send a letter to a man in Massachusetts who worked for that company, detec-tives were sent to talk to him.

The man's name was William Hogardt. He was 17 years old and for the past six summers had stayed in East Poestenkill, near Sand Lake with relatives named Feathers. The house he stayed in was not far from where the Bly family lived. Hogardt told the detectives he met Hazel along with some of her friends the previous summer at the Post Office in Averill Park. They later met at dances and at parties. He said Hazel was a "nice, quiet, refined girl" and he was deeply saddened by her death.

Hogardt claimed that Hazel and he had written to each other several times over the past year. He kept Hazel's letters and turned them over to the detectives. Hazel had sent the postcards and written her letters in September and November of 1907, then again in January and February of 1908. They were sent from Troy, Schenectady and Providence. The content of the writing was casual and showed no sign of romance or intimacy.

The following were all reprinted in the July 21, 1908 edition of the Troy Press.

Sept. 9, 1907
From Schenectady, Hazel wrote:
"Having a fun time here."

A few days later Hazel sent a postcard from Troy showing Rensselaer Polytechnic Institute (RPI):
"Just a step from where I live."

Other postcards were sent from Troy on November 15, December 2, and December 21- all were signed only H.I.D.

January 8, 1908:

"Owing to illness, was unable to get you a New Year's card. But I wish you a very happy New Year. Thank you for your kind remembrance. I remain H.I.D."

February 3, 1908:

"I received your card. Am taking a few months vacation. I never hear from Gordon. I hope to see the girls soon but I have not seen any of them lately. We are having a very cold winter. I will be up to Poestenkill with Bell this summer. My address at the present time is 400 4th St. Troy, NY H.I.D."

March 7, 1908

"Received your postal. I like my new home very much indeed. It will be very lonely here in the summer. We are having quite cold weather here for this time of year. I never hear from Gordon. H.I.D. Whitman West Troy NY"

The last card Hazel sent from Troy was in early April. The date was unreadable but it was written after Easter. Signed only H.I.D.

The last postcard that William Hogardt received from Hazel was sent on April 22 from Providence, Rhode Island. This, presumably was the card that Hazel asked Mina Jones to mail for her.

William Hogardt did not know why Hazel suddenly stopped writing.

(II)

The Times Record on July 20, 1908 reported:

During Saturday there was another visit made to the Cary residence on Whitman place and a diligent search was made for anything that might possibly be found to aid in the unraveling of the mystery. It was thought that Hazel may have thrown away some letters or postals before she left the employ of the Carys and the result was not fruitless. Refuse that had been thrown away and was ready to be burned was carefully sifted and separated.

The letters and postcards revealed the names of more of Hazel's friends. Among the assorted pieces of correspondence, detectives found a torn piece of paper with the name John Magner and the address 449 Lexington Avenue, New York City. John Magner, they learned, worked as a conductor on the Pullman cars that ran from New York City to Montreal, Canada. His train made stops in Albany and Troy.

An Evening World reporter located John Magner at Union Station. The following interview was printed in the July 20, 1908 edition.

The Pullman car conductor whose name was found among Hazel Drew's effects today told an Evening World reporter that he passed through Troy at 1:25 P.M. the day Hazel Drew was last seen here on his way to Montreal, and that on his return trip the day following he departed at 4:40 P.M.

The conductor was seen at the lunch counter in the Union Station. He denied all knowledge of Hazel Drew.

"How long have you been running through Troy?" he was asked.
"A month."
"Where before?"
"Making trips to the coast."
"Did you run through Troy July 6?"
"Yes I did."
"What time?"
"Got here at 1:25 P.M."
"Meet anybody?"

"No, sir. I didn't."

"Did you stop at Saratoga or Lake George?"

"No, sir. I went through to Montreal and returned next day at 4:40 P.M."

"Did you know Hazel Drew?"

"No sir, nor any other girl in this place."

"Know any of her friends?"

"Never heard of her."

"How was your name and address found among her effects?"

"I cannot explain it."

At the Pullman Company's office, Park avenue and Forty first street, Assistant Superintendent Grant verified the conductor's statement concerning his train runs.

(III)

Detectives pieced together another torn letter found in the pile of papers that Hazel had put in the Cary's cellar to be incinerated. It was reprinted in The Thrice-A-Week on July 22, 1908.

June 20, 1908
Troy, NY

Young Women's Camp, Altamont, NY

I saw your advertisement of a summer boarding place and I enclose stamp for which send me a circular (sic).

Miss Hazel Drew

Hazel received a reply from the camp along with a circular. Altamont is located outside Schenectady, approximately 15 miles west of Troy in the opposite direction of Sand Lake. Detectives wanted to know if Hazel may have spent the night of July 6 there. The camp was run by a Mrs. Christie. When interviewed, she told detectives she never heard of Hazel Drew and allowed the investigators to check the ledger. Hazel was not listed. She did not spend July 6, or any other night at the camp.

(IV)

The July 20, Evening World reported:

> Detectives Powers and Unser, working on the Hazel Drew murder mystery, to-day searched about Taborton for a charcoal burner who dropped into a hotel there on July 7 and in a half-drunken way exclaimed, as near as the hotel man can remember: "Too bad, too bad, but it had to be done."
>
> The man gulped down four glasses of whiskey in rapid succession and then disappeared.

The detectives were informed that the stranger arrived at the hotel around 8:30 on the night of July 7. He told some of the patrons that he had come from Troy which means he would have traveled up Taborton Mountain Road.

(V)

The content of the letters that Hazel wrote to William Hogardt don't reveal a sense of romance. The tone is plutonic, two friends merely keeping in touch. But information can still be obtained from the correspondence.

In Hazel's January 8th postcard she revealed that she had an illness. Based on the timing, this illness was the one that brought her to William Taylor's farm for three weeks.

On February 3 Hazel revealed that she was planning to take a few months vacation. Because she posted her parents' Fourth Street address, the Tuppers must have terminated her employment but she had not yet begun to work for the Cary's. At the same time, she informed Hogardt that she was planning to spend the summer in Poestenkill.

Based on her March 7 letter, Hazel had secured employment with the Cary's and wrote that she was happy but accepted the fact that she would be staying in Troy for the summer and would not be visiting Poestenkill as she had previously hoped.

The February 3 and March 7 letters refer to a Gordon. Hogardt told the investigators that the young man was Gordon Hull, one of their friends who lived in Sand Lake. Investigators interviewed Gordon Hull and eliminated him as a suspect.

Hazel and Hogardt were very consistent with their letters to each other. They began corresponding in September 1907 and continued until the following April when Hazel, for some reason, abruptly stopped writing. Something may have occurred in her life at that time that caused her to refocus her energies. She could have been distracted by romance. But why did Hazel keep Hogardt's letters when so many others were earmarked for incineration? Why was she keeping some people in her life and discarding others?

The discovery of John Magner's address presents another mysterious facet to an already complex case. Magner claimed he never met Hazel and did not know who she was. Why, then did Hazel have his name and address among her belongings? Could he have been the reason for her two trips to New York?

Hazel spent a lot of time at Union Station on July 6 and 7. Based on Mary Robinson's statement, it is possible that Hazel took a train to Albany on July 6. John Magner's train came through both stations on those days. Could Hazel have been planning to meet him?

After talking with Mary Robinson, Hazel presumably boarded the 11:30 train bound for Albany. She would have arrived about noon. John Magner, traveling north on his way to Montreal, would have reached the Albany depot at 12:25. Whereas it is possible the two met at the Albany station, the timing makes it unlikely. Hazel was back in Troy in time to place her order with the Westcott Company at 1:15. That means she would have had to have been on the 12:30 train back to Union Station. She could not have boarded John Magner's train because it did not arrive at Union Station until 1:25, ten minutes after Hazel placed her order. It would not make sense for Hazel to take the train to Albany to meet John Magner if she knew he would be coming through Union Station a short time later.

If Hazel did meet Magner at Union Station at 1:25, she could have boarded his train for the trip to Montreal. The problem, though is the return. Magner's train went to Montreal and returned to Union Station on July 7 at 4:40 in the afternoon. Hazel checked her suitcase at 1:49 on that day.

Based on the established times, although Hazel and Magner were in the same places around the same time, they could not have spent any time together. The question still remains how did Hazel get Magner's name and address and why did she have them?

Like many promising leads, the Altamont Camp request proved to be of little value. The timing however, may be significant. Hazel's letter requesting information on the camp was dated June 20, 1908, just two weeks before Hazel's Fourth of July debacle. It appears that Hazel was already preparing to spend time in a summer boarding place but not in Sand Lake. Altamont is approximately thirty miles from Sand Lake. In Hazel's February 3 letter to William Hogardt she said she was planning to spend the summer in Poestenkill. Something caused her to change her mind. How long was she planning to stay in Altamont? Had she already decided to leave the Cary's? How would she be able to afford it?

Criminologist Confounded

Another story has been advanced by a so-called criminologist, that the girl was strangled to death by the use of a small pink ribbon a quarter of an inch wide, which was interlaced through the top of a corset cover. District Attorney O'Brien scoffed at this theory and further declared that in his opinion Dr. Boyce, one of the doctors to whom this theory is ascribed by the criminologist, would not substantiate any such story on the witness stand. At the request of the newspaper men, the clothing taken from the body was spread this morning on the floor of the district attorney's office and every piece carefully examined. The pink ribbon was intact, except where the corset cover had been cut to get it off. It was not and could not have been knotted about the neck. That it was tight about the neck was wholly due to the swollen condition of that part of the body. The protruding tongue and eyes, the district attorney was satisfied, were the result of gases from the body. (The Troy Press, July 20, 1908)

William Clemens, the "so-called criminologist" from New York made his first controversial statement by supporting Dr. Boyce's unlikely assumption that the ribbon found tied around Hazel's neck came from her corset. This would not be the last time that Jarvis O'Brien would have to contend with William Clemens' public statements in the press.

TUESDAY
JULY 21, 1908

Taborton, NY

"Hazel Drew's slayer has not been found. She was last seen on the road to Taborton about a mile and a half beyond Chris Crape's hotel Tuesday evening July 7. Her body was taken from the old mill pond Saturday afternoon, July 11. These are the only facts so far established in the hunt for her murderer."

The Troy Record July 21, 1908

The papers on July 21 announced yet another potential breakthrough in the case. Investigators found and interviewed William and Elizabeth Hoffey who were on Taborton Road the night Hazel was last seen alive. The couple claimed that as they drove past Teal's pond they saw two men who were acting very strangely.

The Hoffeys lived on Taborton Road about three miles past Teal's pond. They were returning from Troy on the evening of July 7. Soon after they turned onto Taborton Road by Crape's Hotel they passed Henry Rollman and his wife. Henry called out to them saying he did not recognize their horse. The Hoffeys usually had a black horse but on this evening they were breaking in a colt.

After a brief conversation, the Hoffeys continued up the mountain, eventually passing the raspberry bushes. They continued a short distance and passed through a grove of chestnut trees. Frank Smith and Rudy Gundrum approached from the opposite direction. They nodded at the two men as they passed and continued on through the Hollow then passed the turn to Taylor's farm. When they arrived at the road leading to Glass Lake, William climbed down from the wagon to give the colt a break. He continued on foot and Elizabeth took the reins.

The Hoffeys said they reached Teal's pond between 7:30 and 8:00. As they approached, they saw a man sitting in a wagon, tightly clenching the reins. The wagon had light colored wheels and a dark box seat. It was parked on the side of the road, facing down the mountain. William thought the rig came from a livery stable and was more conducive for use in a city. The horse had a dark tail and a mane that was bobbed. The man attempted to pull to the side of the road to give the Hoffeys more room to pass. Mrs. Hoffey told investigators she saw something in the back of the the wagon. It was not a bundle but she didn't know what it was.

A description of the man was printed in the July 21, 1908 Troy Times.

> ...the man in the wagon wore a straw hat. As to the color of the clothing, Mr. and Mrs. Hoffey do not remember very well. They agree that his complexion was light, that he was slender in build, and might have been five foot six or seven inches in height. Mr. Hoffey was not sure about the moustache, but Mrs. Hoffey thought he had one and that it was light colored.

The New York Times on July 21 added that he had light hair and was about twenty five years old.

As the Hoffeys continued past the wagon, Elizabeth motioned to her husband to look across the pond. William looked and saw a man standing in the water by the dam, brushing back some high weeds. He appeared to be looking for something. Due to the fading light William could not get a good look at the person but he was sure it was a man and that he wore a light colored shirt and a straw hat.

The Hoffeys continued past the pond and waved to Gilbert Miller who was out doing chores. They continued to the top of the mountain then began the drive down. They arrived home around 9:00.

The detectives realized the importance of the two men the Hoffey's saw around the time they believe Hazel was murdered. They now had a potentially vital lead and a possible description of the killers.

Based on the Hoffey's description of the horse and rig, detectives visited every livery stable in Albany, Troy and places in between. They had a description of the horse, the wagon and of the person driving it. William Powers thought he made a breakthrough when he found a potential match. The story was printed in the July 21, 1908 Evening Telegram.

> Chief Detective Powers roused a young man living in Troy out of bed and made him explain where he had been on Tuesday night with a livery stable rig answering the description given by Hoffey even to the color of the horse and his mane and tail. The man frankly admitted that he had been to Sand Lake, but said he had gone no nearer to Teal's Pond than the road that turns off by Crape's hotel.

> This is about a mile and a half from the pond. The man said he had been out riding with a young woman whose name he gave. His story is being investigated. The carriage was returned to the livery stable at half-past ten o'clock Tuesday night.

The following day another potential lead based on the Hoffey sighting was investigated. The story was written in the July 22, 1908 Troy Press.

The hiring of a rig at William T. Shyne's livery has been thoroughly explained. It had nothing to do with the mysterious death of the Drew girl. The facts are that Fred W. Schatzle, embalmer for the undertaker Thomas H. Neulon telephoned to the livery Monday night, July 6 for a horse and carriage for a friend William Cushing, the Republican committeeman for the eleventh ward. Mr. Cushing and a young woman went driving the following night. They were at Sandlake, but not in the vicinity of Teal Pond.

(II)

Investigators wanted to find out more about John Magner and asked Minnie Taylor if Hazel had ever mentioned a train conductor. Minnie said she had a faint recollection that Hazel did mention a conductor that she met on the train on one of her New York vacations. She said he was very nice to her and Hazel referred to him as her conductor friend.

Minnie said that when Hazel arrived in New York she called on the conductor at his residence but the conductor didn't have time to show her around. Minnie told the investigators that when Hazel recounted the story to her, she spoke in the plural saying such things as "we" called on a conductor, that he was glad to see "us" but wouldn't be able to show show "us" the sights because he had to get up early the next morning for an early train run.

Magner had previously told an Evening World reporter that he never met Hazel or any other woman in Union Station. His statement was contradicted by George Peterson who managed the Westcott Express Company and William Harper who worked in the baggage area of Union Station. Both men told detectives that John Magner was in the habit of meeting a young woman at Union Station who, they said bore a resemblance to Hazel.

Armed with this information, John Lawrenson and John Murnane re-interviewed Magner. The conductor confessed that he did meet a young woman at the station but was adamant that it was not Hazel. He said he didn't know Hazel, had never met her and until he read about the affair in the papers he never even heard of her.

(III)

When investigators searched through the contents of Hazel's trunk they discovered a photograph of an unidentified man, well proportioned and not more than twenty one years old. He had a smooth, short, round face, heavy light colored hair and prominent features. The picture was taken in a studio in Troy. The detectives spent several days trying to identify and then locate the man that Hazel must have liked enough to have kept his photograph.

Investigators also looked into a letter that Mina Jones wrote to Hazel on June 12, 1908. Mina was venting about her life in Waterville, Maine and the absence of her husband, Frank who was staying in Troy. Mina asked Hazel to find Frank and remind him not to forget his wife in Waterville.

The detectives were curious why Frank was in Troy. They paid Mina another visit to find out. In the course of their discussion Mina produced a letter she had just received from Minnie Taylor dated July 16, 1908, five days after Hazel's body was discovered. In the letter, Minnie asked Mina to please destroy all correspondence that Hazel had written her.

(IV)

Trying to track Hazel's movements along Taborton Road the night of July 7 is, of course, an inexact science and much is left to speculation. It is nearly impossible to get from the witnesses an exact time when Hazel was seen. However it is an important element in researching the tragedy to determine approximately how far up the mountain Hazel was able to go before she was murdered. Based on the Rollman and the Smith and Gundrum sightings, compared with the times and places that the Ryemillers and Hoffeys passed them, it is possible to figure out approximately where Hazel was on the road when she was seen and where she should have been when she wasn't. It also allows the researcher to examine other possible avenues Hazel may have taken to get to her unknown destination.

Henry Rollman and his wife were the first known people to pass Hazel on the road that night. They said she was standing by a patch of raspberry bushes between 7:00 and 8:00 as near as they could tell.

The raspberry bushes were approximately one quarter of a mile from the Hollow where Smith and Gundrum would later pass Hazel (New York Times, July 18, 1908). So when she was seen by the Rollmans, Hazel had already passed the so-called New Road and was almost halfway between Crape's Hotel and the turn to Taylor's farm.

The Rollmans continued down the mountain and passed the Ryemillers near the New Road which was about a quarter of a mile from Crape's hotel (Troy Daily Press July 27,1908).

The Ryemillers went up Taborton Road and did not encounter anybody until they passed Rudy Gundrum and Frank Smith on the Taborton side of Teal's pond.

Smith and Gundrum confirmed that they rode past the Ryemillers near the top of the mountain. Smith had just left the Brown's farm. He looked at his watch. It was 7:11. Smith and Gundrum continued down the mountain, drove past the turn to Taylor's farm and met Hazel in the Hollow.

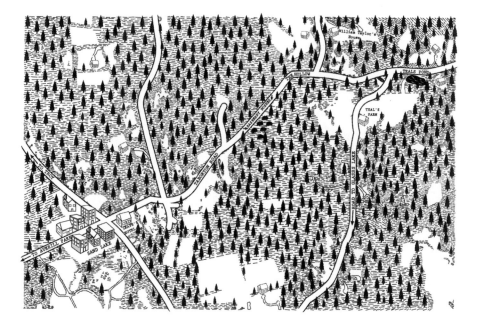

Map by Mikhail Vainblat

Hazel would have traveled approximately one quarter of a mile between the time that the Rollmans saw her at the raspberry bushes and Smith and Gundrum saw her in the Hollow. It was within that quarter of a mile that the Ryemillers should have seen Hazel, but didn't.

Depending on her exact location, the Ryemillers would have travelled between a half and three quarters of a mile after passing where Hazel should have been when they passed Smith and Gundrum. Smith and Gundrum traveled approximately a half mile from that point before passing Hazel in the Hollow. The approximate time was 7:20-7:30. Whereas it is true that both the Ryemillers and Smith and

Gundrum were riding in carriages and Hazel was on foot, they still travelled a combined mile to a mile and one quarter before Hazel travelled one quarter of a mile on her own.

Smith Gundrum continued through the Hollow and passed the Hoffeys near a grove of chestnut trees. The grove was in the same general area as the raspberry bushes, approximately one quarter of a mile from the Hollow.

The Ryemillers were making better time than the Hoffeys. From the time they passed the Rollmans to the time they passed Smith and Gundrum, the Ryemillers travelled approximately one mile. From the time the Hoffeys passed the Rollmans to the time they passed Smith and Gundrum they travelled approximately one half mile.

The Hoffeys continued up Taborton Road and saw the two men and the wagon near Teal's pond. They did not see Hazel. Perhaps the biggest mystery and most important missing piece is what happened to Hazel after she passed Smith and Gundrum?

Although it is possible that she made the left turn and headed towards her uncle's farm, it is unlikely based on the testimonies of William Taylor, Frank Richmond, his wife.

> William Taylor said he sat in a rocking chair smoking on the night of Tuesday, July 7. He did not leave the house and went to bed around 9 o'clock. Hazel did not call at the house and he did not know she had been met on the road until the next morning when Richmond told him. (Troy Record July 28)

> Frank Richmond, who works on the William Taylor farm, said he left the house between 15 and 20 minutes after 8 o'clock the Tuesday night Hazel was last seen alive, and with his wife walked to Averill Park, reaching the station about 9 o'clock. He walked over the Taborton road to Crape's hotel and then across the flats. He did not meet anybody on the road. (The Troy Daily Press, July 28, 1908)

> Mrs. Richmond fully corroborated the story of her husband. She declared positively that Hazel was never at the house while she was there. (The Troy Daily Press, July 28, 1908)

Frank Richmond, his wife and William Taylor were all at the farm when Hazel would have arrived if she was going there. Taylor claimed he was on his porch and never saw his niece. Mr. and Mrs. Richmond left the house, went down the road and turned right onto Taborton Road. They never saw Hazel. Based on these statements, it is not likely that Hazel was on the road to Taylor's farm that night.

After Hazel left Smith and Gundrum, she continued up the mountain and went past the road that led to her uncle's farm. She was not going at a very fast pace but neither were the Hoffeys who were coming up the road behind her. One of five possible scenarios would have happened.

The first is that Hazel, for some reason ducked into the woods before the Ryemillers and then the Hoffeys went past.

The second possibility is that Hazel encountered the person or persons who murdered her. The timing would have been right and would explain why the Hoffeys did not see her, but would not explain why the Ryemilers didn't.

The third possibility is that Hazel met with someone who gave her a ride. The wagon or car could have come from the road that Taylor's farm was on. It would have had to have come after Smith and Gundrum passed the road but before the Hoffeys reached it. The person driving the vehicle may or may not have been the murderer.

The fourth possibility is that Hazel continued on foot and went past Teal's pond. At some point, before the Hoffeys caught up with her, she either arrived at her destination, was murdered, or both.

The final possibility is that Hazel continued on foot and went down the road that leads to Glass Lake, the road that the Teal's farmhouse was on. Hazel may have had enough of a head start to have reached the road before the Hoffeys had a chance to catch up with her. No other witnesses came from that road so it could explain why no one reported seeing her including Gilbert Miller who was out doing chores.

(V)

There is no doubt that Elizabeth and William Hoffey were on Taborton Road the night Hazel was last seen. Their presence was confirmed by the Rollmans and by Smith and Gundrum. What is remarkable is that the Hoffeys, like the Ryemillers, never saw Hazel on the road that night. When looked at wholistically, the two groups traveling down the mountain, the Rollmans and Frank Smith with Rudy Gundrum both saw Hazel. They all said she was casually strolling up the mountain, carrying her hat. At the same time, neither of the two families traveling up the mountain, the Ryemillers nor the Hoffeys reported seeing Hazel. The Rollmans saw Hazel at the raspberry bushes and later they passed the Ryemillers. The Ryemillers did not see Hazel but later passed Smith and Gundrum. Smith and Gundrum passed Hazel in the Hollow and later passed the Hoffeys. The Hoffeys never saw Hazel. So where did she go? Jarvis O'Brien had a theory that was printed in The Troy Times on July 21, 1908.

> Another theory that District Attorney O'Brien believes of some importance is that Hazel may have had a companion along the road that Tuesday night when she was seen by Smith and Gunderman and the others. They all agreed that she was loitering along the road, and some say she was picking berries. The idea is that her friend may have stepped into the bushes to avoid the gaze of the passersby.

The wagon parked alongside Teal's pond also raised questions. Why were the Hoffeys the only ones who saw it? Where did it come from? What were the two men doing? Were they somehow involved with Hazel's death? Why didn't the two men come forward and talk to investigators? Could the Hoffeys have seen the two men who murdered Hazel? They were at the pond around the time Hazel would have been if she made it that far up the mountain.

The two men could be the killers but the timing would have had to have been miraculous. Based on where the Hoffeys passed Smith and Gundrum they could not have been more than two or three minutes behind Hazel. Hazel would not have been able to get to Teal's pond in that short amount of time. When the Hoffeys saw the men at the pond, the wagon was facing down the hill and one of the two men was on the other side of the pond. That would not leave much time for the two men to come across the young woman on the road, accost and murder her get up the hill turn the wagon around, and one of them get to the other side and dump Hazel's body in the water. In all likelihood Hazel would have struggled. This would have taken more time. Her clothing and body revealed no evidence of a struggle. Unless she was killed immediately she would have screamed, yet no one around heard a woman scream, not Frank Smith, Rudy Gundrum, Gilbert Miller, or the Hoffeys.

So if they weren't the killers, what were the two men doing at the pond? The answer may be very simple and innocent. They could have been there catching live bait. The area was known for its good fishing spots. In fact, Rudy Gundrum was on his way to town that night to pick up two friends to take them fishing.

Conrad Teal said that people used to come to his door and ask if they could catch bait fish in his pond and he would always allow it. Some of the people would catch bait for their own use and others would sell it to tourists. Teal claimed he stopped allowing people to use his pond after New York passed a bait tax. If the two men were catching bait in Conrad Teal's pond they were doing so without his knowledge or his permission.

This may explain why the two men never came forward. Detectives were combing the area looking for a murderer. If the two men were caught avoiding a tax they probably thought they would be fined. It was much easier for them to remain anonymous.

William Hoffey thought the wagon looked like it came from a livery and was the kind commonly used in cities. This was why William Powers and the other detectives were checking the livery stables in Troy. Hoffey said the man in the wagon held the reins tightly. He appeared to be either nervous or inexperienced which suggests that the two men, or at least the driver, was not comfortable handling the rig. This implies that the driver was not from the country and thus not local.

The wagon was facing down the hill. If they came up the mountain and turned the rig around, they would have been seen by the Rollmans or by Smith and Gundrum. They could have come from the direction of Taborton. There are two large ponds there, Big Bowman Pond and Little Bowman Pond, both were popular places for fishing. If the two out of town men were staying in Taborton, intent on fishing there, were told of the baitfish available in Teal's pond, they could have gone to catch bait without getting Conrad Teal's permission. This would make them strangers, trespassing on Teal's property, stealing the bait and avoiding a tax. In the scope of the investigation these are minor but to the two men the reality of their actions could have made them anxious and unwilling to talk to authorities.

The problem with the scenario is that the Ryemillers, who were ahead of the Hoffeys, would have passed the two men on the road if they came from the direction of Taborton. They did not. The Ryemillers stated more than once that the only people they saw on the road that night were the Rollmans and Smith and Gundrum.

The only other possibility is that the two men reached Taborton Road by taking either the road that William Taylor's farm was on or, more likely, the road that led up from Glass Lake. They would have had to arrive on Taborton Road after the Ryemillers passed going up the mountain and after Smith and Gundrum passed going down. The timing would have had to have been precise and makes it likely that depending on Hazel's destination, the two unidentified men would have seen Hazel on the road.

John Magner apparently lied to the Evening World reporter when he said he didn't meet any women at Union Station. The question is why he lied? Was it simply a defense mechanism, hoping that the reporter would not dig any further or that the truth would not be discovered? Could it be that his meetings were more intimate and he wanted to protect the identity or the reputation of the girl he met? If he lied about meeting the girl could he have lied when he said he never met Hazel?

If Minnie Taylor is to be believed, then Hazel met a conductor on the train while traveling to New York. Minnie said Hazel went to his home but he didn't have time to show her around. The address that Hazel had in her trunk was Magner's, a conductor who stayed in New York City. The evidence is too strong to assume it is a mere coincidence, and it does support Minnie's statement. But Minnie told investigators that Hazel spoke in the plural. Who was the other person who accompanied Hazel to New York?

Carrie Weaver is the only person known to have gone to New York with Hazel. But Carrie claimed they didn't meet anybody while they were there. This means that either Carrie was not telling the truth or Hazel visited the conductor's home with some other person.

If what Minnie said was true and Hazel met the conductor on the train and he gave her his address at that time, the person who accompanied Hazel could not have been Carrie because she and Hazel took a boat to New York. Also, if the conductor gave Hazel his address on the train, he would not likely have turned her away when she went to his boarding house.

So if Hazel did go to the conductor's apartment as stated by Minnie Taylor but not verified by anyone else, she either went on her first trip to New York or she did not get the address on the train, but at some other point. But to keep this in perspective, if Hazel did in fact go to Magner's apartment as Minnie stated, it is completely out of character from what every other person who knew Hazel said about her. Perhaps it was Hazel's companion who was seeking John Magner and Hazel was merely tagging along.

The woman that Magner met in Union Station was Anna LaBelle who knew Hazel, although to what extent is debated. Anna worked at the lace counter at Frear's Department Store in Troy. The following possible explanation was printed in the Troy Times on July 23, 1908.

> The conductor story is now susceptible of a complete explanation. A young lady living on Third Street and employed in one of the department stores in this city knew Magner and was accustomed to meet him when his train came into the station. Several times they met for a short talk. He admits it and so does she. The girl was a friend of Hazel Drew, and one time when the latter was going to New York the former gave her Magner's name and address and told Hazel to go to his home and surprise him. She went there, but he was away on his train. It was in that manner Hazel obtained Magner's address. She had thrown the slip into a waste paper receptacle, where it was found in searching for clews.

Anna LaBelle admitted to knowing Hazel but said she only knew her casually. According to LaBelle, Hazel would sometimes go to the department store where Anna worked but the two did not meet socially. The following account was printed in the June 22, 1908 Albany Times Union.

> A Times Union reporter called on Miss La Belle at her place of employment, she being a clerk in a dry goods store but when questioned became embarrassed and asked to have the interview occur at her home. The reporter went there and surrounded by her family Miss La Belle easily denied having any knowledge of Hazel other than having met her in the store. However, she showed that she did know quite considerable about her (sic) for when informed of the new discoveries she indignantly defended the memory of the girl and said she wouldn't believe it. She advanced no information and said she couldn't understand how it was that Hazel had the name and the address of Magner.

That Hazel had Magner's address cannot be disputed. What remains a mystery is how she obtained the address, why she had it, and if she acted upon it. If Magner gave Hazel his address it must have been because he was interested in her. The two apparently did not get together either time she was in New York and there is no evidence that they ever met in Troy. The fact that Hazel threw the address in the trash indicates that she had no interest in Magner.

Hazel's friends and family were unanimous in vouching for her character. Not a single person even insinuated that Hazel was the type of girl that would casually meet a stranger and go to his apartment. So if Magner did give Hazel his address, it does not make sense that she would have acted on it. It would have been more likely that she would have politely accepted the address then discarded it soon after. This may have been what happened. But Hazel traveled to New York in early May. She went there again with Carrie Weaver at the end of May. The slip of paper containing Magner's address was not discarded until early July. Therefore, it is unlikely that Magner was the person who gave the address to Hazel.

It is more likely that Anna LaBelle was the one who gave Hazel the address. She and Magner met on a regular basis in Troy. How serious that relationship was is unknown. If Anna knew that Hazel was going to New York, as a joke she may have asked Hazel to knock on Magner's door just to tell him that Anna said hello. That would give them all something to talk about and laugh about later.

Another possible explanation is that LaBelle was the one who accompanied Hazel on her first trip to New York. Magner and LaBelle both admitted that they knew each other and had, at the very least, a flirtatious relationship. While in New York ,LaBelle, perhaps by design, could have arranged to meet Magner at his boarding house. Somehow Hazel was in possession of the address and later, while sorting through her belongings at the Cary's, came upon it and put it with other items to be incinerated. Although LaBelle denied being close to Hazel, it appears that she was quick to defend Hazel's character against certain allegations.

LaBelle was interviewed by the Times Union reporter in front of her family. Perhaps she did not want them to know about the depth of her relationship with Magner. Perhaps she did not want to reveal to thousands of readers her affair with the train conductor. Anna LaBelle had sufficient reason to distance herself from Hazel and not be forthright with reporters.

The man in the photograph found in Hazel's trunk was identified as Fred W. Schlafflin. He worked as a packer in Albany. He met Hazel three years earlier at the skating rink at Rensselaer Park in Troy.

Schlafflin was with a friend and so was Hazel. The two spent the rest of the day together at the park and she allowed him to call on her. They went out several times and went to church together. Schlafflin said he enjoyed her company, that she was always a lady and he treated her as such. He hadn't seen Hazel in a couple of years. The relationship, he said just faded for no apparent reason. He said he must have given her his photograph although he didn't remember doing so.

Hazel's relationship with Fred Schlafflin was innocent. Although it shows that Hazel did have a penchant for meeting men it also shows she followed the rules of dating that were in place at that time. She allowed him to call on her and at least part of their relationship centered around church. Why she kept Schlafflin's photograph years later is unknown. The fact that the relationship simply ended without an explanation is consistent with Hazel's relationships with William Hogardt and Edward LaVoie.

Mina Jones' husband, Frank had been in Troy for about a month and a half and apparently was not keeping in contact with his wife in Maine. He was employed as a laborer at the Fuller and Warren Stove Works and boarded with Mrs. Martha Fuller on First Street. Mrs. Fuller said he never went out at night and spent most evenings reading. On July 3 Frank told Mrs. Fuller he was going to Boston to spend the Fourth of July. He was expected back on the sixth but never returned. Letters from Mina Jones after July 6 however, refer to her husband being with her in Waterville.

Minnie Taylor's request to Mina to destroy Hazel's letters is suspicious yet consistent with Minnie's actions. From the very beginning Minnie never fully cooperated with the investigation. She stated that once people's names were dragged into the papers their reputations suffered and their lives were changed for the worse. She did not want to be responsible for disrupting the lives of her friends.

If this was truly the reason that Minnie refused to assist the detectives, it is difficult to understand her priorities. Her niece who she was supposedly very close to was brutally murdered. Rather than help the authorities catch the person responsible, Minnie felt it was more important to protect the reputations of her friends.

Minnie appeared closer to Hazel than probably any other relative. She claimed she and Hazel met several times a week and the two spent the last weekend of Hazel's life together. If Hazel was keeping some secret it can assumed that she would have confided in her aunt. This, of course is only speculation but also a possible explanation why Minnie wanted Mina to destroy those letters. The question left to be asked is what secret could Hazel have had that may have led to her death and a possible cover-up by her aunt?

WEDNESDAY
JULY 22, 1908

Troy, New York

"The authorities are practically without a single clue to fasten the crime to any individual."

The New York Times July 22, 1908

The July 22 papers announced that Detective Lawrenson and Officer Murnane found another credible witness in Troy who saw Hazel at Union Station. The woman, Jeanette Marcellus was in the station on July 7 between one and two o'clock. She was waiting for a friend to arrive on the 1:45 train from Schaghticoke, NY. Marcellus, who was a friend of Hazel, saw her in the waiting room. She called, "Hello, Hazel" and Hazel returned the greeting. A short time later, Marcellus went into the ladies room and saw Hazel looking in the mirror, adjusting her hat and fixing her hair. Hazel was wearing a black skirt, white waist, and fancy black hat presumably the one with the plumes. She did not have her suitcase with her.

(II)

Investigators continued to pour over the letters and postcards that Hazel had stashed in her trunk and the ones she set aside to be incinerated. One letter in particular caught their attention. From it they learned that Hazel, in addition to staying with the Bly family the previous summer, also spent a week with the family of John Link at Snyder's Lake. While staying there Hazel met a man, apparently an artist who made of sketch of her. The letter, sent from Albany, was published in The Thrice-A-Week World on July 22, 1908.

To my lady of the blond hair:

I am taking the great liberty in addressing this letter to you, my lady, but considering what a pleasant time you afforded us I cannot help but express our deepest sympathy for the loss of your glasses. We feel that we were partly to blame for had we not been as forward in our actions you probably would not have been in our boat. Still I do not wish you to have the impression that we are heartless flirts even though we have come from the city. We noticed that you were somewhat agitated upon leaving the car, and we have thought it was because he and I have made such a peculiar appearance and as though you were ashamed of us. If we had suspected that we were to meet such charming young ladies we would have dressed accordingly. I trust that your wrists are not injured for I could not forgive myself if I had caused even the slightest bruise. T'is true that I had to use force on some occasions, but I tried not to be rough or rude in my actions. My friend and I have more mental than physical work in our business and a week's outing in your and your friend's company is worth more than a month in the mountains.

It is very possible that a pretty girl like you has many admirers and you understandably have a preference among them. I shall always remember the happy scene enacted on Snyder's Lake and dream of my lady of the blond hair. I have sketched your face and shoulders and I cannot get the proper expression of your eyes as they looked to me while you were holding my hands on the beach. I hope you will forgive me for taking possession of your napkin but I really had to take something as a souvenir.

It seems strange to me that we should both take to you more than to your girl friends but somehow you seemed to belong to a higher sphere, and considerably more sensible, modern, and have more pleasing ways. If we send postals we shall expect others in return. 'If Knighthood were in Flower I should live only for and have fond clinging memories of my lady of the blond hair and be faithful unto death under the names of your
KNIGHT OF THE NAPP KIN AND YOUR ARTIST FRIEND HARRY

(III)

The relationship between Hazel and her "Knight of the Napp Kinn" may or may not have been little more than a flirtatious teenage rite of passage. There was another couple seen in Averill Park that summer that definitely caught the attention of many of the local residents. The man, whose name was reported to officials but never printed in the papers, was an insurance agent who may also have dealt in real estate. He frequented the finer establishments in the area and was seen driving around with a very attractive, unidentified blond woman.

Following the discovery of Hazel's body on July 11, witnesses claim the man showed more than a usual interest in the case. He left the area and wasn't seen for three days when he appeared in Utica, New York. He made so many inquiries at the Utica newspaper offices about the progress of the Hazel Drew case that they became annoyed and contacted the local police. The police couldn't arrest the man but they reportedly placed him under surveillance.

(IV)

William Taylor's credibility was challenged when John Abel, a local hackman in Averill Park, claimed he drove Hazel and another woman from the train station to Taylor's farm in early April. Taylor had repeatedly told investigators that he had not seen his niece since the first week in February when she left after recuperating from her illness.

Abel was adamant. He claimed he knew Hazel and had driven her to Taylor's farm in the past, including the time in January when Hazel was ill. He said he remembered picking up the two girls during the first week of April. He remembered the date, he claimed, because it was the first time he used the new wagon. He told the women that he would charge them one dollar (approximately $25 in today's currency) to take them to Taylor's farm. One of them said they only had seventy five cents (approximately $19) and asked if Abel would take them anyway. He said he agreed.

The station agent, A.C. Hogoboom corroborated Abel's story. He remembered talking about the two girls and even recalled that one of them wore a blue dress, the other wore brown.

Armed with this new accusation detectives went back to Taylor's farm to confront the eccentric uncle. Try as they may Taylor steadfastly stuck to his original story that he had not seen Hazel in over five months.

John Abel told investigators that on the night of July 7 he was at the train station waiting to take customers to their destinations. He recalled seeing a young, attractive women get off the 7:00 train. She walked very quickly in the direction of Crape's Hotel.

(V)

Jarvis O'Brien was in a bind. The investigation had been going on for more than a week and he was meeting with one disappointment after another. He still had no motive for Hazel's murder and no suspect. The story had made national news and the pressure was mounting to find the killer.

For O'Brien, the details of Hazel's movements during her last few days were becoming a distraction. Every potential lead turned out to have a reasonable explanation. There were blank spaces in Hazel's movements and who she may have seen, but O'Brien realized that he needed to take a different approach. If he simply concentrated on Hazel's last few minutes, maybe he could work backward and fill in the missing pieces. By doing so he hoped to find the motive.

Based on scores of interviews and the physical evidence available, O'Brien theorized that Hazel was out walking alone on the isolated road. She came upon one or more deranged people who attacked her. Try as she may she was unable to fend him or them off and she died in an unsuccessful attempt to save her honor. She was murdered after being violated.

Having a theory is one thing, being able to prove it is another. The doctors who performed the autopsy, to O'Brien's frustration and disappointment, were not unanimous in their findings. To make matters worse, the Evening World had exposed and exploited the doctor's differences of opinion and presented it to the public as incompetence. O'Brien knew he had to talk to the doctors. He had to be confident that the autopsy was credible. The time had come for a final decision. He had to know, beyond a reasonable doubt, exactly how Hazel died and if she was the victim of a sexual assault. If there was even the slightest possibility that errors had occurred in the autopsy, O'Brien had the authority to disinter Hazel's body to conduct a more thorough examination and he was prepared to do it.

The meeting was held at the home of Dr. Reichard in Averill Park. In attendance were Jarvis O'Brien, Duncan Kaye, Morris Strope, Harry Fairweather, Elmer Reichard and Elais Boyce. The meeting was held behind closed doors and lasted for over an hour. When it was over O'Brien addressed the reporters who were anxiously waiting outside.

The reporters wanted to know the reason for the conference. O'Brien told them, as quoted in the Troy Times on July 22, 1908, that "he had not talked with the doctor's collectively since the autopsy and he desired to question them relative to the condition of the body and the cause of death and gain any other information that might be of help in solving the mystery."

O'Brien's answers to the reporter's questions were printed in the Troy Record on July 23, 1908.

> "Will the body be exhumed?" he was asked and he replied, "No."
> "Why not?"
> "Because there is no reason for it."
> "Who says so?"
> "The doctors."
> "Wouldn't it help to solve the cause of the girl's death?"
> "The doctor's say it will add nothing to the result of the autopsy as to detail."
> "Do the doctors still maintain it was murder?"
> "They say that life was extinct before the body was thrown or fell into the water."
> "How about the wound on the back of the head; how was that caused; did they say?"
> "No."

The District Attorney told the reporters that, beyond any doubt Hazel was killed by the blow to the back of her head, it was not a case of suicide. She died instantly and was placed in the water after death. Strangulation did not play a role in the murder. Hazel was not pregnant and the doctors agreed that her character was "undisputed". "Hazel", he said for the Troy Press, "was a good girl."

The Doctors' conclusions created a serious problem for Jarvis O'Brien and made his theory untenable. There was no way he could prove that Hazel died following a sexual assault when the doctors would not testify that an assault had occurred. He was now at a loss for a motive and was even more desperate. While his team of investigators continued to follow up new leads, he announced that there would be a Coroner's Inquest to officially determine the cause of death. It was a desperate move by a desperate man. The only possible advantage that O'Brien could gain from an inquest was that he would be able to call any person under surveillance or suspicion, or anyone in any way associated with the case, place them under oath and give them a thorough examination.

(VI)

Jeanette Marcellus was waiting at Union Station for a friend to arrive on the 1:45 train. That means she must have seen Hazel around 1:30 first in the waiting room then in the ladies room. This was the fourth time in two days Hazel was known to have been at Union Station. The question still to be determined is what was she doing there?

There are four possible reasons for Hazel to have been at Union Station when Jeanette Marcellus saw her. She could have been preparing to go somewhere by herself, she could have been preparing to go somewhere with someone else, she could have been seeing a friend off, or she could have been waiting for someone to arrive.

Hazel was not showing signs that she was about to travel by herself. She was not carrying her suitcase when Jeanette Marcellus saw her. Hazel checked the suitcase at 1:49 which was fifteen to twenty minutes after Marcellus saw her so she must have access had to it at the time. If she was intending to travel somewhere, possibly to New York, what would have stopped her? The contents of her suitcase were not conducive for an extended stay anyway. The day before, circumstantial evidence suggests that Hazel took a short trip to Albany. Was Hazel simply making short day trips?

There is no indication that Hazel was planning to travel with somebody else. Marcellus did not see her with anyone and if that was the plan, why didn't Hazel and her traveling companion leave? Why did she check her bag at 1:49?

Hazel did not appear to be seeing a friend off. She was alone when Marcellus saw her in the waiting room and again in the ladies room. And again, she would not check her bag if her purpose at the station was merely to say goodbye to a friend.

The most likely reason that Hazel was at Union Station then, was that she was intending to meet somebody. She was dressed nicely and was doing some last minute primping in the ladies room. Although she must have had her suitcase with her, she was not carrying it when Marcellus saw her.

The fact that she checked her bag means either the person she intended to meet did not show, so she checked her bag to have it at a later time or she did meet the person and for some reason, she didn't want to take it with her.

To put the events in perspective, Hazel left her job on Monday morning wearing a brand new shirt and carrying a suitcase with clothes sufficient for an overnight but not an extended stay. After deceiving her aunt about her destination, she went to Union Station and apparently took the train to Albany but returned a short time later. She put in an order for her trunk to be picked up and delivered to her parents house but at no time did she go there. Instead she went somewhere and spent the night with the clothes she was wearing and some overnight apparel in her suitcase. Although she could have gone to her parents or her brother's house, she never did, nor did any of her friends come forward to say that Hazel had stayed with them.

The next day she was again at Union Station, wearing her same new waist and carrying her suitcase with the same overnight attire. She was fixing her appearance in the mirror, very mindful of how she looked. She was most likely waiting for someone to arrive but something happened and at 1:49 she checked her suitcase. She was still wearing the same clothes she wore the day before but was no longer in possession of her overnight attire. At what point was she planning to go to her parent's house to retrieve more clothing from her trunk? It is unlikely that she planned to be out in Sand Lake as late as she was, so how did she get there? She had to have been influenced by somebody else's schedule.

The details of Hazel's stay in Sand Lake and Snyder's Lake the previous summer in all likelihood will never be known. Why she spent some time with the Bly family and other time at the home of John Link and who these families were may or may not be significant.

The letter Hazel received from the "Knight of the Napp Kin" provides some insight into her flirtatious behavior. Hazel's friends and family all stated that Hazel did not have a steady boyfriend. It seems, based on her relationships with Fred Schlaffin, William Hogardt and the "Knight of the Napp Kin" that she preferred more casual, less serious relationships. Reading into the letter, it is evident that Hazel's effect upon the writer was powerful even if she herself didn't appear to take the relationship very seriously.

The fact that Hazel was in a boat with the "Knight" and his friend apparently at an early stage of their acquaintance is telling. It was while she was in the boat that she lost her glasses. The somewhat immature behavior of the young men appeared to have gotten her agitated.

Hazel was not alone when she met the two young men but, as usual she was the one who made the greatest impression, the one everyone wanted to be with. Somehow due to some playful shenanigans, the young man bruised Hazel's wrists but only gave a halfhearted apology. He seemed to defend his use of force on her. He also made a sketch of her as he recalled holding her hand on the beach insinuating the relationship was more than platonic.

It is possible that the attractive blond woman seen driving around Sand Lake with the insurance agent was Hazel but it is not and cannot be known. Hazel was not the only attractive blond woman that frequented Sand Lake. There are no witnesses that came forward and stated for certain that Hazel was the woman seen with the man. The fact that the man, while in Utica showed an interest in the case is not unusual as the story was compelling and was making headline news around the country.

The authorities were aware of the man and his curiosity in the case. The police in Utica had reportedly placed him under surveillance. If he was somehow involved with Hazel's murder and the police were aware of him, it is likely they would have discovered it and dealt with him accordingly.

If Hazel was at her uncle's farm in April as John Abel claimed it means that William Taylor lied. If he did, what would be his motive?

And if he lied about her being there in April, could he have lied about her being there on July 7?

The case of Hazel being at Taylor's farm in April seems strong. Not one but two witnesses claimed to have seen her along with a friend. John Abel and A.C. Hogoboom were even able to describe the clothes the girls were wearing. Abel recalled negotiating a price for the ride and bringing them up the mountain, right to Taylor's farm house. He even remembered it was in early April.

Could Abel and Hogoboom have been mistaken or were intentionally misleading investigators? Taylor was not a popular figure in Sand Lake and there was a reward for information leading to an arrest. Taylor never wavered in his claim that Hazel had not been to his farm since she left in early February. Frank Richmond and his wife moved in with Taylor on April 1. They claim that Hazel was never at the farm while they stayed there and they had never met her.

John Abel told investigators that he witnessed a young attractive woman depart the 7 o'clock train at the Averill Park station and proceed toward Taborton Road. The insinuation is that it was Hazel. If so, it means Hazel arrived in Averill Park by train, alone, at 7 pm.

The woman Abel claimed he saw that night was not Hazel. In the first place, Abel apparently knew Hazel but he didn't identify this woman as her. Abel may or may not have been mistaken about taking Hazel to Taylor's in March or April but he did take her in January.

If the woman that Abel saw was Hazel, she would have had to have walked a mile to Crape's then another approximate three quarters of a mile up a mountain road to the Hollow where she was seen by Smith and Gundrum at 7:30. No one else saw her on the road except for the Rollmans who said she was leisurely standing by the side of the road picking raspberries. She did not appear to be out of breath or perspiring. She would have had to walk all that way, in heeled boots. Frank Smith was unable to sprint from Crape's to Averill Park and back in fifteen minutes so it is doubtful that the woman seen by Abel was Hazel. There would not have been enough time for that person to leave the train station at 7:00 and travel that distance on foot in thirty minutes.

William M. Clemens

The first time William Clemens' name appeared in the local papers in connection with the Hazel Drew investigation was on July 17. He was reportedly the world's foremost criminologist, a title he either gave to himself or was given by the New York Evening World newspaper. In an attempt to boost sales, the World may have granted Clemens the title to promote the so called expert to give the appearance that the paper had an experienced and knowledgeable investigator working for them. Using his criminologist title, Clemens investigated and claimed to have solved several cases, some of which were cold cases. He published his findings in the Evening World which were later reprinted in other newspapers.

William Montgomery Clemens was born in Paris, Ohio on January 16, 1860 to Sarah (Flickinger) and John Clemens. He was educated in the Akron public schools and attended Buchtel College (now Akron University). He married Rosa Garfield on July 2, 1881. The couple had four daughters, Rhea (1884), Nina (1886), Marian (1888) and Florence (1890). Sometime after the birth of Florence, Rosa passed away. On April 25, 1891, William married Edna Graves.

William Clemens had a long and successful career as a journalist and editor but was not educated in criminal justice and had no experience working in law enforcement. Between 1876 and 1884 he wrote for newspapers in Akron, Pittsburgh, and Cleveland. In 1884 he took a job as a correspondent for the United Press to cover the presidential campaigns for the upcoming election. He moved to California and wrote for the San Diego Sunday News and later for the San Francisco Chronicle. In 1894, Clemens returned east and began writing for the New York Evening World and as an editor for Literary Life. In 1898 he began writing for the American Press Association.

In addition to his work as a journalist, Clemens was also the author of several books. His first nonfiction book was The Life of Mark Twain (1891). (William was a nephew of Samuel Clemens more famously known as Mark Twain). His other works of nonfiction include, The Life of Theodore Roosevelt (1898), and The Life of Admiral Dewey (1898). His novels, included The Gilded Lady, published in 1903 and The House of the Hundred Doors in 1906.

In 1904, beginning as a freelance writer and later hired by the Evening World to be their expert criminologist, Clemens began publishing accounts of famous murders which he claimed to have investigated and solved. His first series of articles involved the 1841 murder of Mary Rogers, made famous as the inspiration for Edgar Allen Poe's The Mystery of Marie Roget. In 1904 Clemens claimed to have solved the mystery surrounding the death of Martha Laimbeer (Margaret Lynch). In 1907 he identified the body of Lena Whitmore and testified at the trial of her husband who was charged with her murder. In March 1908 he investigated the disappearance of some tools from a defense plant in Brooklyn that nearly caused an international incident between the United States and Germany. On July 17, 1908 William Clemens arrived in Troy to investigate the murder of Hazel Drew. His reports were not without controversy and the reliability of the evidence he claimed to have found would be disputed.

William Clemens developed a pattern in his writing. His style was effective and convincing but his information was based on evidence he claimed he discovered but would not share with others. As he investigated and then published articles on the Hazel Drew murder, his pattern would be repeated. It thus becomes necessary to examine the writings of William Clemens to establish a comparison to his controversial Hazel Drew findings.

(II)

The Case of Mary Rogers

On July 28, 1841 the bruised and battered body of Mary Rogers was discovered floating in the Hudson River near Hoboken, New Jersey. Rogers with her jet black hair and strong features was a beautiful young woman. At the time of her death she helped her mother run a boarding house on Nassau Street in New York City.

Rogers was last seen alive on Sunday morning July 25. She told her fiancé she was going to visit her aunt, Mrs. Downing and that she would be home later that evening. She left the boarding house carrying her parasol and wearing a white dress, silk scarf and a leghorn hat. When a violent thunderstorm moved into the area late in the afternoon and Mary didn't return home, her mother and fiancé assumed that she had stayed with her aunt. The next day when Mary had still had not returned home Mrs. Rogers contacted her sister. She was surprised to learn that not only had Mary not been to see her but Mrs. Downing was not even expecting a visit from her. "What she did, with whom, and why, remain cast in mystery, the subject of much conjecture, the story behind the story that became the Mary Rogers mystery." (Srebnick p. 16)

The police were contacted and an extensive search for Mary began. Three days later her body was pulled out of the Hudson River. Dr. Richard Cook, from Hoboken performed the autopsy and provided a detailed account of the extensive and horrific damage done to Mary Rogers' body.

> "Her features were scarcely visible, so much violence had been done to her. On her head she wore a bonnet-light gloves on her hands, with the long watery fingers pointing out- her dress was torn in various portions- her shoes were on her feet- and altogether she presented the most awful spectacle that the eye could see." (Srebnick p. 76)

Dr. Cook announced that the girl had not drown. He stated,

> "There was frothy blood still issuing from the mouth, but no foam, which issues from the mouth of persons who die by drowning. Her face was swollen, the veins were highly distended. If she had drowned there would not have been those particular appearances that I found in the veins." (Stashower, p. 93)

Cook noted bruising around the neck.

> "He discovered a deep bruise about the size and shape of a man's thumb on the right side of the neck, near the jugular vein, and several smaller bruises on the left side resembling the shape of a man's fingers. These marks, Cook stated 'led me to believe she had been throttled and partially choked by a man's hand." (Stashower, p. 94)

When Dr. Cook prodded the back of Mary's head he felt a small mass. "I observed a crease round the neck (and) passing my hand behind her ear, I accidently felt a small knot; and found that a piece of lace...was tied so tightly round her neck as to have been hidden from sight in the flesh of the neck; this was tied in a hard knot under the left ear." (Srebnick p. 79). His conclusion was that strangulation was the cause of death.

Dr. Cook proceeded to undress the corpse. When he examined the clothing he discovered that the lace chord that was used to strangle Mary Rogers had come from the trim of her underskirt.

> This finding, coupled with the thumb and finger marks around her neck, led the coroner to conclude that Mary Rogers had, in essence, been strangled twice. First, he reasoned, the attacker had grabbed her by the throat with one hand, choking off her air until she lost consciousness. Then, as she lay senseless, the attacker tore a strip of fabric from her skirts and pulled it, 'fast round her neck'- so tightly that the thin cord sank deep into the flesh- insuring that she would never regain consciousness. (Stashower, p.94)

When Dr. Cook examined Mary's "feminine region" he noted a series of abrasions and bruises. He concluded that Mary had been sexually assaulted by no fewer than three assailants before they ended her life.

> A grim sequence of events now came into focus. The dead girl's arms, Cook concluded, were positioned 'as if she had raised her hands to try to tear something from her mouth and neck, which was choking and strangling her.' Abrasions on the left wrist, along with corresponding marks on the upper side of the right wrist, confirmed that her hands had been lashed together with sturdy rope. 'The hands had been tied, probably, while the body was violated,' Cook concluded, 'and untied before she was thrown in the water.' Though the ropes had been removed, a loop of fine muslin-carefully torn from another of the undergarments- was found hanging loosely at the young woman's throat. Cook reasoned that the fabric had been used as a gag. 'I think this was done to smother her cries,' he said, 'and that it was probably held tight around her mouth by one of her brutal ravishers.' (Stashower, p.95)

Mary's back revealed raw skin and bruises around the shoulder blades. Dr. Cook believed Mary was on her back on some hard surface when she was assaulted. The back wound, he believed was the result of her desperate effort to resist her attackers.

A strip of her white dress, twelve inches wide had been ripped from the hem to the waist, then wound around the body and tied "as a sort of hitch." Dr. Cook believed Mary was dragged to the water by the strip of cloth which the killer used as a sort of crude handle.

Dr. Cook did not think Mary Rogers was wearing her hat at the time of the attack. He believed it was carefully placed back on her head and tied carefully following the assault. The string was not tied in the typical way a woman fastens her bonnet and resembled a knot much like a sailor would use.

Frederica Loss, the mother of three sons owned and operated Nick Moore's Tavern just north of where Mary Rogers' body was discovered. On November 25, 1841 four months to the day that Mary Rogers walked away from her boarding house, Loss sent two of her sons into the nearby woods to collect sassafras bark. The two boys, Charles Kellenbarack, age 16 and Ossian Kellenbarack, age 12 (named after their father) went into a thicket of overgrown vines and boulders about a quarter of a mile from the tavern. As they searched the woods they discovered a woman's petticoat, a silk scarf, some strips of fabric, a handkerchief embroidered with the initials MR and a parasol. The items showed signs of having been out in the elements for several weeks. The boys brought the findings back to their mother. She later brought the clothing to the police. For the next several months police continued to investigate the death of Mary Rogers. Several suspects were interviewed but no one was ever charged.

In November 1842 Frederica Loss was accidently shot in the leg by one of her sons. He claimed he was cleaning a shotgun when it slipped from his hands and discharged. For nine days Mrs. Loss lay in agony. When it became apparent that she did not have long to live, she asked one of her sons to get a police officer so she could make a deathbed confession .

Mrs. Loss told the officer that Mary Rogers had been to the tavern the day she was last seen alive. She was with a man who Mrs. Loss described as "swarthy". She claimed that the man was a doctor and that Mary Rogers had gone to the tavern to get an abortion. Something went wrong during the procedure and Mary died from the complications.

In 1904 from seemingly out of the blue, William Clemens wrote an article in the New York Evening World claiming to have solved the famous murder. Writing as an expert criminologist, he claimed to have proof that Mary was killed in Nick Moore's Tavern. Clemens claimed that Mary Rogers was murdered by Mrs. Loss' sons to prevent her from talking after they robbed her. They dumped her in the Hudson River as a convenient way to dispose of the body. Clemens claimed that Mrs. Loss' death was no accident. She was murdered by her sons because she would not keep quiet about the Rogers affair.

To support his claim, which he presented as indisputable fact, Clemens wrote that he had a sworn affidavit from Gilbert Merritt who was coroner at the time of Mary's death. The affidavit stated that the Kellenbarack boys were responsible for Mary's death. Coroner Merritt characterized the brothers as "worthless and profligate and that their tavern was one of the most "depraved and debauched houses in New Jersey." (Stashower, p. 249)

Clemens claimed that in 1904, when he published his article and sixty three years after the murder, he found five people who lived in the area at the time Mary was murdered that distinctly remembered the tragedy. Clemens wrote that one of them was a constable. Every one of the witnesses, Clemens' claimed, believed that the Kellenbarack boys murdered Mary Rogers.

Clemens wrote that he uncovered evidence that was missed by the investigators at the time of the murder and that, in addition to Mary Rogers, there was a second victim. His evidence came from the August 5, 1841 edition of a New York newspaper. The body of an unidentified man about thirty five years old was found floating in the Hudson River near Barclay Street. According to Clemens the man was tall and swarthy. He wore a white shirt, silk vest, dark pantaloons, and morocco shoes. The body was badly decomposed due to being in the water for several days.

"The mystery is no longer a mystery" wrote Clemens. "Mary Rogers and the tall man went into Nick Moore's Tavern to escape the storm. They were killed on Sunday and their bodies were thrown into the river on Wednesday. Both Mary and the tall man were higher class than the rest of the patrons, wearing nicer clothes and jewelry. Because nothing of value was discovered on the corpses, Clemens claimed, is proof that robbery was the motive." (The Scrap Book, p. 817)

> "...and, in further investigating the case and talking with these old people, I proved to my satisfaction that both the man and the woman were killed in the road house for their money and both thrown into the boat, and the girl's apparel placed in the thicket to attract attention." (The Scrap Book, p. 817)

Clemens did not include any physical evidence to support his claims and except for the man's body being discovered in the Hudson River, he did not introduce any new evidence.

There is no evidence that the man pulled from the Hudson River in August had any connection to the the Rogers case. Bodies found in the Hudson River were almost a common occurrence as Amy Srebnick points out in her outstanding work on Rogers' murder.

> "It was not unusual for bodies to be found floating in the waters around New York, the new nation's largest and most busy city. These were almost ordinary occurrences, attesting to the frequency of suicides, accidental drownings, or even foul play." (Srebnick p. 4)

What's more, Clemens did not take any of the documented evidence into consideration. His theory lacked common sense and reasoning. For example if the Kellenbarack boys murdered Mary and for some unexplained reason tossed her clothes and parasol in the thicket, why would they pretend to discover them later? The longer the clothes remained unfound the better for the killer(s).

Clemens did not explain why Mrs. Loss would turn the clothes over to the police. If she was aware that her sons murdered Mary, as Clemens stated, she would have simply destroyed the clothes or tossed them in the river.

Clemens claimed that robbery was the motive but Mary was not a wealthy young woman. She quit her job in a cigar shop to help her mother run a struggling boarding house. Clemens never explained why Mary's face was so bruised and battered if robbery was the motive. Why would Mrs. Loss' sons tie Mary's hands and place the garrote around her throat? It is obvious that Mary's death had a brutal sexual component to it, yet Clemens never mentioned this fact. Either he did not know the autopsy evidence or, more likely, it didn't fit nicely into his accusations so he simply ignored it.

Clemens claimed that Mrs. Loss' death was not accidental. He reported that she was intentionally murdered by her sons to silence her. Yet Mrs. Loss was shot in the leg and it took her ten days to die.

While she lay dying, not only did her sons allow her to speak to a police investigator, they were the ones who went to get the officer.

Mary Rogers' murder remains unsolved. Cold case enthusiasts continue to delve into the records, creating new theories and testing old ones. The murder continues to haunt and fascinate the American conscience. Amy Srebnick holds to the belief and provides credible evidence to support her theory that Rogers died as a result of a botched abortion performed by an incompetent doctor. The damage to Mary's "feminine region" was not the result of a sexual assault, she maintains, but rather the work of an abortion gone horribly wrong.

Daniel Stashower doubts the abortion theory and although he presents no definitive suspect or motive, unlike Clemens and Srebnick he focuses on the sexual assault evidence.

William Clemens claimed he spoke to witnesses who had information not available to the public at the time of the murder. This convinced him, he claimed, that they were reliable. But Clemens never discussed any of the information he purported to have learned nor did he identify by name any of the so called credible witnesses. He would consistently repeat this pattern in future investigations.

His assertions are not supported by the known facts of the case. Clemens developed a creative and thought provoking theory, reported it as fact and presented it the public. He asked his readers to believe him because he was considered the world's foremost criminologist. The trusting reader would be swayed by his title and the presentation of his work. Clemens' clever use of unnamed witnesses, including a supposed constable gives him an undeserved sense of credibility.

(III)

The Laimbeer-Lynch-Fream Mystery

On a bright and sunny Monday afternoon on April 11, 1904, the body of a young woman was discovered in some woods near Greenfield Cemetery in Freeport, New York in Nassau County, Long Island. It was estimated that the woman had been dead for three to five days by the time she was found.

The victim was fully dressed, wearing a green shirtwaist. She had a small cut or contusion above her left eye which had occurred prior to death. Her pocketbook containing 17 cents, a gold pen bearing the initial "O.M.", and a pearl handled pocket knife were discovered near the body. An empty vial that had contained carbolic acid was found at the scene.

A motorman named Herman remembered a woman on his train who wore a green waist. She boarded the train in Queens, New York City on April 6 and went to Freeport. After leaving the train, Herman saw her walking near the cemetery in what he described as an agitated state and he later saw her sitting by the side of the road.

An autopsy was performed but apparently District Attorney James Niemann was not satisfied with the results and ordered a second one be conducted. The second autopsy was done by Dr. J.H.B. Denton. District Attorney Niemann also requested the assistance of William Clemens who was beginning to make a name for himself.

The body showed no signs of trauma or sexual abuse. However, it was discovered that the victim was pregnant. Dr. Denton noted the victim's lips were black, caused he believed, from ingesting the carbolic acid, traces of which were found in her system.

The District Attorney believed the evidence clearly pointed to suicide. He theorized that, based on the women's clothing and possessions, she was probably employed as a servant.

> A theory which may lead to the identification of the dead woman has been advanced recently. This was that the woman was a servant girl or seamstress employed to some wealthy family. Discovery of her delicate condition possibly led to her dismissal or retirement it is believed. Having no home to go to she may have wandered off and being without funds to seek a hospital or pay for her board during her unanticipated illness she determined to take her life. (The Brooklyn Daily Eagle, April 16, 1904)

Facing an unwanted pregnancy and an uncertain future, District Attorney Niemann theorized the women took her own life by swallowing the poison. She received the small cut or contusion either by walking through the woods or falling down when the carbolic acid took effect.

When William Clemens examined the evidence, he announced that the woman was a victim of homicide. He claimed that the body was in a stooped position which convinced him that it had been moved after death. The cut over her eye was caused, he claimed, when she attempted to defend herself from her assailant.

By April 14 the victim had still not been identified. Plans were being made to bury her in a pauper's grave when a letter arrived at Dr. Denton's office. The letter, dated April 13 and sent from Brooklyn had a $100 bill enclosed. It read,

> Dear Sir,
>
> In the name of charity, in the name of your noble profession and of distracted relatives who shun public disgrace, I beg of you to spare the poor woman from a pauper's grave. Please give her a decent burial with the one hundred dollar bill enclosed.

Purchase a grave and coffin for her and retain sufficient to repay you for your trouble. (sic)

Please put an advertisement in Friday morning's New York Herald personal column, saying '$100. Will do as directed.' Bury her under the name of Martha Laimbeer. The body will be claimed in the future. Please do not publish this letter. The poor woman had often threatened to kill herself. God will reward you for your kindness.

Dr. Denton as requested placed the advertisement in the New York Herald and used the $100 to give the victim a proper burial. As instructed, the victim's headstone read Martha Laimbeer. District Attorney Nieman, contrary to Clemens' so called findings, stated officially that the woman took her own life.

Several Laimbeer families lived in Brooklyn. However, none of those families reported any of their relatives missing. For the time being the case was considered closed.

Five Months Later

In September, 1904, William Clemens published an article that renewed interest in the case. He repeated his original theory that the woman did not take her own life but was the victim of homicide. He asserted that the woman died as the result of a blow to the head even though no medical evidence supported his assertion. He went even further and stated that the woman's husband killed her while the two were out riding in a carriage. Ignoring motorman Herman's testimony that the woman was a passenger on his car, Clemens' claimed the husband drove the body ten miles to the cemetery to dispose of it. He arranged the body and clothing and poured the carbolic acid in the dead woman's mouth, never explaining how the carbolic acid made its way into her system. He placed the vial nearby to give the appearance of suicide. Clemens claimed that the husband later wrote the letter to Dr. Denton and sent the $100 to give his wife a respectable burial.

Clemens continued. He wrote that the same man that killed the woman went on to murder his mistress in Chester, Pennsylvania because he admitted to her that he killed his wife. Clemens did not include any other details on the Chester, Pennsylvania murder, including the name of the victim or anyone associated with that case.

In his article, Clemens stated that he knew the identity of the killer, and he was not alone. The District Attorney, he claimed, also knew who the killer was as did the victim's family. He did not reveal the killer's name but stated that the husband was very wealthy and lived in Brooklyn. The killer had powerful political friends in New York that were protecting him. He had previously fathered one child with the victim and was responsible for her latest pregnancy.

September 28, 1904

District Attorney Niemann was convinced that there was more to the Martha Laimbeer story than what appeared and was able to get a court order to exhume the body. He had undisclosed evidence that the victim was a woman named Margaret Lynch.

The body was exhumed in the presence of District Attorney Niemann, Margaret Lynch's pastor, her mother and two sisters, Annie and Catherine. Dr. John Shea, Margaret's dentist was also present and had with him her dental records. When the casket was opened, the pastor and the three Lynch women all agreed that the victim was Margaret. Dr. Shea examined the victim's teeth and the dental records confirmed that the deceased woman was Margaret Lynch, the daughter of Edward Lynch.

When the developments were reported in the papers, William Clemens responded. He claimed that for some time he had known the identity of the victim but had not intended to reveal her name until more leads had been investigated. In particular, he claimed he wanted to learn the identity of the person whose "O.M." initials were on the gold pen that was found with the body. He still clung to his assertion that the woman had been murdered and the killer's family had strong political connections in New York. (The Seattle Daily Times, October 1, 1904)

Three Years Later: September 6, 1907

Shortly after 5:30 on the morning of September 6, 1907 the body of Stephen T. Fream was discovered in a chair on the front porch of his brother-in-law, L.G. Daniels' house in Hackensack, New Jersey. Fream died from a single gunshot wound to the right side of his head. He was holding a pistol in his right hand, his raincoat and suitcase were nearby. The death was ruled a suicide.

Fream was a Lieutenant in the New Jersey National Guard and a veteran of the Spanish American War. At the time of his death he was working for a printing firm in Manhattan. He had taken the week off from work and went to Sullivan County, New York for a vacation. He borrowed some fishing equipment and appeared to be in good spirits. His mother wanted to go with him but he told her he would rather be alone to rest and unwind. He did, however invite Addison Burroughs, his friend and ranking officer, to join him later in the week. Fream had sent Burroughs a postcard from Sullivan County.

For unknown reasons, Fream cut short his visit and without telling anyone, returned to Hackensack the same day that Burroughs was supposed to meet him. Fream had $60 (approximately $1500 in today's currency) when he began his vacation but returned with only 30 cents (approximately $6). Police could not account for Fream's expenses or figure out how he could have gone through so much money so quickly.

Fream arrived by train in Hackensack at 10:43 pm. It is not known where he was between the time his train arrived and the time his body was discovered nearly seven hours later but he did not go to the places he usually went.

At 3:00 a milkman made a delivery to Daniel's home and did not see anyone on the porch or anything unusual. At 5:00 a baker walked by the residence and saw a man sitting in the chair on Daniel's porch but thought he was sleeping. At 5:30 a witness claimed to have heard a gunshot.

Shortly after the discovery of the body, William Clemens wrote an article about Stephen Fream's relationship with Margaret Lynch. Clemens based his article on dozens of meetings he claimed to have had with Fream. He wrote that Fream confided in him that he and Lynch had dated for three years and were at one time engaged to be married. Fream, Clemens wrote, allowed him to read the love letters Lynch had written and showed him a large photograph of the former girlfriend. Clemens wrote that Fream told him that Lynch ended the engagement when she became interested in another man. The man who led her astray, Clemens claimed, was the politically connected man from Brooklyn that he had written about earlier, and who was responsible for Margaret's murder.

Clemens told his readers that Fream believed Margaret Lynch was still alive and that some other woman's body was placed in the cemetery to conceal the identity of the guilty party. Clemens reported that he had proof that the person found in Freeport died as a result of a fractured skull. He never revealed his proof.

The real victim, he said was the wife of a man living in Brooklyn. Clemens now claimed the man killed her at home by fracturing her skull. He placed her in a bag and then drove her body out to Long Island. Clemens claimed that the knife found at the scene contained blood and fibers from the bag. After placing the body near the cemetery, the husband proceeded to pour the carbolic acid down his wife's throat. He never explained why the husband would have done this if the woman had a fractured skull.

To support his claim that Margaret Lynch's death was staged, Clemens claimed to have received from a priest a suicide note written by Lynch. Clemens said that the priest told him the letter had been mailed to Margaret's mother. Clemens wrote that he knew immediately that the priest was a fraud and the note was a forgery. He said the ink had not yet dried and the paper had not been folded. Clemens never allowed investigators to see or read the letter he claimed to have been given, nor did he reveal the name of the fraudulent priest.

Reporters and detectives interviewed Stephen Fream's family and his closest friends but were confused by what they learned. Those closest to Stephen knew that he had known Margaret Lynch but claimed that it wasn't a romantic relationship much less that the two had been engaged. Fream told his friends and family that William Clemens was the one who told him that Lynch was still alive but he did not believe the criminologist.

The friends and family said that, to their knowledge, Fream had met with Clemens only one time and not the dozens that Clemens claimed. They added that they were not satisfied with the District

Attorney's report and were not convinced that Stephen took his own life.

Clemens again made reference to people associated with the case known only to him but never identified which conveniently makes confirmation of the evidence impossible. He again asked his readers to trust his findings because he was the world's expert. His conclusions were based on ideas that he alone created and reported as fact although the evidence did not coincide with those ideas. By introducing an unnamed priest who he claimed presented him with fabricated evidence, never shown to anyone in position of authority, Clemens attempted to distract his readers into believing that he was dealing with a sophisticated conspiracy that he alone had the ability to see through. By including information he claimed was given to him personally by the now deceased Stephen Fream, Clemens positioned himself as a foremost authority armed with inside information, subject to evidence that he alone was able to obtain, even though no one close to Fream would corroborate, confirm, or even support.

As with the Mary Rogers case, Clemens presented controversial theories in a persuasive and compelling style that fascinated the reader. His inclusion of unverified evidence which he presented as fact made his writing even more believable. Only with an examination of all the evidence, not available to the public at the time, researchers can now see the self-serving bias and manipulation of facts that William Clemens utilized to further his own career at the expense of the truth.

(IV)

The Case of Lena Whitmore

On the frigid morning of December 26, 1907 the body of a woman was discovered in a swamp near the Passaic River in Harrison, New Jersey. The attractive 5'4" victim with auburn hair was estimated to be about 30 years old. She was nude but her clothes, including a scarlet red coat with military style braids were discovered not far from her body. Based on the style and quality of the clothing found, investigators reasoned the woman was from the middle class.

Three days after the discovery, William Clemens was hired by the New York World to discover the identity of the victim. Focusing on the coat's braids, Clemens claimed he visited textile factories and clothing shops all over New York City. After four days, Clemens said he was able to track the bill of sale to Mrs. Lena Whitmore. Theodore Whitmore, Lena's husband, was later arrested for the murder.

Clemens testified at the trial of Theodore Whitmore. In painstaking detail, he provided an account of his work running down leads that ultimately led to the identification of the coat and then the victim. His testimony, printed in the New York Sun on Thursday May, 28, 1908 provides a glimpse into the arrogance of the "world famous" criminologist.

> William M. Clemens, who described himself as a criminologist and the founder of a brand new school of criminal investigation, took the stand. Mr. Clemens was got up after the style of Mr. Gillette's Sherlock Holmes. He left his short bulldog pipe on the prosecution's table. After Clemens outlined his investigation of the murder for a New York

newspaper and the aid he had furnished the prosecution Lawyer Simpson pounced upon him gleefully.

"What method do you employ, Mr. Clemens, that of Lombroso?"

"By no means," said the criminologist eagerly. "I am violently opposed to the theories of Lombroso. My methods are entirely my own.

"How do you judge a man, by his looks?"

"Oh no. By his actions and admissions."

"Do you ever make a mistake?"

"Oh very rarely," said the criminologist.

"What! Very rarely?"

"Well seldom. I am nearly infallible."

"Didn't you make a great mistake in the Margaret Lynch case some years ago when you insisted the body was that of another girl although the mother and other relatives of the dead girl had identified the remains positively as those of Margaret Lynch."

"I alone was right," said Mr. Clemens firmly. "The others were all wrong."

William Clemens had investigated several cases involving the deaths of beautiful young women. He would continue that pattern in the summer of 1908 when he traveled to Sand Lake to investigate the death of Hazel Drew. Before that, however, Clemens would investigate the disappearance of some tools from a factory in Brooklyn. He would again employ controversial and unethical methods in his reporting. This time, however, the consequences were nearly catastrophic.

(V)

The Case of William Esser: March 1908

The E.W. Bliss Company in Brooklyn manufactured, among other things, the Bliss-Leavitt torpedo used at that time by the US Navy. In 1908 the company discovered some of the tools used in one of the machine shops were missing and called William Clemens. Clemens investigation led to a former Bliss employee named William Esser.

William Esser was a German immigrant who arrived in the United States in 1902. Described as plump and dirty, Esser began working for the Bliss Company in 1904. He stopped working for the company in the summer of 1907 after he built a workshop at his residence and began working from his home.

Clemens searched Esser's shop and discovered $40 worth of tools that the Bliss Company reported missing. However during the search, hidden in some boxes under a pile of rubbish, Clemens claimed he discovered blueprints and a model of the Bliss-Leavitt torpedo.

Clemens then announced that for some time he had been part of an international investigation that was beginning to come together. The larger investigation was an extension of an espionage conspiracy that he stumbled upon, he claimed, while traveling in Europe. Of course he would not reveal any of the details but said he had been working very closely with the Bliss Company as part of the investigation.

Clemens claimed that William Esser had been negotiating with the German government to sell them the secrets of the Bliss-Leavitt torpedo. Clemens, when hired to locate the missing tools, worked in conjunction with the Brooklyn Police Department and specifically Captain August Kuhne. Clemens claimed that he found a letter in William Esser's pocket that he shared with Captain Kuhne. The letter, written in German had the seal of the German government on the top proving, he said, that it was official. Clemens said he had the letter translated and it provided details about the secret sale of the torpedo plans.

Captain Kuhne confirmed to the press that Clemens had been hired by the Bliss Company to find the stolen tools and had kept the police informed of his progress. Kuhne told reporters that Clemens told him about the letter but never showed it to him and did not provide him with a copy. Kuhne also stated that he was not aware that any plans for the torpedo were found at Esser's residence.

When Clemens learned of Kuhne's statements he said that he found another letter in Esser's house warning the German to lay low, that he was under suspicion. The letter, Clemens claimed, was postmarked from New York and as a result, Esser must have hidden or destroyed the plans before the police could search his house. To strengthen his assertions, Clemens claimed he was in possession of dozens of letters written in German that he took from Esser's house. The letters are proof, Clemens stated, of the relationship between Esser and the German government. None of the letters were turned over to Captain Kuhne or to any other law enforcement agency.

As Kuhne and other investigators delved more deeply into the facts, Clemens case began to fall apart. The German government, angered and insulted by Clemens allegations launched their own investigation. They officially denied any knowledge of William Esser or any attempt to procure the plans. They emphatically denied that any German official had been in contact with Esser and stated that no letters with official German letterhead had been sent to him.

The German government made it clear that they had no interest in the Bliss-Leavitt Torpedo. They were confident that their own torpedoes were far superior and more accurate than the Bliss-Leavitt.

As the investigation continued, Captain Kuhne announced that the Bliss Company had, for years, been willing to sell the plans of their torpedo to any country upon request. There was no need for the German government to enter into secret negotiations or espionage with Esser. The plans were not secret. The Bliss Company had patents all over Europe, including Berlin and the German government could purchase the weapon simply by asking.

Captain Kuhne also revealed that Esser did not work in the part of the factory that handled torpedos or torpedo technology. In addition, the Bliss Company confirmed that none of the plans had been compromised and none were missing.

Clemens stories had evolved from sensationalized and manipulative reports involving the murders of pretty young women in the area around New York City into explosive accusations involving foreign governments. Clemens' confidence had soared but perhaps he realized he had gone too far and needed to find the kind of story that didn't involve powerful political forces and veteran Metropolitan police officials. If he could return to the kind of cases where people were more easily swayed by his outlandish accusations, perhaps in a more rural area with so-called country investigators and doctors, maybe he could regain the reputation that he once believed he had.

He found his opportunity on July 12, 1908 when the Northern Budget reported the discovery of a young woman's body on a desolate mountain top in rural upstate New York. On July 17, hired by the New York World, the world's foremost criminologist arrived at Union Station ready to solve the mystery surrounding the death of pretty Hazel Drew.

Clemens' spent several days working with Jarvis O'Brien's detectives and then began working independently. It must have come as a relief to the investigators when Clemens broke from them and began working on his own.

Clemens began writing his articles on July 20, 1908. The first was published two days later in the Thrice-A-Week World.

The Thrice-A-Week World
Wednesday, July 22, 1908

Letters Received by the Girl Murdered at Teal's Pond Shows that She Was a Favorite of Men

---

By William M. Clemens
The World's Expert in Criminology

Troy, N.Y., July 20- Light is beginning to break in the Hazel Drew case. There would never have been such a black wall of mystery in this case had Hazel herself been less secretive and more frank and honest with her friends and relatives. The fact that she made her young life so secretive has brought about the puzzling problem of her death. She was her own worst enemy. I have already eliminated the only two suspects in the case, old man Taylor and young Frank Smith. I have shown the real cause of death and the peculiar condition of her clothing. The next step is the girl's personality, and then her habits, her movements prior to her death, her friendships and her love affairs.

When Hazel packed her trunk at the home of Prof. Carey on Monday, July 6, she filled a hat box with torn letters, postcards, photographs, bills, receipts, circulars, visiting cards, and a mass of stuff that had accumulated in her room. The police secured her trunk, searched her room and found a few letters. The hat box filled with scraps had been carried to the cellar of the Carey home and lay there overlooked. Here is where I found it and there are some few clues now in hand that may by merest chance lead to the solution of the mystery. Hazel kept an address book in which she wrote down the names and addresses of her particular friends and correspondents and the list she apparently revised once a month.

Crossed Off Names

As friends dropped out of her young life, she crossed off their names, entering the names of newly formed intimates. The more recent lists contain the names of something like sixty friends and acquaintances, a majority of them young girls of her own age and station of life, but there are addresses of numerous men. There are letters from her Aunt Minnie Taylor, her married friend Mrs. Mina Jones, from a man at Hyde Park, Mass., from her younger sister and from her sweethearts of the past. There is a photograph of Hazel taken last year, the torn photos of two young men, an invitation to a wedding in Schenectady, visiting cards bearing the names of a dozen young men in Troy.

There is a group photograph of four young women and three young men taken at Prospect Park two years ago. The four girls are seated, Hazel at the left, the young men standing. The personnel of the photograph is as follows Hazel Drew, Arthur Phillips, Lillie Robertson, John C. Stagmayer, Anna Coma(?), Bert Bruns, and Margaret Westfall. These young people I have interviewed but they belong to a period long since past in Hazel's life.

Hazel was a flirt. She was vain of her beauty and clothes, and during the last year she dropped, one by one, her girl friends and the young boys of her life and began making acquaintances of the more worldly sort. Every time she made a trip to another city she made a new acquaintance. When she visited Providence, R.I., she added a young man from Hyde Park, Mass., to her list of correspondents.

New York Men Involved

In May when she went to New York, she brought back the names of New York men and she had male friends in Albany, Schenectady, Cohoes, and other towns.

Her mother had said that she did not have a beau, whereas she had many of them. Her mistress, Mrs. Carey, who had believed in her thoroughly, told me Hazel seldom received a letter but my proof shows she received letters daily and not a few of them from men. Some of those letters are dated within a few weeks of her death and sooner or later may have an indirect bearing on her death.

She was a girl of more than average intelligence but of slight education. Her writing is like that of a country school girl with little regard for spelling and punctuation and with noticeable lapses in the grammar. Hazel before sending letters to anyone invariably wrote a first copy in pencil before writing her letters in ink and of these edited copies I have a large number. There are letters to department stores in New York, Chicago, and Albany asking for circulars and catalogues; letters to girls and her relatives, and a number addressed to men, some in New York and Massachusetts. One of these letters after being patched together from the fragments found in the Carey cellar, reads as follows.

"June 20, 1908. Troy, N.Y. Young Women's Camp, Altamont, N.Y. saw your advertisement of a summer boarding place, and I enclose stamp for which send me a circular.

Miss Hazel Drew

This letter is dated June 20, less than three weeks prior to the murder. It would seem that Hazel had made her plans to leave Troy at least for a vacation and seemingly preferred Altamont to Sand Lake or Averill Park. Altamont is a station on the Delaware and Hudson Railroad about twelve miles from Troy. To this letter a reply was received together with a circular.

Planned to Go Away

There is no doubt Hazel had made plans to go away from Troy, at least ten days before her death.

The week prior to July 4 she had all her best clothes in the laundry, all her shirt waists, and was preparing even then to leave, for on Wednesday, July 1 she spoke to Mrs. Carey about getting another girl. On Friday morning, July 3, she received a letter in a man's handwriting written in pencil and within an hour were carrying articles of clothing from her room to her trunk, which she kept in the cellar of the house. It would appear that an elopement might have been planned. She went away on the morning of July 4, Mrs. Carey having given her a two day holiday.

With her aunt, Minnie Taylor, she went to Rensselaer Park and in the evening to the house of a friend in Schenectady where they remained until Sunday evening. Hazel was home at the Carey house by 11 o'clock Sunday night. Early the next morning she abruptly informed Mrs. Carey she was going to leave and began at once to complete the packing of her trunk. At 10 o'clock on Monday, July 6, she left the house never to return.

Yesterday, while at the home of Prof. Carey I discovered in a closet the family ragbag and Mrs. Carey was astonished at its size and the quantity of its contents. She was still more surprised when the bag was emptied on the floor for there were found many articles of clothing belonging to Hazel which she had discarded in her haste to get away.

These articles were not worthless many of them being neither ragged nor torn. There were white skirts, gloves, underwear, stockings, handkerchief, shoes, aprons and the like. Three undervests were included one of them having been washed only the week before according to Mrs. Carey's statement. When it is remembered that no undervest or shirt was found on the body of Hazel Drew when it was taken from Teal's Pond, we wonder why these three undervests were discovered at the Cary home.

Expected Other Money

It is more than theory to assert that Hazel Drew was expecting to leave Troy with other money than the few dollars in her purse, and that she expected to replenish her wardrobe at a very early date, necessarily with money furnished by the person whom she expected to accompany her in flight. There seems to be no question here that Hazel Drew was expecting to leave Troy by train during the afternoon or evening of Monday July 6.

As an instance of Hazel's flirtations and the sort of men she attracted by her honesty and personality I am going to break the sacredness of her life by publishing the following letter mailed from Albany.

To my lady of the blond hair:

> I am taking the great liberty in addressing this letter to you, my lady, but considering what a pleasant time you afforded us I cannot help but express our deepest sympathy for the loss of your glasses. We feel that we were partly to blame for had we not been as forward in our actions you probably would not have been in our boat. Still I do not wish you to have the impression that we are heartless flirts even though we have come from the city. We noticed that you were somewhat agitated upon leaving the car, and we have thought it was because he and I have made such a peculiar appearance and as though you were ashamed of us. If we had suspected that we were to meet such charming young ladies we would have dressed accordingly.
>
> I trust that your wrists are not injured for I could not forgive myself if I had caused even the slightest bruise. T'is true that I had to use force on some occasions, but I tried not to be rough or rude in my actions. My friend and I have more mental than physical work in our business and a week's outing in your and your friend's company is worth more than a month in the mountains.

A Case of Flattery

It is very possible that a pretty girl like you has many admirers and you understandably have a preference among them. I shall always remember the happy scene enacted on Snyder's Lake and dream of my lady of the blond hair. I have sketched your face and shoulders and I cannot get the proper expression of your eyes as they looked to me while you were holding my hands on the beach. I hope you will forgive me for taking possession of your napkin but I really had to take something as a souvenir.

It seems strange to me that we should both take to you more than to your girl friends but somehow you seemed to belong to a higher sphere, and considerably more sensible, modern, and have more pleasing ways. If we send postals we shall expect others in return. 'If Knighthood were in Flower I should live only for and have fond clinging memories of my lady of the blond hair and be faithful unto death under the names of your
KNIGHT OF THE NAPP KIN AND YOUR ARTIST FRIEND HARRY

This or similar letters may have been the beginning of bringing Hazel's little narrow world something of the vanities and flattery that men and women know so well in the rapid civilization of city life. She, poor, rural, innocent, whose beauty was a real danger, soon became the moth before the flame, and fate had marked her for the fire.

Remembering that William Clemens had, in the past, introduced unsubstantiated evidence to support his claims, it is difficult to trust any evidence that Clemens professed to have discovered. The Troy Record on July 20, 1908, two days before Clemens published his first article on the case, implied that it was O'Brien's investigators who discovered the items sent to be incinerated in the Cary's basement. The article states,

During Saturday there was another visit made to the Cary residence on Whitman place and a diligent search was made for anything that might possibly be found to aid in the unraveling of the mystery. It was thought that Hazel may have thrown away more letters or postals before she left the employ of the Carys and the result was not fruitless. Refuse that had been thrown away and was ready to be burned was carefully sifted and separated. There was disclosed a few more of Hazel's friends. Scraps of letters were found and a postal card that had been torn in two was obtained These were collected, pasted together and from them several names of her former friends were brought to light.

The article did not state directly that it was O'Brien's men who discovered the letters and postcards. It is possible that it was Clemens who made the discovery in the Cary's basement. It is also possible that Clemens was with the detectives when the letters were discovered. There was very little new or vital evidence that he purported to have gained from those letters. He would have no real reason to lie about his role in their discovery except possibly to enhance his ego and his self proclaimed reputation.

However, John Magner's name and address was found in the incineration pile. Clemens did not mention John Magner's name in his article. It is difficult to believe that he would have turned the information over to O'Brien before he, himself would have investigated and then written about him.

It's a minor point and perhaps even irrelevant to know who discovered the letters. It is more important to examine the content and follow up on the assertions made in Clemens' articles. For example, he claimed that Mrs. Cary said Hazel seldom received any letters yet he claimed she received daily correspondence, many from men. If this is true, Mrs. Cary, Carrie Weaver, and everyone else who was close to Hazel was in error about her relationships and Clemens alone was correct.

Clemens wrote that Hazel informed Mrs. Cary on July 1 that she was planning to leave, yet Mrs. Cary never mentioned this to the investigators or to any other reporter. According to her July 17 interview with the Thrice-A-Week World, Mrs Cary stated,

> "I was nonplussed when she told me after breakfast on the morning of July 6 that she was going to leave us. There had been no trouble nor even slight unpleasantness. I did not question Hazel and she departed without giving any explanation of her leave-taking."

These do not sound like the words of an employer who had, according to Clemens, been told on July 1 to start looking for someone to replace her.

Clemens stated that after receiving a letter on July 3, written in a man's handwriting, Hazel immediately began packing her trunk. There is no way to verify this, only the word of William Clemens. But why would Hazel keep such a life changing secret from everyone she was close to? She saw her best friend Carrie Weaver that same day. They laughed and joked as usual. She saw her favorite aunt the next day. She spent the weekend with her cousins, yet she never told any of them about her plans or intentions.

Clemens claimed that Hazel discarded much of her wardrobe at the Cary's before she departed on Monday morning July 6. He claimed that he personally went through the items, many of which were in excellent condition. If true, why would Hazel do this? Why not pack the clothes in her trunk? She had room. Or, why not pack some of the clothes in her suitcase? Again, she had room. Why pack a suitcase with only enough clothes for an overnight visit, pack the rest of her clothes in her trunk, and discard others when there was no reason to do so?

William Clemens may have been telling the truth, he may have exaggerated or even created the stories he published. What in his writing is accurate and what is made up? Unfortunately the world's foremost criminologist continued to publish articles and the contemporary reader is left to decide what is to be believed and what is not.

On July 21, 1908 William Clemens wrote the following article for the New York World which was printed the following day.

The New York World
Wednesday, July 22, 1908

HAZEL DREW'S FRIENDS ARE NOW TALKING.

Murdered Girl's Family Tell Why She Spent A Month In Seclusion in Her Uncle Taylor's House.

HER DOWNFALL CHARGED TO A MARRIED MAN.

Bracelets and Other Articles Evidently Taken from the Teal's Pond Victim.

William M. Clemens
The World's Expert in Criminology

Troy, N.Y., July 21- To All Pawnbrokers. Arrest man who attempts to pawn one or pair of heavy, solid chained gold bracelets, one-half inch wide, with small looped chain three inches long attached. These were stolen from body of Hazel Drew, murdered near Troy, N.Y., July 7.

The above notice should be reprinted and circulated by the authorities in every town and hamlet, especially in New York State. I discovered today that Hazel Drew wore a pair of valuable bracelets at the time of her disappearance in Troy on Monday, July 6. She received these bracelets as a present from an aunt now deceased. They were of solid gold, heavy, and valuable. Hazel always wore one of the bracelets, and sometimes the pair.

Miss Mary Sharp, her most intimate friend who lives at No. 21 Hawthorne avenue, told me to-night that she last saw Hazel on Friday, the day before July 4. She called on her. Both girls had been intimate during the last few months and had twice visited Albany together. Miss Sharp is positive that Hazel carried the bracelets in her shopping bag wherever she went if she did not wear them. She guarded them so carefully that she would not leave them in her room when she went out of the house.

It was also learned to-day that Hazel carried a small clasp coin purse which she invariably kept inside the shopping bag, which was of brown imitation leather, six inches long, four inches across and shirred with a brown ribbon.

Miss Sharp also told me it was absolute nonsense to think that Hazel would, at anytime go without an undervest. It would appear, then, that when Hazel Drew was murdered the assassin carried away with him the brown shopping bag, two gold bracelets, coin purse and the check for her dress suitcase.

What a Friend of Hazel Says.

Mrs. V.H. Huntley of No. 383 Third Avenue, Watervliet, N.Y., quickly verified the statement of Miss Sharp when I saw her to-night. She was one of Hazel's closest and dearest friends.

She said: "I have been astonished that the police have been stupid enough to overlook the gold bracelets that Hazel wore. I never saw her when she did not wear one or both of those bracelets, and she was proud of the fact that she wore no rings, not caring for them. I became acquainted with Hazel a year ago while we were both boarding at the Bly's summer home on the mountains. She was here at my house only a few weeks ago, and was happy and contented, and I am sure she did not have a care in the world.

"As to the missing undervest, I cannot understand it. I am positive that Hazel would never dress without wearing such a garment. She had a large bust and her corset necessarily had to be laced tightly. In this warm weather the perspiration would have rusted her corset steels and ruined the corsets if she had worn them next to the skin. She was the neatest, tidiest girl I ever knew and was over-fastidious in her dress.

Her back combs were worn just as mine are, and if I stoop to pick anything from the floor my combs fall out. It would have been impossible for Hazel to have received a wound five inches in diameter, as the doctors say, on the back of the head without either breaking them or knocking them off. I am convinced Hazel was not murdered out of doors, but in a room."

Beginning to Talk

These two interviews today mark the beginning of the end. The human dams of Troy are commencing to open, and we will soon know the truth concerning the mysterious murder at Teal's pond. During the last week the police and the District-Attorney have been finding fault because they could get no information from any of Hazel Drew's relatives and could find no trace of her friends and intimates. The District-Attorney caused a $1000 reward to be offered last Friday with the hopes that information would walk in upon him every hour of the day. In this he has been disappointed and to-day realizes that to obtain information he must send his sleuths out to hustle for it.

For instance, I interviewed Joseph Drew, a brother of Hazel the other day, and he told me that not a single detective had been to see him. I questioned other members of the Drew family today and learned for the first time the real secret of the Drew attitude of silence and unconcern over Hazel's tragic death. It will be recalled that Hazel's father and mother have been morose and non-committal; that Aunt Minnie Taylor would not be interviewed; Uncle William Taylor did not seem to take any particular interest in the case.

All of this reticence and queer behavior are explained at last. The secret could not have been kept much longer and I succeeded in obtaining the truth from a member of the Drew family today. In January last, when Hazel Drew sought her Uncle William's house near Teal's Pond in the dead of winter, with the thermometer at twenty below zero and snow drifts everywhere, she went there for a purpose. Her sister-in-law, Eva Drew, wife of Joseph was keeping house for Uncle Taylor, and Hazel remained there in seclusion for nearly a month, and was very ill and without a physician being called. For one week no one was allowed to enter Hazel's room but Eva.

In his July 22 article, Clemens both subtly and overtly criticized the handling of the investigation. He did so in part to assert himself as the expert criminologist who had more expertise than others who were working the case. Typical of Clemens, most of his assertions that can be checked proved to be false and much of the rest cannot be verified.

For example, Clemens attempted to expose the incompetence of the authorities by pointing out their failure to investigate Hazel's missing bracelets. He sarcastically began his article by calling on all pawn brokers to be on the lookout, a subtle technique used by the writer to both entice and empower his readers and at the same time expose a part of the investigation that he claimed the authorities had failed to follow up. He skillfully introduced two of Hazel's friends to verify her attachment to the bracelets, even getting one of them, Mrs. E.V. Huntley (Clemens mistakenly called her Mrs. V.H. Huntley), to refer to the police as stupid for not looking into the matter more closely.

Clemens' tactic may have worked on the more removed New York readers in 1908 but not as well on the local capital district readers, nor on the contemporary researcher. Hazel did possess two gold bracelets but both had been accounted for when Clemens wrote his article. The July 22, 1908 Troy Times, in response to Clemens' article, printed the following.

> The bracelets belonging to Hazel Drew and not found when the body was discovered have been accounted for. One was in the possession of Minnie Taylor, and the other was found in Hazel's trunk.

Hazel's trunk was searched on Monday July 13 and O'Brien's men had been consistently interviewing Minnie Taylor beginning that same day. Hazel gave Minnie one of the bracelets, possibly the last time the two women met. Hazel's jewelry had been accounted for long before William Clemens arrived in Troy and printed his accusations. His criticism was groundless but gave the appearance that he had discovered a flaw in the investigation and that he alone was actively and competently working to solve the case.

Clemens used the fact that a reward was offered as a ridiculous and unfair criticism against the detectives, accusing them of being lazy. Clemens argued that the reward was established so that the detectives would not have to go out and look for clues, preferring instead, that witnesses to come to them.

The July 16 newspapers reported that Rensselaer County offered the $1000 reward. The same day an unnamed Troy newspaper posted a $500 reward. The offers were generous and well intended. However, the rewards also created much more work for the detectives. Witnesses began to appear with stories that investigators knew to be false. As information was updated in the papers, unscrupulous reward seekers came forward with fabricated stories in an effort to collect the reward money. Their greed cost investigators precious time and manpower as each tip had to be investigated.

Why Clemens devoted time focusing on Hazel's undervests is a mystery. An undervest was used by women as a way to protect the corset and shirtwaist from perspiration. Clemens used two sources to say that it was unusual that Hazel was not wearing such under-wear, yet in his previous article he was quick to point out that Hazel discarded three such garments. If Clemens was implying that Hazel's not wearing an undervest was evidence of a sexual assault, he does not follow through with the argument. It is more likely that Clemens was again enticing his readers, this time with women's underwear. His inclusion of Mrs. Huntley's statement about Hazel, "She had a large bust..." was an unnecessary inclusion but used as sex appeal to attract more readers.

His last paragraph is typical Clemens. He cleverly teased his readers with information that he alone had discovered. He mentioned vague yet unnamed sources, this time family members, purported to be reliable. Unbeknownst to his readers at the time, it was an unethical tactic that Clemens had used in the past.

On July 24, 1908 the Auburn Semi-Weekly Journal published the secret that, according to William Clemens, the Drew family had kept from everyone except him.

Auburn Semi-Weekly Journal
July 24, 1908

HAZEL DREW SECRET OUT

Story of Downfall of Murdered Girl and Her Attempt to Hide Her Shame

---

By William M. Clemens
World's Expert in Criminology

Secret of Her Visit.

The regrettable truth, now confessed by the family, is that Hazel went to her uncle's house in the mountains to hide her shame. I suspected as much the other day when I found certain medicines among her effects that bore the imprint of a quack medical concern in Chicago. These were with the torn letters and photographs thrown aside in the rubbish heap at the home of Prof. Cary. This suspicion was fully confirmed Tuesday by a member of the family, Tuesday. (sic) In January last, when ment in the case (sic) cannot but have an important bearing on the murder mystery; in fact, it confirms suspicions already aroused in a certain direction.

Joseph J. Sonev of No. 380 First street, was one of Hazel's acquaintances. He last saw her on Halloween night at a party to which she invited him and he told me in detail of his three year acquaintance with her. There was nothing as far as he knew, to her discredit.

A young lawyer who lives in Green Island confided to me Tuesday night that he had known Hazel for several years. He said she was a respectable girl as far as he knew, although he got acquainted with her by "picking her up" in the street. He also met her and another girl by appointment at the Union depot. He said that as long as three years ago Hazel was well known to the young men about town as a flirt.

Other intimate girl friends of Hazel Drew who broke their silence to me Tuesday were Margaret Burns, Martha Hildebrandt, Lillie Robertson, Jeannie Mason and Mabel Mackie.

There is now no question of the double life that poor Hazel had been living for a year before her death. Her downfall dates to the time she met a married man last year. Before that time her friendships had been confined to boys and girls and her pleasures and amusements were devoid of real wrongs. Not until the schooled worldly villain of middle age came into her young life did Hazel Drew take the first step that led to a bewildering maze of crooked byways leading on and on to the shores of Teal's pond, where death overtook her. The villain, too, doubtless is not sorry that Hazel is out of harm's way and will trouble him no more. She gave him all her love, her hope, her dream of future happiness and last of all she gave her very life for him.

Clemens once again came up with unnamed witnesses close to the source to reveal important and potentially embarrassing information. He claimed Hazel went to her Uncle William's farm the previous winter to abort a pregnancy. His proof, he claimed, was his discovery of medicine in the Cary house that was among the effects that Hazel brought to the basement to be incinerated. He added that unnamed family members confirmed his suspicion. It is unusual that Hazel's family would reveal such a personal and intimate secret to an out of town reporter, but to no one else. It is also unusual that, if true, Hazel used the medicine in late January and kept it for five months only to leave it in the Cary's basement for them to incinerate after she left.

Clemens supposed discovery of the medicine missed by other investigators is very similar that of the William Esser case where he discovered evidence that investigators working on the case had not seen and were unaware of. In both cases Clemens claimed the evidence was confirmed by unnamed sources that he alone was in contact with but disputed by the investigators working the case.

Clemens used a similar technique when he claimed that Hazel was murdered by a married man so she "will trouble him no more". Earlier, Clemens reported that the married man who supposedly murdered Margaret Lynch also murdered his mistress in Chester, Pennsylvania because she, too had become dangerous to him. Mrs. Loss too, he claimed, was murdered to silence her. Not by a married man but by her own sons.

What is frustrating about Clemens' assertions is that they are logical and cannot be ruled out simply because the writer had, in the past, used questionable methods. However, because Clemens had a history and a reputation for unscrupulous reporting the same must be assumed for his handling of the Hazel Drew case. It is possible that Hazel did go to William Taylor's farm to have an abortion. The reliable evidence does not rule it out. What is questionable however, is that family members confided in Clemens and that he stumbled across medical evidence that was missed by the dedicated investigators who had been working the case from the beginning. Likewise, the reported relationship that Hazel may have had with a married man can not be ruled out but neither can it be confirmed as fact based on Clemens' writing .

The same day that the Auburn Semi-Weekly Journal published Clemens article, the Thrice-A-Week World published another Clemens report.

The Thrice-A-Week World
Friday July 24, 1908

HAS HAZEL DREW'S AUNT MINNIE TOLD ALL SHE KNOWS

William M. Clemens Declares There is Reason to Suspect that She Could Clear the Pond Mystery

---

William M. Clemens
World's Expert in Criminology

Troy N.Y. July 22- For several days District-Attorney O'Brien and his sleuths have been scouring the town to verify a report that Frank Jones, of Providence R.I. had been in Troy on July 6 and 7. O'Brien seems to connect the presence of Jones in Troy with something or other. Mr. Jones is the husband of Mrs. Mina Jones of Providence the chum and intimate of Hazel Drew, and in some manner the names of Jones and Aunt Minnie Taylor are mixed up in the undercurrent of the murder mystery.

I can throw some light on Jones through a letter written by Hazel to her friend Mrs. Jones only a few days before her death. Hazel's first draft copy, written in red pencil, contained the sentence, "I received your letter and was surprised to learn that you live in Maine. I have not been down to see Mrs. Shigsheimer but I hear from another that Mr. Jones was boarding at Mrs. Schuler's. I do not know her address. Perhaps you may know. I am sorry I could not see Mr. Jones but no doubt you have heard from him. Two young people are coming here this afternoon, one to stay a week and one all summer, I think one of them is a student. I haven't much love for them.

This seems to show that Mr. Jones was hereabouts and may be still. While on the subject of Jones the following extracts of letters may prove of interest. A letter from Mrs. Jones to Hazel dated Providence says: "Everything here is on the bum. Mr. Jones hasn't had any work for three weeks. Do you ever see Mrs. Hamm and how are Mr. D and his love getting along?"

"Come and Bring Your Friend"

Another letter from Mrs. Jones dated May 1 says: "You wanted me to tell you about the boats from New York to Providence. Take the Joy line from New York. I hope you will make up your mind to come and bring your friend with you."

Another letter from Mina Jones, dated Providence May 3 contains this: "Mrs. Smith is here yet. They got after him and gave her seven dollars. Mr. Isleps(?) called on me Thursday. Get that address for me just as soon as you can.

On Dec. 30 last, a few days before she went into retirement at Uncle William Taylor's farm, near Teal's pond. Mina Jones wrote from Providence the letter containing this suggestive paragraph: "I am very, very sorry for you dearie. I know just how to feel for you."

Some comments on the church in Troy and the minister, Mr. D., close like this. "How do the people (?) out now? Love doesn't seem to agree with Mr. D. He must have it bad. What do you think?"

A letter to Hazel from her friend Jeanie Mason, makes the inquiry: "Are there any fellows down there? I suppose you have one.

A letter to Hazel from her friend, "Margaret" dated Troy, Jan. 14, 1908, was written while Hazel was ill at Uncle William Taylor's. It read in part: "I was very sorry to hear of your illness and going away. We were wondering what happened to you. I wouldn't tell what was the matter."

The announcement in The World this morning that Hazel's two gold bracelets were missing, started the county detectives on a hot-foot chase, and one of the bracelets was found in Hazel's trunk at her father's house. The detectives found at the same time a cheap photograph of a stockily-built young man: having overlooked the photo as well as the bracelet during the careful detective work of the last ten days. Then, to-day, they found that Aunt Minnie Taylor was in possession of the other bracelet. She said Hazel had made her a present of it sometime ago.

All this appears very strange to the looker-on in this Troy drama. No one in this town had mentioned bracelets either publicly or privately until The World announced this morning that the bracelets were missing. Yesterday Aunt Minnie was at the home of Drew's and said nothing about the bracelets, nor had she spoken of them at any previous time.

To-night John Drew put in an appearance rather unexpectedly at the house of Prof. Cary in Whitman Court and was in a somewhat joyous state of mind and body. He insisted upon repaying Mrs. Cary the amount she had paid Hazel for the two days, July 4 and 5, she was absent on a holiday from the Drew house. Although Drew kept on insisting that Mrs. Cary take the money, it was refused. John Drew said he had also called to learn if anything new had developed. He said he was getting anxious about the case, and found fault with the authorities because they had not solved the mystery.

Referring again to the bracelet in the possession of Aunt Minnie Taylor, she is quoted today as saying that Hazel had only loaned her the bracelet. On the Friday before Hazel's disappearance she wore both bracelets when she called on Miss Sharp and Miss Weaver, on Hawthorne avenue. It being Hazel's custom to wear either one or both of the bracelets on all occasions. It looks strange that one should turn up in her trunk and one in the possession of her Aunt Minnie.

Traces of the bay mare and the run-about that has figured in the romance coming from the wonderful highway that passes Teal's Pond were found to-day at Shayne's livery stable, in Third street. Monday night, July 6 at 7 o'clock a telephone call came asking that a rig be sent at once to Seventh and Congress streets.

Mr. Shayne told the man at the phone that he would have to come to the stable in person. In a few moments a stranger came, gave his name as D. Shaitus, and drove away. He did not return until after midnight. There is no man named Shaitus in Troy and none of the hotels harbored a man of that name on Monday July 6.

Mr. Shayne describes the man as rather short, stout, full smooth face, and of light complexion.

Description Fits Photo

This description fits exactly the cheap photograph of the unknown man found in Hazel's trunk by the detectives to-day. When they searched the trunk it was not there, and it looks to me like a plant.

I am making no comments on the missing bracelet found today. Mr. Shayne's record of the Shaitus livery rig is on his books in black and white. The admissions made to me yesterday by a member of the Drew family that Hazel had gone to Uncle Taylor's last winter to hide her shame aroused the authorities, doctors, and all hands to-day. Aunt

Minnie Taylor, it seems, had written about Hazel's condition to Mrs. Jones in Providence.

That Miss Taylor wanted to conceal all that would bring the past to light was indicated in a letter that she wrote to Mrs. Jones after it became known that Hazel's body was found in Teal's Pond.

In that letter, Minnie directs Mrs. Jones to destroy all correspondence she had had with Hazel. Why Miss Taylor had made such a request, the District-Attorney wants to find out, and if necessary drastic measures will be resorted to to compel her to give forth the information that will lead to an eligible clue.

Miss Taylor must have known of the condition Hazel was in last January beyond a question of a doubt. Ever since the investigation as to the cause of the murder as well as who committed the crime it has been a matter of comment the reticence displayed by this woman.

On Monday July 13, when a reporter saw her, she snapped at him: "She was a good girl. I won't tell you who her friends are, because it could get a lot of girls in trouble. It's none of your business, anyhow."

Now the admissions of the family show, in a measure, why there was so little desire on the part of her acquaintances to tell what they know of her. As the aunt was constantly with her and partook in most all of the excursions and outings that Hazel went to it is believed that she should be compelled to tell everything. If she should do this it is believed that the man who committed the crime could be found in a short time.

Miss Taylor did not know Mrs. Jones personally, but procured her address from the District-Attorney. Through this means she communicated with Mrs. Jones and made the request to destroy the letters.

Mrs. Jones in her first letter to Minnie said that she had a feeling of unrest, and in a second letter that Minnie had written she evidently asked what was the cause of this feeling. Mrs. Jones replied that it was not on account of the Hazel affair, but because she had removed to Waterville, Me.

The physicians in the case, who made a superficial examination of Hazel's decomposed body will doubtless aver that Hazel had never met with misfortune. This medical exposition reminds me of the Lena Whitmore case. Three days before my identification of Mrs. Whitmore's body at the Harrison Morgue, I wrote in The World that the unknown body was that of a Brooklyn woman and that she had been a mother. Three eminent Jersey physicians reported to the Coroner of Hudson County that Mrs. Whitmore had never had a child. Afterward it was shown that a child had been born in Albany fifteen years before.

Thus we see what doctors can do when they don't try. To-day's developments have only added additional interest to this interesting case. Tomorrow promises that things may happen worthwhile, and I repeat my prediction of a few days ago that light is breaking.

William Clemens' article was the only time in any newspaper that claimed two young men were going to stay at the Cary's for the summer. If true and Clemens was forthright in his article then Hazel didn't care for at least one of the two. This could have affected Hazel's decision to leave the employment of the Cary's on July 6. But because the information was not reported or verified in any other place, and the author had a reputation for fabricating evidence, it becomes unusable.

Clemens attempted to support his accusation that Hazel went to William Taylor's farm because she was pregnant and wished to hide her shame. He introduced two letters that, like the Cary visitors, were not printed in any other newspaper. One was reportedly written by Mina Jones who stated, "I am very, very sorry for you dearie. I know just how to feel for you." The other was supposedly written by a woman known only as Margaret who, according to Clemens wrote, "I was very sorry to hear of your illness and going away. We were wondering what happened to you. I wouldn't tell what was the matter." Both letters, if authentic, provide circumstantial evidence that Hazel was pregnant, thus conveniently supporting Clemens claim. But Clemens' history of fabricating letters and other evidence leaves doubt to the overall integrity of the evidence.

William Clemens continued his attack on the investigation, first by attempting to counter the bracelet evidence, and then by criticizing the doctors who performed the autopsy. He accused the investigators of not looking for the bracelets until after he exposed their incompetence in his New York World article. He wrote, "No one in this town had mentioned bracelets either publicly or privately until The World announced this morning that the bracelets were missing." Investigators from the beginning had knowledge of and were in possession of the bracelets. They were not mentioned because they were not newsworthy.

The autopsy doctors were the next victims of Clemens calculated attack. He claimed that because the doctors were negligent when they performed the autopsy they would not be able to testify that Hazel had been pregnant. It was necessary for Clemens to preemptively malign the doctors' reputations because they alone could discredit his accusation that Hazel had been pregnant in January.

Clemens claimed that he alone discovered that Lena Whitmore bore a child fifteen years before her murder. Like most things Clemens wrote, this too is doubtful. He printed the assertion, for the first time on July 24, 1908 as a way to show his readers that he had experience in such matters. His claim was never published or supported in any other newspaper at any time, including while the Whitmore case was still ongoing and receiving headline attention.

Clemens supposedly knew she had been a mother "three days before (his) identification of Mrs. Whitmore's body at the Harrison Morgue. (He) wrote in The World that the unknown body was that of a Brooklyn woman and that she had been a mother". However, according to his court testimony, he spent the first four days on the case tracking down the scarlet red jacket with the military style braids. The doctors at that time did not believe Lena Whitmore was, or ever had been pregnant so Clemens could not have used them as his source. Clemens could not have spoken to other witnesses about Lena Whitmore's past because at that time she was still unidentified. Therefore it would have been impossible for Clemens to have known that Lena Whitmore had ever been pregnant. So his use of that particular case as a justified reason to attack Hazel's autopsy doctors is totally false. Once again, Clemens was providing unsubstantiated and misleading reports to deceive his readers, enhance his own credibility and destroy the reputations of the authorities who were in position to discredit him but who were striving to find the real murderer.

Clemens continued undermining the investigation when he informed his readers that even John Drew was becoming anxious about the case. Clemens wrote that Hazel's father "found fault with the authorities because they had not solved the mystery". This may or may not have been true but again, Clemens article is the only place that it was published.

THURSDAY
JULY 23, 1908
Troy, New York

"If the murderer of Hazel Drew escapes the penalty of his atrocious crime, Rensselaer County citizens will have official inactivity to blame. Promptness and thoroughness has been sadly lacking in the efforts of Troy's authorities to unravel the mystery."

The Evening World, July 23, 1908

Jarvis O'Brien had been very busy preparing for the Coroner's Inquest which was scheduled to begin on Monday July 27. Duncan Kaye served nearly fifty subpoenas to witnesses scattered throughout Rensselaer County. To accommodate so many people who were spread so far, O'Brien arranged to hold the inquest in two separate locations. The first phase of hearings would be held in Averill Park, the second in Troy. He estimated a full week would be needed to thoroughly interrogate the witnesses. The other detectives continued to investigate and follow up on new leads.

With the lull in the investigation and with little to report, both the Evening World and the Times Union printed scathing articles that criticized the overall handling of the investigation. The papers were especially critical of what they called a superficial autopsy and a lackluster investigation conducted by an incompetent District Attorney.

The Evening World claimed that valuable information that was available early in the investigation was mishandled. Opportunities were missed by investigators who became distracted by irrelevant and meaningless evidence. The papers criticized the detectives for taking three days to locate Hazel's suitcase. Why, they asked, did it take so long for Hazel's letters and postcards to be discovered in the Cary's basement? The insinuation may have been missed but the Evening World, William Clemens base newspaper, implied that O'Brien's men were the ones who discovered the letters, albeit late, and not Clemens. Investigators were criticized for squandering their best lead of all, identifying the two men seen lurking around Teal's pond by William and Elizabeth Hoffey. This like all other leads, they claimed, went nowhere because the investigators were not up to the task.

The Evening World continued to attack the handling of the case when they stated that almost two weeks into the investigation, "...not one official can say positively as to the manner of Hazel's death" (The Evening World, July 23, 1908).

One reason, they wrote, was due to the incompetence of the four doctors who couldn't even agree on Hazel's "condition". If Hazel was in fact pregnant, they argued, the motive for her murder may have simply been for her killer to avoid an unwanted future.

> Without a known motive, without positive assurances of why the girl was slain, easily ascertainable from a careful autopsy, detectives willing but at sea have lost almost two weeks of time in their search for the murderer. (The Evening World, July 23, 1908)

The Times Union was critical of O'Brien's decision to trust the opinions of the doctors rather than exhume the body and eliminate all doubt.

> Whether or not she was in otherwise than a perfectly nor-
> mal condition or had suffered an operation does not matter
> to the district attorney. (The Times Union, July 23, 1908)

Until the conference at Dr. Reichard's house, O'Brien and his detectives kept open the possibility or even the likelihood that Hazel took her own life. The conference was called so O'Brien could force the doctors to commit to the cause of Hazel's death, which they did. O'Brien relied on the expertise of the doctors to guide him to his decision that Hazel was the victim of homicide. The Evening World was critical of O'Brien's decision to direct the course of the investigation based on the findings of four doctors who, they argued were far from competent.

The Evening World used William Clemens' "findings" as fact and continued to criticize the investigation.

> And the rattling of the family's skeleton has at least exposed
> secrets which, if earlier revealed, would have saved two
> weeks of aimless rambling about the county in search of
> clues and perhaps deprived the slayer of Hazel Drew of that
> chance to escape. (The Evening World, July 23, 1908)

The article continued to attack O'Brien, specifically for his inability to get those closest to Hazel to talk.

> ...because an over-cautious District-Attorney did not break
> at once the obstinate silence of the victim's relatives and
> friends. (The Evening World, July 23, 1908)

Many questions that O'Brien and his detectives had worked tirelessly to find answers to but never could were publicly exposed in the Evening World. For example, the paper questioned how Hazel arrived in the Hollow. What the motive was for her death and where Hazel spent the night of July 6. The paper questioned if Hazel was murdered at the pond or at some other location, why she destroyed so many of her letters and other mementos, why she visited her relatives the Saturday and Sunday before her death, and why she was at Union Station so often. O'Brien's inability to find answers to these questions, they argued, highlight the incompetence of the investigation.

The Evening World then broke down Hazel's presence on the mountain.

> Either Hazel Drew walked to the Taylor turnpike or she was carried there. One points irresistibly to a farewell visit to her uncle; the other to a secret meeting, a romance or a denouncement and death. The one indicates the slayer as a stranger or strangers met on the road; the other directs the finger of suspicion to her guilty lover. The one means that she was murdered near the pond; the other that she was murdered elsewhere and her body carried there. (The Evening World, July 23, 1908)

FRIDAY
JULY 24, 1908

Sand Lake, New York

"Every clue which might point toward someone as the perpetrator of the crime has thus far been explained, with the exception of a story about a camp at some distance from the pond. The death of the pretty domestic is as much a mystery as ever and not much pointing toward a solution has been unearthed."

The Troy Times, July 24, 1908

Jarvis O'Brien and his team of detectives had investigated hundreds of leads in their effort to capture Hazel Drew's killer. Every clue was checked and followed up, even those clues whose likelihood of being associated with the case was minimal. On July 24 the local papers followed the developments of a story that O'Brien's men were investigating which involved a camp in the Alps Mountains located about three miles from Teal's pond.

The camp, owned by Henry Kramrath a successful businessman from Albany, was active during the summer but the locals were very suspicious of the activities believed to have been going on there. Girls were rumored to be brought to the camp by men who offered them rides. Once there the girls were stranded. Stories of sexual manipulation and orgies were rumored to take place at the camp.

William Powers went to see if the rumors were true and if the camp may in some way be connected to Hazel's murder. He interviewed Mrs. William Clifford and her husband who lived near the camp and at one time had worked there as caretakers. Mrs. Clifford told Detective Powers that on the night of either July 6 or 7 she was awakened by a woman's scream. She woke her husband and said, "You had better get up; they are liable to be killing that young girl over there." (The Troy Record, July 24, 1908). Mr. Clifford got up but because he did not hear any commotion he ignored the potential problem and went back to bed.

Mrs. Clifford told Detective Powers about another incident which the Evening Telegram published on July 24, 1908.

> "Early in May two young women came up to visit the camp. One, who had light hair and a slight build but a well developed figure, came over shortly afterward to buy butter of me. This girl said her aunt, who was with her at the camp, was ill. Afterward she came again and begged me to let her take our team, as she said she had an engagement to spend Decoration Day with friends and afterward to go to Lake George."

> "She also said that her life had been threatened by one of the men, who was intoxicated, and who, because she did not blow out a light when he ordered, threw her against the wall with great violence. If she could borrow our team, she said, she wanted to go to Brown's Hotel, at Crooked Lake to telephone for someone to take her home."

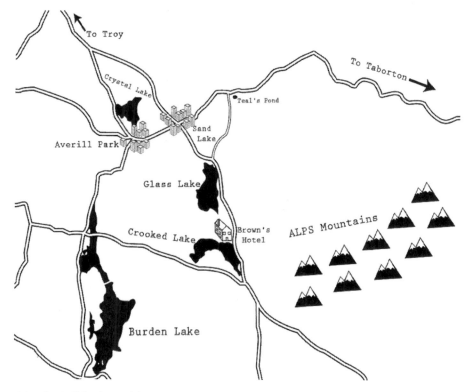

Map by Mikhail Vainblat

Miss Mabel Brown who worked at her family's hotel on Crooked Lake recalled the story of two young girls who showed up in May and possibly corroborated Mrs. Clifford's account. The story was printed in the same Evening Telegram newspaper.

> "(The girl) wore a man's coat and was only partially dressed from which the inference was drawn that part of her clothing had been hidden to prevent her from leaving the camp. Miss Brown remembered the name of the man the girl called on the telephone which was that of one of the owners of the camp. The girl, she said, asked that a physician be sent to the camp as her aunt was ill."

"Later the girl came again to the hotel accompanied by another girl. She wore a man's trousers and her friend, to conceal the absence of outer clothing, wore a heavy blanket around her shoulders, although the day was very hot."

The girls asked to use the telephone, Brown reportedly said, because they were without money and desperate to get home. They said they had accepted a ride from some men and ended up at the camp. They were stranded. They had no money and the men refused to take them back because the girls would not promise to keep quiet about the activities that had occurred at the camp.

The most direct way to get to the Alps Mountains from Sand Lake is to continue straight (southeast) past Crooked Lake and up the Stephentown Heights. It is possible to get to the Alps from Sand Lake by driving up Taborton Road and turning right onto the road that leads to Glass Lake, and after passing Brown's Hotel at Crooked Lake, take the road to Stephentown Heights. This however, would have been a roundabout route and not an efficient way to get to the Alps from Sand Lake.

On the night July 7, Mrs. Neusteil (not known if this is Beverly Neusteil) who lived near the pond, claimed she heard an automobile drive by late at night. Chris Crape's report of a car that drove up Taborton Road was recalled. Crape had originally said the automobile drove past his place on July 4 but sometime later, probably after the reward was offered, changed his story. According to the July 24, 1908 Troy Record, "Chris Crape later said that he never told the exact date that the machine passed his hotel and he did not intend to until the proper time arrived."

Investigators discussed the possibilities. The young girl mentioned by Mrs. Clifford matched the basic description of Hazel. The places she said she was planning to visit and reportedly told Mrs.

Clifford were the places that Hazel either travelled to or attempted to, New York on Decoration Day and plans for Lake George shortly after. The girl told Mrs. Clifford that she was at the camp with her aunt. Investigators wondered if the aunt could have been Minnie Taylor.

Because much of what Mrs. Clifford described was information that had already been printed in the newspapers, detectives were aware that Mrs. Clifford may have been yet another of the many people who kept abreast of the details of the case in order to collect some of the reward money.

Could Hazel have been in the car that drove past Crape's Hotel as first thought? Could she have been taken to Henry Kramrath's camp, walked away or escaped and was on her way to her uncle's for help? Could Hazel have been at the camp and at some point, either in the car, at the camp itself, or on the road, resisted the man or men who brought her there and was killed during the struggle?

None of the scenarios make sense. In the first place, if Hazel was fleeing the camp and going to her uncle's for help she would not have been walking up Taborton Road. Hazel knew the area and would have taken the route from the Alps that goes past Teal's farm and then down Taborton Road.

Hazel was not in distress when she was seen by the Rollmans or by Frank Smith and Rudy Gundrum walking up Taborton Road. If she was fleeing a precarious situation at the camp she wouldn't be loitering around the side of the road casually picking raspberries or pleasantly saying hello to Frank Smith sitting in Rudy Gundrum's wagon.

Chris Crape did not revise the date of seeing the car speed past his hotel on July 4 until after the newspapers reported that Hazel was seen and accounted for on July 7. The fact that he changed his story and his refusal to provide the specific date that he claimed he saw the car lessens his credibility.

The condition of Taborton Road also lessens the likelihood of a car taking that route to or driving away from the camp. As stated in the Troy Record on July 24, 1908,

> Mr. O'Brien also said that it was not reasonable to suppose that a person would drive a touring car over the Taborton mountains, although it could be done. Relative to the automobile and the camp figuring in the case, he said that the machine would have to ascend a big hill and mountainous country, country almost impassible. A car could be driven from the camp at the Alps to Teal's pond without passing Crape's hotel, as the road from Glass Lake would lead to it. This road is least popular on account of the roadbed in places being rough and dangerous to the shoes on the cars.

Neither Jarvis O'Brien, William Powers, nor any other investigator believed that the camp in the Alps had anything to do with Hazel's death. O'Brien promised to fully investigate the camp and if illegal activities were being conducted he would take appropriate measures.

(II)

Meanwhile, the July 24, 1908 Evening World continued to attack the District Attorney.

> District Attorney O'Brien is to be a candidate for reelection this fall, and his seeming indifference relative to the case is thought by many the result of politics.

The Troy Daily Press asked O'Brien to comment on the attacks. The following response was published on July 24.

> District Attorney O'Brien was amused this morning when he read that he was a "$100,000" politician, "large, tall,

impressive, wears a goatee, strikes military attitudes and smokes cigarettes," he said to The Press reporter. "I never had a goatee and I don't know that I want one. As to cigarettes, I don't use them. A cigar is good enough for me, and I don't smoke them very often."

O'Brien then used the opportunity to discuss the unusual behavior of William Clemens, although not mentioning him by name.

Referring to his critic, who poses as a criminologist, the district attorney said, "He wanted to sleep with the Drew girl's clothes, but I wouldn't let him. He was permitted to see the clothes, and had to ask my stenographer what each article was called."

SATURDAY
JULY 25, 1908

Troy, New York

"It has proven one of the most difficult mysteries that the authorities of Rensselaer County have ever been called upon to unravel to find out how she came to her death."

The Troy Times, July 25, 1908

From the time the letters and postcards were discovered in Hazel's trunk and others later found in the Cary's basement, investigators had been exhausting all resources in their attempt to learn the identities of the writers. The task was extremely difficult because very few of the letters included the name of the writer. Almost all of the correspondence were signed only with initials.

The content of most of the postcards was platonic, little more than friends writing to each other to keep in touch. Very little information was gained from the messages themselves but the detectives understood the importance of identifying each writer knowing that any one of them could provide information that could lead to the long awaited and much needed breakthrough in the case.

In order to identify the writer, detectives were forced to rely on events or anecdotes written in the letters. If a third person was

231

mentioned by name investigators had a specific starting point from which to work. If an event or incident was mentioned, they would learn what they could about the event and talk to people they knew were there and learn the names of others who may have information.

By July 25, almost all of the people whose letters Hazel had saved had been identified and interviewed. There were still some letters, however whose content had not divulged enough useful information and investigators were still laboring to learn the identities of those writers. Hazel received at least one such letter from a man who at one time had worked as a waiter in one of the restaurants in Averill Park.

The July 25 newspapers focused on the story of a man that Duncan Kaye brought to the courthouse who was believed to have written one of those letters. The man worked as a conductor on the trains that ran from Albany to New York but had previously worked as a waiter in Averill Park. Remembering Minnie Taylor's statement that Hazel had called on a conductor in New York and knowing that Hazel probably went to the Albany train station on July 6, O'Brien realized the importance of this potential suspect. The fact that the man now lived in Troy and was familiar with Averill Park added to O'Brien's investigative interest. The man arrived at the courthouse with his wife and the two were interviewed at the same time in separate rooms.

The man's name was Samuel LeRoy. He was small, weighing about 110 pounds. He was 38 years old and married to Rose LeRoy. They had two sons, Martin, age 16 and Harold age 13. The family lived on Seventh Avenue in Troy.

Samuel and Rose LeRoy confirmed that they used to work in a restaurant in Averill Park. Samuel had been the waiter in charge of the dining room and Rose was a waitress. The couple moved from Averill Park ten years earlier when Samuel accepted a position with the railroad. They had never been back to Averill Park.

Mr. and Mrs. LeRoy were both open and straightforward with their answers. He told the investigators that he began working at Union Station and, although it took a long time, he worked his way into the service of the Pullman cars. He became a conductor in March. His first route was from Kansas City to Texas. He was then transferred and worked on the Albany to Chicago run and recently became a conductor on the Albany to New York route. LeRoy said he was familiar with who John Magner was but only as a fellow conductor. LeRoy claimed he didn't know and he never met Hazel Drew or Anna LaBelle.

O'Brien and Kaye were specifically interested in Samuel's whereabouts on July 6 and July 7. He told them that on July 6 he took the 12:05 pm train from Albany to New York. It arrived at Grand Central Station at 3:45. He went to his boarding house, took a nap and then returned to Albany on the early train which arrived at 5:50 am.

Rose LeRoy independently verified her husband's story. She said that Samuel spent July 7, an oppressively hot day, lounging on the couch. Sometime in the early evening they sent their son, Martin to the home of a neighbor, Mrs. Coleman, to see if she would be interested in playing cards that night. Mrs. Coleman told young LeRoy that she couldn't because she was waiting on a call from Miss Whitney, a boarder who was getting married the next day. Mrs. Coleman was planning to help Miss Whitney prepare for the wedding but told Martin to tell his parents that she would be glad to play cards another day. Samuel said he went to bed that night between 10:30 and 11:00.

While the duel interrogations continued, Detective Kaye left the courthouse to visit Mrs. Coleman on Seventh Avenue to verify the statements. Kaye met not only with Mrs. Coleman but also her mother Esther Prangley who lived with her. Both women provided the same story as Samuel and Rose. Detective Kaye then spoke with young Martin LeRoy who also verified his parents' story.

(II)

In their continued effort to locate the place where Hazel spent the night of July 6, detectives examined the registries of the Hudson River night liner boats. They discovered that, on the night of July 6, a "Miss Drew" obtained a stateroom on the steamship *Saratoga* in Albany. A watchman on board recalled that "the woman was a blonde, but not one of the bleached variety." (Troy Daily Press, July 25, 1908)

Officers Murnane and Lawrenson visited every Drew family in the area and not one of them was aware of a relative that reserved a stateroom on a boat bound for New York on July 6.

The steamship Saratoga. A Miss Drew reserved a stateroom on the ship the night of July 6. The woman had blond hair but it is not known if she was Hazel. Photo courtesy of Images of America:Troy, by Don Rittner

(III)

Could Samuel LeRoy and Hazel Drew have been involved in a relationship? If Hazel planned to meet LeRoy on Monday morning July 6, Union Station would have been a logical place. He would have to be at the station to catch the train to Albany in time to make his 12:05 connection to New York. At the very latest, he would have had to have caught the 11:30 train, but is more likely that he would have taken an earlier one. Mary Robinson saw Hazel at Union Station between 11:20 and 11:30, the latest possible time that LeRoy could have passed through. Hazel told her friend that she was "going down the river, maybe as far as New York." If so, she most likely would have been a passenger on LeRoy's train.

Hazel would have arrived at the Albany train station around the time that LeRoy's train was departing for New York. If she saw him before he left they could have made arrangements to meet back at Union Station the following day. Hazel could then have returned to Union Station in time to place her order at the Westcott Express Company.

When all of the components are examined however, the scenario does not makes sense. It is still not known where Hazel spent Monday night. If she wasn't planning to meet LeRoy until the following day, there would be no need for secrecy. She could have spent the night with her family or some close friend and returned the next day.

LeRoy returned to Troy the following morning at 5:50 and spent the rest of the day at home lying on his couch. This was confirmed by his wife and son. If he had arranged to meet Hazel, why didn't he? And what was Hazel doing? She was seen at Union Station by Jeanette Marcellus and possibly Adelbert Atwood later that day.

There is no evidence that Hazel Drew and Samuel LeRoy ever met, much less that they were involved in a relationship. O'Brien quickly exonerated Samuel Leroy; yet another promising lead lost. The Troy Record stated on July 25, "In the end the incident proved another expedition into the realm of the rainbow chasers who are supplying all sorts of dreams calculated to involve innocent persons."

The fact that investigators never discovered the identity of the "Miss Drew" who travelled on the *Saratoga* leaves open the possibility that the woman may have been Hazel. Based on Mary Robinson's statement, it appears that Hazel did have an interest in traveling south possibly as far as New York. Hazel even used the term "going down the river," an unusual choice of words if she was planning to travel by rail. Hazel was familiar with traveling by ship on the Hudson River as that is how she and Carrie Weaver traveled to New York. If William Clemens is to be believed, Hazel also inquired of Mina Jones how to travel by ship from New York to Providence. She could have taken the train to Albany with plans to travel down the Hudson River on the *Saratoga*.

Reason and timing however, once again present problems. If Hazel was going to New York why would she take a boat when trains are faster, more accessible and presumably more affordable. If she was traveling on the boat with a male companion, she would not have registered as "Miss Drew" as that was not acceptable behavior or protocol of the era and may not even have been permitted by the steamboat company. Instead she would have signed in as the wife of the man she was traveling with.

Assuming however, that it was Hazel, the ship would have had to have travelled most of the night to reach New York. Hazel would then have had to get off the ship and very soon after, catch a train back to Troy in time for Jeanette Marcellus to see her in Union Station. The blond haired Miss Drew that was seen aboard the *Saratoga* in all likelihood, could not have been Hazel Drew.

SUNDAY
JULY 26, 1908

Troy, New York

*"Many false rumors have been set afloat by sensational newspapers and the
wildest of stories have been printed for the sole purpose of exciting the people,
creating sensations and to make it appear that the officials of the county and
city have been amiss in their duties."*

The Northern Budget, July 26, 1908

While Jarvis O'Brien and his investigators continued to
prepare for the Coroner's Inquest, The Northern Budget
responded to the personal attacks on the District
Attorney and defend the actions of the officials who, they argued
were fully committed to bringing a murderer to justice. At the same
time, the local newspaper criticized the unethical and unscrupulous
tactics employed by the New York newspapers and those who used
Hazel's murder to advance their own agendas or sought personal gain
and profit.

At least one of the papers, citing an unnamed source, claimed
that Hazel's killer had strong political connections in Troy and that
Jarvis O'Brien would not pursue charges against him for political

reasons. The accusation was reminiscent of William Clemens charge against District Attorney James Niemann in the Margaret Lynch case.

The Northern Budget responded to the attack.

> ...but where politics comes in they, of course, fail to point out. Those who know District Attorney O'Brien, know very well that no politics would prevent him from bringing to justice the murderer of Hazel Drew if he could find him.

The Northern Budget pointed out that the investigative reporters and criminologists from New York had full access to all of the information and evidence that the District Attorney and his investigators had.

> These sensational metropolitan papers have sent their most 'brilliant' reporters here, backed by their criminologists, sleuths, photographers and all of the paraphernalia they can command, yet they have failed to find the slightest clew to the murderer of the girl. Now that they have so signally failed in their efforts, and they have been given every courtesy and assistance within the power of the office of the District Attorney, they try to cover up their failure by criticizing the officials of the county and city.

When the reporters and the famous criminologist from New York failed to uncover any evidence that could reveal the identity of the killer, they changed their tactic and became more critical of the investigation itself. They criticized O'Brien for being unable to capture the killer when the list of suspects was so small and the evidence was so obvious. They failed to mention that even William Clemens had eliminated William Taylor and Frank Smith, two of the most publicized suspects, in his July 22, Thrice-A-Week World article.

The Northern Budget addressed the unscrupulous tactic used by the New York press.

The same papers are clamoring for the arrest of someone even though there is not the slightest bit of evidence against them. District Attorney O'Brien said yesterday that he did not think it proper to place people under arrest who were merely acquainted with the girl, and who saw her just before the time of her death, when there is nothing to prove that they had anything to do with her death. "Some people have been clamoring for the arrest of William Taylor, the uncle," said Mr. O'Brien. "There is no evidence against him; no motive has been shown for his murdering the girl. Others have been advocating the arrest of Miss Taylor, the aunt. She has answered all our questions, apparently in an honest manner, and has assured us over and over again that she will do anything possible to fix the responsibility for the crime. Of course, no one suspects her, but some think she knows more about the girl's previous whereabouts than she has told. We have no reason to believe that she does. Others have clamored for the arrest of Smith and Gunderman, (sic) but there is nothing in a sense of fairness and justice, which would warrant out placing a stain upon their lives by taking them into custody."

O'Brien summed up his frustration and irritation.

"All is being done that can be done. If others can come to this city, from New York or any other place, and capture the murderer, I will be glad to have them do it. We are not looking for glory in this case. All we want is to see the guilty party or parties brought to justice."

MONDAY
JULY 27, 1908

Averill Park, New York

"It is a peculiar coincidence in the Hazel Drew case that the principle, if not the only grounds for suspicion against William Taylor, the girl's uncle, and Frank Smith is the indifference of both after the body was found."

The Troy Times, July 27, 1908

T he first phase of the Coroner's Inquest was held at the dance hall pavilion in the rear of Warger's Hotel in Averill Park. In the past the pavilion served as a place where politicians campaigned and gave rousing speeches. Jarvis O'Brien himself had spoken there in 1904 when he endorsed President Theodore Roosevelt and other prominent Republicans. The pavilion was a place where summer vacationers danced late into the night. Weddings, parties, dances, and other joyous gatherings were held at Warger's over the years. But on July 27 the gathering was more somber.

Coroner Morris Strope was the presiding officer. He would listen to witness testimony and examine all of the evidence in order to officially determine the cause of Hazel Drew's death. District Attorney O'Brien would call and interview the witnesses who were sworn to tell the truth or face perjury charges.

Approximately fifty people were in attendance, including twenty six who had been subpoenaed. William Taylor was among the first to arrive. Wearing a dark suit, white shirt, dark blue cravat and a light colored fedora, he sat silently by himself off to the side, staring at the floor, his feet crossed.

Frank Smith also arrived early. He did not wear a coat, but his shirt was freshly washed. He wore a soft hat and smoked a cigar. Unlike Taylor, Smith seemed to revel in the attention and the notoriety he was receiving.

Coroner Strope called the Inquest to order at 1:00 pm. Lorenzo Gruber, George White, George Alberts, and Gilbert Miller respectively were the first four witnesses called. Each of the young men recounted how they discovered and then reported finding the body on July 11 and how they later assisted in removing the corpse from the pond.

Conrad Teal was called next. He testified that he owned the property on which the body was found. When he heard of the discovery in his pond, he along with his family went to investigate. His house, he said, was close enough to the pond to hear talking and other commotion but he did not hear anything the night of July 7.

Mrs. and Mr. Henry Rollman were the next two witnesses called. They each told their story of passing the blond woman picking raspberries by the side of the road the night of July 7. Mrs. Rollman remembered the woman's stunning appearance and took particular notice of the black hat with the three large plumes. The Rollmans both told of passing the Ryemillers and later the Hoffeys on their way down the mountain.

Henry Ryemiller and his wife both testified that while travelling up Taborton Mountain on July 7, they passed the Rollmans and later Frank Smith and Rudy Gundrum. They stated under oath, however that they did not encounter any woman walking along the mountain road nor did they see a wagon or any people lurking around Teal's pond.

Elizabeth and William Hoffey each told their version of passing the Rollmans and later Smith and Gundrum. Neither saw a woman walking along the road but they told of the wagon parked by the pond. They also testified about the two men they saw, one in the wagon, the other on the far side of the pond near the dam. To be clear that it was not Hazel that William Hoffey saw on the other side of the pond, O'Brien asked him if he was sure it was a man that he saw.

"Well, if it was a woman, she wore pants, announced the witness. A man would have to be pretty drunk to mistake a man for a woman." (Troy Daily Press, July 27, 1908)

Rudy Gundrum was called and recounted his story of riding down the mountain with Frank Smith and meeting Hazel in the Hollow. He told the District Attorney that Hazel said hello to Frank, calling him by name, as they passed.

Frank Smith was called and repeated the story of meeting Hazel on Taborton Road. He testified that, later that night he ran into Frank Richmond at the train station and asked him about Hazel. He later discussed taking bets at Crape's hotel, including the one where he ran to Averill Park in an attempt to obtain a postcard from Wright's Pharmacy.

Smith admitted that the day after he saw Hazel he made inquiries about her whereabouts. He said he was interested in calling on her, that she was the prettiest girl he knew. He said that one of the families he visited in his search was the Sowalsky's. O'Brien recalled that Frank and Edward Sowalsky were two of the young men who had camped along the bank of Teal's pond with Lorenzo Gruber and George White.

William Taylor was the most anticipated witness of the day. He repeated under oath that he had not seen Hazel since February when she left his farm following her illness. He said that John Abel, the hackman who said he brought Hazel to his farm in the spring was either mistaken or lying.

O'Brien questioned Taylor about his unusual behavior following the discovery of the body and his apathy when he was informed that it may be his niece. Taylor testified that the first he heard that Hazel may be in the area was on the morning of July 8 when Frank Richmond asked if she was there. Richmond, Taylor learned, had encountered Frank Smith at the train station on July 7 and Smith mentioned seeing Hazel on Taborton Road.

On July 11, the day the body was discovered in the pond, Frank Smith's father stopped by Taylor's farm and told his neighbor that the person his son helped pull from the pond may be Hazel. On July 12, Frank Smith saw Taylor in Averill Park and personally told the uncle that he believed the girl in the pond may be his niece. Still after all these notices, Taylor never took any action. He did not go to Averill Park to identify the body and he did not use the telephone at Crape's hotel to call family members in Troy. O'Brien felt this lack of interest was very peculiar under the circumstances and demanded answers.

William Taylor was a peculiar man. He had no friends and his family had all but abandoned him. On the stand, he attempted to explain his apparent lack of interest following the discovery of the body in the pond. He said he heard that the body was in such a state of decomposition that it could not be identified. The only way to know if the victim was Hazel would be by recognizing the clothing. Since he did not know Hazel's wardrobe, he said, he could be of no assistance in helping with the identification.

Jarvis O'Brien had no reason to believe Taylor had anything to do with the death of his niece nor did he have any evidence. The fact that he was peculiar did not mean he murdered Hazel. The Troy Record on July 27, 1908 stated,

Taylor was questioned along with other ones and told a straightforward and plausible story and at the conclusion, the district attorney stated that Taylor henceforth would be practically eliminated from the case. The district attorney gave as his opinion that Taylor is a taciturn man, with no interest in anything except his little farm and the money he makes. He thought that was the reason he did not go to visit the body after it was found. He simply had no interest in the matter; no curiosity.

If John Abel was being truthful when he said he brought Hazel and a friend to Taylor's farm in April, then Taylor had to have been lying. This was a critical point that O'Brien needed to address. As such he called Eva Drew to the stand. She provided the following account as printed in the Troy Record on July 27, 1908.

"John Abel is mistaken about driving Hazel and another girl over to Uncle Taylor's house. How do I know he is mistaken? Because I was at Uncle Taylor's at the time. I remember it all quite well. I remember that John Abel drove up to Uncle Taylor's house with his carriage. In it were seated two girls, also my husband, Joe Drew, and Philip, a young man from Troy. One of the girls in Abel's carriage wore glasses. She is Miss Stella Carner of Troy. The carriage held five persons, Stella and Kate Carner, sisters of Troy who were to spend the day with me. My husband and Philip were also in the carriage and with the driver, Mr. Abel, makes five persons. Stella Carner wears glasses and Mr. Abel may now suppose it was Hazel. Stella Carner is right here in the house, now," said Miss Drew. "I will call her." Stella came from another room...

O'Brien cross-examined Stella Carner. The Troy Record continued.

"I went out to Uncle Taylor's in March with my sister Kate Carner. My young man Philip was also expected there that day. Kate, my sister and myself arrived at the Averill

Park depot about 2 o'clock Sunday afternoon just before St. Patrick's day. At the depot we arranged with Mr. Abel to drive us over. We agreed to pay him one dollar. He took us over to Taylor's. At Crape's hotel we met Joe Drew and Philip, my friend. Philip and Joe also got in the rig at Crape's and all drove over to Taylor's."

Averill Park taxi drivers. John Abel, who claimed to have driven Hazel to William Taylor's farm in April is at the far right. Photo courtesy of Images of America:Sand Lake by Mary D. French and Robert J. Lilly

TUESDAY
JULY 28, 1908

Averill Park, New York

"'But I don't believe it was Hazel that Frank Smith or those other people saw on the Taborton road that night walking alone. She was taken out there in an automobile or a carriage by someone maybe from Troy. I believe that it was someone who was well to do and who had Hazel in his control.'"

Julia Drew as quoted in The Evening World, July 28, 1908

The doctors who performed Hazel's autopsy testified at the Inquest on July 28. This was arguably the most important information that could be obtained from the Inquiry.

Dr. Boyce was the first to testify. He told of being at the pond when Hazel's body was removed from the water and placed on the dam. He described the bloated and decomposed condition of the body. He discussed in detail his cutting the ribbon that was wrapped around Hazel's neck. Dr. Boyce described the wound on the back of Hazel's head which he said caused a clot between the skull and the covering of the brain. This, in his opinion was the primary cause of death. The murder weapon was a blunt instrument; one, he said, that would bruise but not cut. There was no water in Hazel's lungs or stomach. The Troy Daily Press on July 28, 1908 reported his testimony.

"Now doctor", asked the district attorney, "in your opinion, was this woman dead or alive before thrown into the water?"

"Dead"

"Was the wound on the head inflicted before death?"

"Yes"

"Was it sufficient to cause death?"

"Yes"

"The distortion of the face indicated that she may have been strangled, but the decomposition was so great as to make a decision indefinite. The clothes on the body were not disarranged. All of the underclothing was in good condition, and none appeared to be torn or out of place."

"What, in your opinion, was the cause of death?"

"I think the contusion on the back of the head was the cause of death, but it might have been assisted by strangulation."

Doctor Reichard's and Doctor Fairweather's descriptions of the decomposed body and the absence of water in the lungs and stomach matched that of Dr. Boyce. Both of the doctors agreed that the body was placed in the water after death. The wound on the back of Hazel's head did, in their opinions, cause her death. The only possible discrepancy between the two doctors was reported in the Troy Daily Press.

Dr. Reichard claimed, "There was a slight rupture in the female organs." He could not tell if it was a fresh rupture.

Dr. Fairweather claimed, "There was no indication that the deceased was not a good girl."

Hazel's good friend Carrie Weaver was scheduled to return to Troy on the First of August. Therefore, she would not be back in time to testify at the Inquest. The following article was printed in the July 28, 1908 Troy Record.

A special dispatch to The Record from Springfield OH says:

Springfield, OH, July 28- The three weeks vacation which Miss Carrie Weaver, close friend of Hazel Drew, who was mysteriously murdered in Troy, NY July 7, has been spending in this vicinity, is fast drawing to a close and she will leave here for Troy Wednesday.

Statements made by Miss Weaver to relatives and intimate friends here disclose two facts. One is that Miss Drew undoubtedly has a friend or friends who made possible for her many social pleasures and diversions. Miss Weaver is essentially a country girl, despite her six months' residence in Troy.

One of Miss Weaver's first remarks to her relatives in Dayton was in regard to Miss Drew's financial ability. It has been, and still is a constant source of wonder to Miss Weaver how her friend managed to live so well, to wear such stylish costumes, to take so many and so extended trips and to enjoy so many luncheons at such expensive hostelries on her wages as a domestic.

Miss Weaver was loud in her praise of Miss Drew and while (?) (?) of the adventures the latter confided in her trips up and down the Hudson on first class boats and trips by rail to Providence, Boston and other neighboring cities, she protested all the while that Miss Drew explicitly stated that she had no men friends.

"I never saw her in the company of a man all the time I was in Troy," said Miss Weaver, "and she told me on more than one occasion that she had no sweetheart. Really, Hazel was a remarkable girl. She could make a dollar go further than any other woman I ever saw. Her wages were only a little more than mine, yet I never could manage to buy as fine hats and as swell costumes as she did, let alone the luncheons at fashionable restaurants and the frequent trips she made out of town."

"From what Hazel told me, she must have had an awfully good time when she went away from home. She said she had dandy dinners and not the slightest attempt was ever made anywhere to offer her an insult any more than if she had been accompanied by a brother or her father. She knew how to take care of herself, all right, but from what our little trips together cost I know she must have spent a great deal of money on pleasures of this kind, and for the life of me I don't see how she managed to save enough from her wages."

When the proceedings concluded, it was announced that the next session would be held on Thursday, July 30 in the courthouse in Troy. A reporter from the Associated Press writing for the Albany Times Union asked Hazel's mother to comment on what she had heard. According to the reporter, Mrs. Drew looked at him, a tear ran down her cheek, with a tremor in her lip she said, "My girl Hazel was hypnotized and then murdered." (Times Union, July 28, 1908)

According to the article, Mrs. Drew told the reporter that ever since the discovery of her daughter's body, she has been rehashing in her mind every possible scenario and motive for her daughter's death.

"I've thought this matter over and I'm sure Hazel did not commit suicide. Why should she? She was happy and had everything she wanted. If anything had been wrong she would have come to me. She always did, and I gave her everything she asked; whether it was money or anything else. She would not have gone to Uncle Will for money, as has been said. That never made her go out to Averill Park on that Tuesday night. But I don't believe that it was Hazel that Frank Smith or those other people saw on the road in the night walking alone. She was taken out there in an automobile or carriage by someone maybe from Troy. I believe it was someone who was well to do, and who had Hazel in his control. He mesmerized her or what you called hypnotized my Hazel, and she did whatever he asked of her. He took her out there while she was under his influence and murdered her."

The next day Mrs. Drew was asked by other reporters to elaborate further on the hypnotism story. She denied making the statement. When they pressed she said, "They came down here and asked me if I knew anything about Hazel being hypnotized. Why, I said she might have been hypnotized and kidnapped." (The Troy Times, July 29, 1908)

The reporters told her the article printed in the papers must have been embellished. A somewhat agitated Mrs. Drew replied, "If you see any of them tell them not to make a big item because I do not know anything about it." (The Troy Times, July 29, 1908)

District Attorney O'Brien scoffed when a reporter asked him to comment on the hypnotism story. When he was told that Mrs. Drew denied making the statement O'Brien said that the Drew's were dignified people and Mrs. Drew was careful in her statements.

WEDNESDAY
JULY 29, 1908

Taborton Mountain

"The dead girl was devoted to her brother (Willie). It is said that she thought more of him than any other member of her family, and the belief is now that on the night she was slain she was on the way to the Sowalsky farm to tell her brother good-bye, she having decided to leave this part of the state."

The Evening World, July 29, 1908

With the completion of the first phase of the Inquest in Averill Park, Jarvis O'Brien used Wednesday to prepare for the second phase which would be held in the Grand Jury Room at the Courthouse in Troy. Detective Unser and Investigator Powers used the day to follow up on leads that were revealed at the Inquest. In particular, they wanted to obtain more information on the Sowalsky family. They knew that Frank Smith had visited the Sowalsky home when he was making inquiries about Hazel the day after he saw her on Taborton Road. Unser and Powers were also reminded at Inquest that two of the Sowalsky brothers had camped with Lorenzo Gruber and George White the night before Hazel's body was discovered.

Edward and Frank Sowalsky lived with their 60 year old widowed mother, Libbie and another brother, Michael on the road that led to Glass Lake. Unser and Powers drove up the mountain to interview the family. They met with Libbie Sowalsky but there is no record of an interview with Frank or Edward.

Libbie Sowalsky told the investigators that Hazel's eight year old brother, Willie had been staying at her house for three weeks and had been there when Hazel was murdered. Willie returned home to his parents the Monday after Hazel's body was discovered. The investigators learned that Hazel was very close to Willie, closer in fact, than to any of her other siblings.

During his stay, Willie told Mrs. Sowalsky that he was expecting to see his sister. If Hazel was intending to leave the area it is likely she would have gone to see her favorite brother to say good-bye.

Mrs. Sowalsky told the investigators that Willie had been talking about his sister the week before July 7, that is, the week before Hazel was last seen alive. He gave Libbie the impression that Hazel would be stopping by to visit him. When it was learned that a well dressed woman was found floating in Teal's pond, Willie exclaimed that his sister was always well dressed. He told Mrs. Sowalsky, "If I thought that was my sister, I would go and jump in the pond and die with her." (The Thrice-A-Week World, July 29, 1908)

On Monday July 13, the day after Hazel's body was identified by her father, Willie returned home to Troy. One of his friends informed him that the body had been identified and it was his sister Hazel. Willie reportedly broke down and cried uncontrollably.

Willie later talked to an Evening World reporter. The exchange was printed in the July 29, 1908 edition of that paper.

> "I went to the officers to-day and told them all I knew about
> my sister's murder. That wasn't much either. I told them I
> knew Hazel would never have gone away without telling me
> goodbye. I am sure she was on her way to Mrs. Sowalsky's

when she started up the road that leads past the pond. She had no other friends in the neighborhood."

Unser and Powers inquired about Libbie's sons. Eventually the investigators concentrated on Michael Sowalsky. He was twenty years old and powerfully built but they learned that there was something strange about him. His behavior was inappropriate and he had a reputation for abusing farm animals.

The detectives asked Willie about Michael. The exchange was printed in The Evening World on July 29, 1908.

> "What sort of fellow is Mrs. Sowalsky's son?" A detective asked the boy.
> "He's big and naughty," the boy answered.

Unser and Powers questioned Michael about his activities on July 6 and 7. As printed in the same Evening World article, he told the detectives,

> "I went to Troy on July 6 but I was not away from home that night or the next. I did not know Hazel Drew's body had been found until the following Monday when Willie, who had been staying at our house, told me he was going to Troy to help look for the murderer."

Michael told the detectives that on the night of July 7 he wasn't feeling well. He said he worked all day in the fields and went right to bed when he returned home.

Mrs. Sowalsky verified her son's story. She said he was working in the fields all day July 7 and was home the entire night. Neighbors who visited Libbie that same night confirmed the story. They claimed they saw Michael in the house and Libbie told them he wasn't feeling well. No witness could be found that saw Michael near Teal's pond or anywhere but in his own house on the night Hazel was believed to have been murdered.

On Monday July 27, 1908 The Evening Telegram-New York printed an article that claimed another Sowalsky family lived on Taborton Mountain. The article states,

> If Hazel had been going to visit her brother the road would have taken her past Teal's Pond, up the Glass Lake road, where it branches from the main highway.

> There is another Sowalsky family living on the branch of the road that goes past William Taylor's house. If this proves the place the new lead will not help much except to provide a possible way for Hazel to have gone up the Taylor road without stopping at Taylor's house.

The implication is clear. It is possible that no one else saw Hazel on Taborton Road after Frank Smith and Rudy Gundrum because she turned onto the road that Taylor's farm was on, but went past her uncle's farmhouse without being seen. The only problem would be why was Hazel going to the other Sowalskys unless she mistakenly believed her brother may have been staying with that family.

THURSDAY
JULY 30, 1908

Troy, New York

"Mrs. Drew last saw her daughter alive July 2, and then told her Willie was at Sowalsky's."

The Troy Daily Press, July 30, 1908

T he Inquest in Troy began precisely at 1:00. Once again Coroner Strope presided and Jarvis O'Brien interviewed the witnesses. Twenty two people were subpoenaed, most of whom had been mentioned and interviewed in the newspapers throughout the investigation.

The first witness called was Hazel's former employer, Professor Edward Cary. He discussed Hazel's responsibilities and her sudden departure. He verified that Hazel began working for the family in February and she voluntarily and unexpectedly terminated her employment on the morning of July 6, 1908. He said around 5:00 that evening a deliveryman from the Westcott Express Company arrived at his house to pick up Hazel's trunk. It was to be delivered to her parents' house on Fourth Street.

Louis Howe, the correspondent for the New York Evening Telegram and John Kelly, the reporter for the New York Evening World

255

both testified that they found Hazel's glasses on the cowpath near the pond on the morning of July 15. The glasses were about two feet from where the hat and gloves were discovered. Dr. Charles Limerick, Hazel's optician verified the glasses were, in fact, Hazel's.

Hazel's mother, dressed in mourning, testified that the last time she saw her daughter was on Thursday, July 2 when Hazel stopped by the house on Fourth Street. Mrs. Drew said that Hazel was excited about her upcoming trip to Lake George.

Hazel did not mention that she was thinking about giving up her job at the Cary's or that she had any plans to visit William Taylor or anyone else in Sand Lake. Mrs. Drew didn't think her daughter had been to William's farm more than three times since the family moved out and that included her stay the previous winter when she was ill. She was not aware that Hazel had left the employment of the Tuppers in February or that she went to stay at Taylor's farm until William later told her. Mrs. Drew said she did tell Hazel that Willie was staying with the Sowalsky's. Mrs. Drew added that she had a good, loving relationship with her daughter and that Hazel did not make a confidante of any other members of her family. She said Hazel had not spent much time with the family recently.

The Courthouse on Congress Street, Troy, New York. From A Nostalgic Post Card Album of Troy, NY

Julia was followed to the stand by her husband, John. Hazel's father stated that the last time he saw his daughter alive was on July 4 he thought around 11:00. He didn't remember where he saw her but thought it might have been at Franklin Square in Troy. Minnie Taylor who was sitting to his right as he testified, had been staring at the floor. When he gave this testimony she looked up at him, forced a smile and shook her head. John had no idea who Hazel may have been going to see in Sand Lake except possibly his brother-in-law, William Taylor.

Minnie Taylor testified next. She recounted the events of July 6 when Hazel returned her clothes. When Hazel left, she told her aunt she was going to visit friends in Watervliet. Minnie said that she and Hazel had become close over the past six months, getting together as often as three nights a week. She said that at one point last winter, Hazel stayed with her for three nights.

Minnie told O'Brien and the court that she visited her sister, on Thursday July 9 and asked if she had seen Hazel. Mrs. Drew replied in the negative but mentioned that Hazel's trunk had unexpectedly been delivered to her house three days earlier. Minnie told Julia at that time she feared Hazel may have lost her position at the Cary's.

Before Hazel went to Taylor's farm the previous winter, she complained to Minnie that she wasn't feeling well. She was working for the Tupper's at the time and Minnie said she would go and assist Hazel in her duties. She did not ask the nature of Hazel's illness. Even after Hazel returned from Taylor's and began working for the Cary's, Minnie never asked Hazel about her illness.

Minnie said that, to her knowledge, Hazel never visited anyone near Teal's pond and as far as she knew, didn't have any friends in that area. The only person she thought Hazel may have been going to see was William Taylor, but she doubted her niece would visit him. Minnie never knew Hazel to have trouble with anybody and as far as she could tell, Hazel didn't fear for her life.

Hazel's brother, Joseph testified to Hazel's being at Taylor's farm the previous winter. He said his sister showed up unexpectedly and spent about three weeks recovering. For the first week, Hazel was confined to her bed and his wife, Eva tended to her. Joseph never asked or inquired about the nature of his sister's illness.

Eva Drew confirmed her husband's story. She believed Hazel arrived sometime during the second week in January, complaining that she wasn't feeling well. Eva escorted her to the bedroom where Hazel lay for the next week recuperating. Eva said she was the only one who attended to Hazel. O'Brien, as far as the newspapers reported, never inquired about the specific nature of Hazel's illness and Eva did not volunteer the information.

Mrs. Mary Robinson testified to seeing Hazel at Union Station between 11:20 and 11:30 on Monday, July 6. Hazel, she said told her that she was going down the river but left to buy a ticket before she could give any more details.

Thomas Carey stated that he saw Hazel walking along Congress Street in Troy on either July 6 or 7. He said she was carrying a suitcase at the time. He was positive it was Hazel because he had known her for several years.

Chris Crape testified that the car he saw racing up Taborton Road late in the night occurred on July 6. It came from the direction of Averill Park, drove up Taborton Mountain, and returned a few minutes later. He was positive it was July 6 although earlier in the investigation he claimed the car drove by on July 4.

Henry Kramrath, the businessman from Albany who owned the camp in the Alps testified next. He emphatically denied that illicit sex parties or any other immoral activities were being conducted at his camp and objected to the negative portrayal in the papers. He couldn't understand why Mr. and Mrs. Clifford made such disparaging comments about his camp. He said he knew the Cliffords very well, he used to go to their house for meals. Mr. Clifford, Kramrath said, was employed at the camp and as far as he knew they all got along. He said that the Cliffords lived about a half mile from the camp and if Mrs. Clifford heard screams in the night, she must have been dreaming.

The last witness called was Miss Mabel Brown who worked in her father's establishment, Brown's Hotel. She testified under oath that she never heard anything derogatory about Henry Kramrath's camp and as far as she knew there was never any problems or unethical activities conducted there. She did remember a girl coming to the hotel in May or June asking to use the phone, claiming she wasn't feeling well but that, she said, didn't necessarily reflect badly on the camp.

The Inquest had lasted four days. Nearly fifty people had been interviewed and Coroner Strope recessed for the day. On Friday he would deliver his verdict on the official cause of Hazel Drew's death.

JULY 31, 1908
RENSSELAER COUNTY
COURTHOUSE

Troy, New York

After four long days of testimony Coroner Morris Strope submitted his report. It was the last act and an anticlimactic end to the exhausting investigation. The 119 word document was brief and to the point. It was a statement officially declaring the cause of Hazel Drew's death. It did not convey the warmth of the popular and beautiful 20 year old who died so violently before her life had really begun. It made no mention of the extensive efforts of the investigators who, in three weeks traveled to five states and interviewed hundreds of people but were never able to figure out Hazel's unexplained and mysterious actions during her last days. It did not reveal the motives of friends and family members who did not and would not fully co-operate with the investigators. And it did not betray the secrets that Hazel had been keeping but were known to a select few.

> State of New York, Rensselaer County- Inquisition taken at
> Averill Park, N.Y., July 27, and continued at the Court House
> in the city of Troy on July 30, 1908, before M.H. Strope, one
> of the Coroners of said county, on the body of Hazel Irene
> Drew, which was found in the pond of Coonrad Teal in the
> town of Sand Lake July 11, 1908. From testimony taken on
> the above dates I find that the said Hazel Irene Drew came

261

to her death from extravasation of blood in the dura mater caused by a blow on the head from some blunt instrument in some manner unknown.

Dated, Troy, N.Y., July 31, 1908.
M.H. STROPE
Coroner

The detectives would now be re-assigned to other cases and although District Attorney Jarvis O'Brien would officially keep the case open, it would no longer be a priority. The reporters would leave. The media circus that had disrupted the lives of countless people and ruined the reputations and careers of others would go off in search of other fresh stories, all in an effort to sell more papers. Life in the small Town of Sand Lake would return to normal. The quaint village of Averill Park would once again rely on the picturesque lakes to bring in tourists. In time the story would be forgotten, her name would be forgotten, but justice would not be served and a killer would never be caught.

A Psychological Profile of Hazel Drew's Killer

Hazel Drew: Photo taken from The Evening World, July 14, 1908

Although the person responsible for Hazel Drew's death remains unknown, clues exist that reveal certain personality traits about that person from which modern researchers can create a psychological profile.

> Profiling does not provide the specific identity of the offender. Rather, it indicates the kind of person most likely to have committed a crime by focusing on certain behavioral and personality characteristics. (Profilers, p.14)

Modern law enforcement agencies, most notably the FBI, utilize criminal behavioral analysts in their efforts to create a psychological profile for the type of person who commits certain types of crimes. These analysts have, for years studied crime scenes and other aspects of individual cases and cross referenced the similarities. They interviewed thousands of criminals as a means to study the behavioral aspects of their personalities, what led them to commit their crimes and the state of mind they were in when perpetrating those crimes. With a high degree of success, these analysts are able to create a behavioral portrait of the criminal that is used by law enforcement to focus their investigation on a particular type of person.

Retired FBI agent John Douglas is perhaps the most famous of the behavior analysts. He was instrumental in creating and managing the criminal profiling program used by the FBI to train their analysts. His experience and success working in famous and well documented cases has helped police around the country narrow their list of suspects and apprehend dangerous criminals. Their methods are based on the combination of clues left at a crime scene and information learned about the victim. When the information is compiled a psychological profile of the unknown subject, which profilers refer to as the UNSUB, is created. Once a basic psychological profile is compiled, experts can determine probable characteristics about their UNSUB.

Try as they may, Jarvis O'Brien and his team of detectives were never able to determine the motive for Hazel's murder. Their inability to do so left the detectives unable to focus on a specific direction to take the investigation. They were forced to keep all options open which caused them to spend valuable time and manpower running down every clue just to figure out a starting point. With an unknown motive, the investigators needed luck as much as they needed skill.

The killer had to have had a reason, that is a motive, to want Hazel dead. Hazel's unusual behavior and secret movements in the days prior to her death are intriguing and may help to reveal the motive but pieces still remain missing. In their book, Journey into Darkness, John Douglas and Mark Olshaker point out the importance of learning the motive.

> "Motive is one of the thorniest issues in criminal investigative analysis. It is also among the most critical. Until you can figure out why a particular violent crime was committed, it is going to be very difficult trying to come to meaningful conclusions regarding the behavior and personality of the UNSUB." p. 43

Without all of the evidence and with an unknown motive, trying to piece together the specific details of what happened to Hazel becomes difficult. The investigator must put all of the knowns together then make logical assumptions about the unknowns and build on the logic. Some of Hazel's movements are known, the rest of her movements and her reasons for secrecy must rely on logic. For whatever the reason, Hazel was on Taborton Road the night of July 7. It is logical to assume she was murdered shortly after passing Frank Smith and Rudy Gundrum. Where her killer was hiding or where he came from is unknown. What is logical to assume though is he knew Hazel was there and he had planned in advance to end her life.

Douglas and Olshaker explain how modern profilers proceed in compiling information even without an apparent motive. In Journey into Darkness they write,

> When law enforcement officials cannot readily determine a motive for murder, they examine its behavioral aspects. In developing techniques for profiling murders, FBI agents have found that they need to understand the thought patterns of murderers in order to make sense of crime scene evidence and victim information. Characteristics of evidence and victims can reveal much about the murderer's intensity of planning, preparation, and follow through. From these observations the agents begin to uncover the murderer's motivation, recognizing how dependent motivation is to the killer's dominant thinking pattern. p. 56

Today's researcher can apply modern advances in crime detection to cold cases. Where a motive is not obvious, behavioral analysts must use other means. These methods were not known to the dedicated team of detectives investigating Hazel death. When investigating cases where the motive is not obvious,

> ...the investigating officer faces a completely different situation from the one in which a murder occurs as the result of jealousy or a family quarrel, or during the commission of another felony. In those cases, a readily identifiable motive may provide vital clues about the identity of the perpetrator. In the case of the apparently motiveless crime, law enforcement may need to look to other methods in addition to conventional investigative techniques in its efforts to identify the perpetrator..." (Profilers, p.15)

With an unknown motive, profilers must look more closely at other clues. As places to start, the crime scene, the autopsy, and background information about the victim (known as victimology) must be thoroughly examined. Trained behavior analysts will use the evidence to compile information about the offender which allows them to develop a psychological profile. Among other factors, the available evidence can be used to figure out the level of risk the offender is comfortable with. The profiler can learn the degree of planning that went into the crime and the offender's emotional state. A close examination, particularly of the crime scene can provide clues to, among other things, the offender's socio-economic status, occupation, intelligence level and relationship status.

As the first step in creating a psychological profile, a modern behavior analyst will categorize a crime scene as Organized or Disorganized. The analyst will then use the findings to classify the offender as Organized or Disorganized.

> Homicide scenes are behaviorally categorized according to whether they are an organized or disorganized scene. No homicide scene is exclusively one way or the other. It is based on a preponderance of the behavioral characteristics observed at the scene.

> The degree of organization or disorganization can provide tremendous insights into the level of sophistication of the offender, including the approach used in accessing the victim, the style of attack, the relationship of the victim to the offender, and the type of interaction that likely took place at the scene between the offender and the victim. (Ressler, Burgess, and Douglas, Sexual Homicide) (Profilers, p.227)

Even without a known motive or a likely suspect, using profiler techniques, information about Hazel's killer can be learned. An examination of all of the facts allows the researcher to determine if the crime scene was Organized or Disorganized.

Characteristics of an Organized Crime Scene:

> The initial observation at the crime scene of an organized offender is that some semblance of order existed prior, during, and after the offense. This scene of methodical organization suggests a carefully planned crime that is aimed at deterring detection. (Profilers, p. 101)

Characteristics of a Disorganized Crime Scene:

> The overall imprint of the disorganized crime scene is that the crime is committed suddenly and with no set plan of action for deterring detection. The crime scene shows great disarray. There is a spontaneous, unplanned quality to the crime scene...

> The death scene and crime scene are usually the same in murders committed by the disorganized offender, with the victim being left in the position in which she or he were killed...

> No attempt is made to conceal the body. Fingerprints and footprints may be found and the police have a great deal of evidence to use in their investigation. Usually, the murder weapon is one obtained at the scene and is left there, providing investigators with evidence. (Profilers, pp.105-6)

Hazel's fully clothed body was discovered in Teal's pond. The doctors estimated the body had been in the water for nearly a week but because she was seen by witnesses, she could have only been in the water a maximum of four days.

Hazel's hat and gloves were stacked neatly on the cowpath in the woods approximately twenty feet from the water's edge. Her glasses were found nearby. There were no footprints on or near the cowpath. There was no sign of a struggle anywhere near the pond. The scene was in such a condition that it is not known if Hazel was struck down near the pond or at some other location. No matter where Hazel's life ended, the killer did not simply leave her body where it was, but took time and effort to place her in the water after death, possibly to conceal or destroy evidence.

Based on the physical evidence, Teal's pond and the surrounding area meet the criteria of an Organized crime scene. The analyst must then check the characteristics of an Organized assailant to create a psychological profile of Hazel's killer.

Characteristics of an Organized assailant:

> Although the organized offender has an average or better than average IQ, he often works at occupations below his abilities, yet he prefers a skilled occupation. His work history is also sporadic.

> Precipitating situational stress, such as problems with finances, marriages, employment, and relationships with women is often present prior to the murder. The organized offender is socially adept and and is usually living with a partner.

> The organized offender may report an angry frame of mind at the time of the murder or state he was depressed. However, while committing the crime, he admits being calm and relaxed. Alcohol may have been consumed prior to the crime. (Profilers, p. 101)

The profile of the person who killed Hazel has begun but more information must be drawn to determine other psychological factors including the amount of planning that went into the assault, the assailant's risk level, and the killer's emotional state at the time of the attack.

> One of the behavioral indicators that can suggest that the offender planned out some or many aspects of the crime is

> the lack of physical evidence found at the scene. The lack
> of physical evidence suggests that the offender considered
> what precautions to take so he or she would not leave a
> forensic trail... A well-planned crime can suggest a sophisti-
> cated and/or experienced offender. (Profilers, p.225)

No obvious clues were left at or around Teal's pond. The killer
was not careless and he covered his movements very well. Being struck
from behind, Hazel did not have the ability to cry out or to put up a
fight. The killer knew what he was doing, leaving nothing to chance.
This does not necessarily indicate that the assailant had killed before
but does give the appearance of advanced planning, self discipline,
premeditation and an above average level of intelligence.

The last known people to have seen Hazel alive were Frank
Smith and Rudy Gundrum, who saw her around 7:30 on Tuesday July
7. Nothing more is known until her body was discovered by Lorenzo
Gruber on Saturday morning July 11. Due to the advanced state of
decomposition, it is likely that Hazel's body was placed in the pond
shortly after being seen by Smith and Gundrum. When the murder
actually occurred and other time factors need to be examined to add
to the profile.

> There are several time factors that need to be considered
> in generating a criminal profile. These factors include the
> length of time required (1) to kill the victim, (2) to commit
> additional acts with the body, and (3) to dispose of the body.
> The time of day or night that the crime was committed is also
> important, as it may provide information on the lifestyle and
> occupation of the suspect (and also relates to the offender
> risk factor). For example, the longer an offender stays with
> his victim, the more likely it is he will be apprehended at the
> crime scene... A killer who intends to spend time with his
> victim therefore must select a location to preclude observa-
> tion or on with which he is familiar. (Profilers, p.23)

Hazel was apparently killed by a single blow to the head. There were no defense wounds and no signs of a struggle. The killer appeared to strike quickly and had no other intentions, sexual or other. He did not take the time to torture Hazel before death or mutilate her body after death. The only extra time that was taken was to place her body in the pond and leave the hat, gloves and glasses on the cowpath. The killer did not appear to linger.

The murder was committed on a weekday, most likely a Tuesday, and most likely after work hours. The implication is that the killer was probably employed. Being an organized offender, he most likely held a skilled or managerial position.

The profile so far compiled suggests that Hazel's killer fits into the Organized category. He was of average or above average intelligence. He appeared comfortable around people but may have had stress in his life at the time of the murder. He may have possibly been depressed and something triggered his rage. What his mental state was at the time of the attack must be examined.

In <u>Journey into Darkness</u>, Douglas and Olshaker write,

> "...it is very important to get into the mind of not only the killer...but into the mind of the victim at the time the crime occurred. That's the only way you're going to be able to understand the dynamics of the crime- what was going on between the victim and the offender." p. 28

Based on the condition of Hazel's clothing and the speed and efficiency in which she was killed, and although the autopsy doctors were not unanimous in their beliefs, it is logical to conclude that Hazel was not sexually attacked prior to her death. Because Hazel had her back to her assailant when she was struck, either she didn't know that someone dangerous was behind her or she did know someone was there but didn't fear him.

The likelihood that a random assailant snuck up on an unsuspecting Hazel on the lonely road and delivered the death blow without provocation or without a typical motive such as robbery or rape is not a reasonable scenario. Hazel knew her attacker and was aware of his presence. Perhaps the two were walking along the mountain road together and her assailant asked Hazel to turn and look at something. Maybe he strategically slowed down to let her get in front of him, when she did he proceeded to strike. Any way that it may have happened, Hazel did not know that she was in peril. She felt comfortable enough around her attacker to have her back to him which indicates a level of trust, a relationship, a person she felt comfortable being around.

Examining the wounds to Hazel's body gives the profiler an indication into the emotional state of the assailant while he was committing the murder.

> Injuries and physical trauma suffered by the victim can suggest the amount of emotion the offender brought to the crime scene or the anger he or she developed once at the scene. For example, if the offender is extremely angry at the victim during the assault, the resulting injuries to the victim will frequently appear to be excessive, extensive, and even lethal. *Overkill,* (Italics original) which is "excessive trauma or injury beyond that necessary to cause death," (Douglas, Burgess, Burgess, and Ressler, Crime Classification Manual) frequently is the result of a very angry offender.

> Escalation of an argument or fight also can be detected at a crime scene. Battery to the victim's face and trauma to other parts of the body, including defensive injuries on the victim, can indicate that there was an escalation of emotion during the crime. Escalation suggests the offender and victim began their interaction with a verbal altercation, followed by a physical assault... resulting in death. (Profilers, p.226)

The only injury to Hazel's body was the wound to her head. The implication is that Hazel was unaware of the danger she was in. There were no wounds to her hands or arms commonly found in victims who resist their attacker. There were no bruises on her body and her face showed no indication of having been beaten. The fact that Hazel did not have defensive wounds and had her back to her assailant suggests that she was not arguing with him when she was struck down. Thus, the attacker did not escalate his mood from anger to rage. He did not "overkill" Hazel. The indication is that the murder had been planned, the assailant had mentally prepared himself, and Hazel was caught completely unaware of the fate that awaited her on Taborton Mountain.

In The Anatomy of Motive, Douglas and Olshaker wrote about the murder of a young woman who, like Hazel was struck down by a killer standing behind her. The two murders can be compared.

> "If the offender knew the victim well, he would have to depersonalize her at this moment, to set himself apart emotionally. It may be difficult to look at her- so he struck her from behind. He would try, at least initially to cover up the crime and get away with it because he convinced himself of the rightness and the justice of his actions." p. 374

Because Hazel was struck from the rear, it could also mean that her murderer was not comfortable with what he was doing and could not bring himself to look at her while he was taking her life. This suggests that, although he was responsible for her death, he did have feelings for her. He did not take pleasure in what he was doing but felt it was the only viable solution available to him.

The profiler now has an indication of the type of person most likely responsible for Hazel's murder and an idea as to his mental state at the time of the attack. To complete the profile, the analyst would then examine the lifestyle of the victim to compare their level of risk to that of the assailant.

> Victimology is the study of the victim(s) of a violent crime or crime series... The profiler must ask how likely it is, considering the victim's family, lifestyle, friends, habits, behaviors, and environment, that this person would have become the victim of a violent crime. To answer this question, the risk level of the victim must be assessed to determine whether the victim is a high-, medium-, or low risk victim. A low risk victim, for example, is the homicide victim with an ordinary background who works during the day inside his or her secured home located in a low-crime area...
>
> A high-risk victim can be a prostitute...or anyone whose lifestyle exposes him or her to exponential dangers.
>
> Understanding the risk level of the offender also is important. How much risk did the offender take in committing this crime, in terms of where the crime occurred, the time of day it occurred, and the type of victim the offender selected?... (Profilers, p.226)

Hazel worked as a governess in the home of a professor in an upper middle class neighborhood. She rarely went out at night, paid attention to her curfew, and was not known to associate with dangerous men. By all accounts she was polite and refined, seemingly a low risk victim.

There are enough exceptions however, to place Hazel in a medium risk category. Hazel appeared to be at ease meeting men. Her introduction and ensuing relationships with Fred Schlafflin, and the "Knight of the Napp Kinn" indicate that Hazel was comfortable going off with men she just met. Her mysterious and unexplained association with John Magner and the possibility that she went to his boarding place while in New York City and her ease traveling either as a single women or secretly in the company of an unknown man show that Hazel, while most of time exhibiting conservative behaviors also had a side to her that was more willing to take risks.

In examining the offender's level of risk, the profiler would pay attention to where and when the murder occurred. Hazel appears to have been lured to the seclusion of Taborton Mountain. The sun was beginning to set on a Tuesday night. The traffic on the road would be lighter than any other time of the day. The person responsible for Hazel's murder had not only planned the murder very carefully, he was not willing to take any chance of being caught. He picked the perfect time and place to commit the murder.

It is possible that Hazel's killer was merely trying to cover up his crime when he placed the body in Teal's pond. On the other hand it might show that, in his mind, he felt fully justified for his actions and the place of disposal may reveal his lack of respect for Hazel. But the disposal of the body might reveal other clues as well.

In The Anatomy of Motive, Douglas and Olshaker explain what profilers can assume about a killer based on his post-murderous behavior and especially what he does with the corpse.

> "If the body is left in plain sight or casually dumped...that tells me the killer had contempt for the victim..."

> "If the body is cared for after death, that's going to suggest that the killer had some tender feelings toward the victim, maybe even remorse." p. 26

Although Hazel's killer could have done anything with her dead body, he took the time to place it in the pond. If he carefully laid her body in the woods or covered her with brush or some other object, it would reveal that the killer had genuine feelings for Hazel and felt remorse for what he had done. This he did not do. Placing the body in the pond indicates that the killer felt contempt and disregard for Hazel.

The fact that Hazel was struck from behind suggests that the killer could not look at her face and thus had feelings for her, seems to contradict his apparent disregard for her by dumping her body in Teal's pond. However, the two emotions can coexist. It is possible that the killer was not comfortable killing Hazel. He was probably not an experienced murderer and at one time he did care for her. However, after she was dead, he was reminded of the reason that compelled him to end her life. The anger and contempt that he felt made him feel justified in not just hiding the body to avoid detection, but to disrespect her by dumping her in the pond.

The killer appeared to have had feelings for Hazel at one time but those feelings no longer existed. Romance was replaced by disdain. Hazel, it seems, became a liability or a burden to him.

Hazel was struck down by a single, powerful blow. She was not the victim of a murderous frenzy. The killer did not exhibit rage or extreme hatred. Although the killer wanted Hazel dead, as contradictory as it may sound, he did not hate her.

This type of killer fits the profile of a dominant male who has little respect and no regard for woman. He feels he has power over them and cannot and will not tolerate any deviation from this belief. Thus it is reasonable to conclude that Hazel was involved in a relationship with a man who had complete control over her. The relationship was likely an abusive one. The abuse she endured was definitely emotional and probably physical. However, the evidence indicates that Hazel was not looking to get away from him. On the contrary. It appears that Hazel spent the better part of two days trying to find this man. Why would a woman spend so much effort trying to locate her abusive partner when she had ample means to get away?

Douglas and Olshaker in <u>Obsession</u> provide some insight into abusive relationships.

> Domestic abusers often reveal their personality defects in subtle ways that don't set off warning buzzers. The future victim (in this case Hazel) may be completely unaware of what she is getting into at first. The abuser can be so manipulative and cunning, the behavior so insidious that she may not realize what is going on until she is enmeshed in a potentially dangerous situation.

> The offender may first appear attentive, which soon reveals itself as truly more possessive and jealous then caring. He tries to control aspects of his mate's life- from picking out her clothes to trying to limit the time she spends away from him (or possibly, in Hazel's case, keeping his existence a secret). He has the most strength if he can keep her off balance and playing mind games is one way he does this.

> His most successful game involves switching moods, loving and tender one moment, angry and violent the next. His partner never knows whom she is dealing with and which she fears and loathes the one side of his behavior, she cares for the other and thrives under his attention.

> To increase his control over his partner, the abuser will try to put his victim in a situation where she is emotionally dependent on him. pp. 336-7.

Hazel abruptly quit her work on July 6 and spent much of the next two days as if she were on some secret mission. She did not contact any friends or family members. She was apparently waiting at Union Station for someone to pass through. She had her suitcase with her, ready to go when she could finally find the person she was waiting to see. If she was in an abusive relationship, she had reason to fear his anger. She must have experienced his mood swings in the past and hoped that her being there for him would bring out his compassionate and understanding side.

Aspects of Hazel's life fit the pattern of a person who is dominated by a strong figure. In <u>Obsession</u>, Douglas and Olshaker discuss the typical lifestyle changes that take place for a person in such a circumstance.

> As an abusive relationship continues, the offender grows increasingly critical of her friends and family, more and more jealous and controlling of the time she spends away from him. She may get to the point where she feels it's not worth the fight to see others. p. 338.

Hazel's social behavior changed in the months preceding her death. She stopped writing friends that she had been steadily keeping in contact with such as William Hogardt and Edward LaVoie. William Clemens wrote in the July 22, 1908 edition of the Evening World that Hazel had been systematically crossing out the names of old friends from her address book.

> As friends dropped out of her young life, she crossed off their names...

Clemens, in the same article discussed how Hazel was in the process of putting her old life behind her and appeared to be beginning a new one. She had a box of letters, postcards, and other memorabilia earmarked for incineration. Clemens described one of those items she intended to destroy.

> There is a group photograph of four young women and three young men taken at Prospect Park two years ago. The four

girls are seated, Hazel at the left, the young men standing. The personnel of the photograph is as follows Hazel Drew, Arthur Phillips, Lillie Robertson, John C. Stagmayer, Anna Coma(?), Bert Bruns, and Margaret Westfall. These young people I have interviewed but they belong to a period long since past in Hazel's life.

Hazel was...vain of her beauty and clothes, and during the last year she dropped, one by one, her girl friends and the young boys of her life and began making acquaintances of the more worldly sort.

The fact that no one close to Hazel, not even the Cary's with whom she spent most of her time was aware that she was in a relationship further supports the controlling nature of the powerful, abusive boyfriend who demanded that Hazel keep their relationship secret.

Douglas and Olshaker in <u>Journey into Darkness</u> take the reader into the mind of an assailant in the moments leading up to his attack. The same conditions are logically what transpired at the time of Hazel's attack.

"Before the attack...there would have been a real or perceived crisis in the offender's life which would have triggered his acting out. He held...this particular woman accountable for his problems and this is how he dealt with his rage." p. 50

"There is generally a triggering mechanism to these types of crimes, some kind of inciting incident in the hours, days or weeks before." p. 350

So what would that crisis have been in the mind of her killer that Hazel had to pay the price with her life? What triggered the assault? Was Hazel in the process of ending her relationship with an abusive boyfriend? Probably not. Her actions, especially at Union Station give the appearance that she was searching for someone, not avoiding him. It is not logical to assume that Hazel would quit her job and secretly search for her abusive lover for two days just to break up with him. Hazel was being held accountable for her killer's problems. What were those problems? What had Hazel done that in the eyes of her killer, he needed to unleash his rage on her? Did he lure Hazel to Taborton Mountain to kill her or did he follow her there? When did he decide that Hazel had to die?

Using all of the evidence available and applying basic profiling techniques, the missing pieces regarding Hazel Drew's murder can logically be explored. Different scenarios can be examined and those that do not take into account all of the physical and psychological criteria can be eliminated. What is left is the most logical account regarding the murder of Hazel Drew.

Theories and Possible Killers

Because the investigators in 1908 were unable to piece together much of Hazel's movements on July 6 and 7, and because they never learned where she spent the night of July 6, the case was never solved. Cold case enthusiasts, with the help of the internet still grapple with the question, "Who killed Hazel Drew?". The identity of the killer may never be learned but using all of the evidence available and applying modern investigative techniques, theories relating to motive and possible suspects can still be explored.

Theory 1: Hazel worked as a Call Girl

When all of the evidence is examined the possibility exists that Hazel may have led a double existence and that prostitution may have played a part in her so called secret life. Two of the autopsy doctors, Dr. Boyce and Dr. Fairweather claimed that tearing in Hazel's "female organ" was the result of sexual activity. Dr. Boyce never wavered in his belief that the cord found wrapped around Hazel's neck came from her corset and that strangulation may have contributed to her death. If he was correct, the killer had access to Hazel when she was at least partially undressed.

A statement by Mrs. E.V. Huntley supports this theory. Quoted in William Clemens article in the July 22 New York World, Mrs. Huntley said,

> "As to the missing undervest, I cannot understand it. I am positive that Hazel would never dress without wearing such a garment. She had a large bust and her corset necessarily had to be laced tightly.

In the same article, William Clemens interviewed Hazel's friend, Mary Sharp.

> Miss Sharp also told me it was absolute nonsense to think that Hazel would, at anytime go without an undervest.

It is not known how Mrs. Huntley and Mary Sharpe knew that Hazel was not wearing an undervest as this information was not public knowledge. They were most likely told by William Clemens whose integrity is known to be self-serving. If their information was correct however, and Hazel's undervest was missing and never located, the killer would logically have had access to it which implies that Hazel had to have been undressed. This in and of itself does not imply prostitution until other factors are considered.

It was widely known that Hazel lived well above her means. In the five months she worked for the Cary's Hazel traveled out of town on at least four occasions and planned on a fifth. She took a boat to New York on one of those trips and had asked Mina Jones for information about how to get from New York to Providence by boat in preparation for another trip as printed in the July 24 Thrice-A-Week World.

Carrie Weaver's letter printed in the Troy Record on July 28 addressed Hazel's remarkable ability.

> One of Miss Weaver's first remarks to her relatives in Dayton was in regard to Miss Drew's financial ability. It has been, and still is a constant source of wonder to Miss Weaver how her friend managed to live so well, to wear such stylish costumes, to take so many and so extended trips and to enjoy so many luncheons at such expensive hostelries on her wages as a domestic.

> "From what Hazel told me, she must have had an awfully good time when she went away from home. She said she

had dandy dinners and not the slightest attempt was ever made anywhere to offer her an insult any more than if she had been accompanied by a brother or her father. She knew how to take care of herself, all right, but from what our little trips together cost I know she must have spent a great deal of money on pleasures of this kind, and for the life of me I don't see how she managed to save enough from her wages."

Hazel's employer, Mrs. Cary told The-Thrice-A-Week reporters on July 17, 1908,

"I could not understand where Hazel got the money to take these outings," Mrs. Cary said. "She volunteered no information and was so enthusiastic to her descriptions of sights seen that my suspicions were disarmed if I ever harbored any. I recall now that Hazel never told me who, if anyone accompanied her when she visited, where she stopped, or whether she defrayed her own expenses. As a matter of fact the trips were such as might be expected from a girl of Hazel's temperament."

Hazel wore fine jewelry and dressed in the latest fashion. It was reported that she frequented the finest restaurants in the capital district as well as in Averill Park. She also had gold fillings in her teeth. For a person working as a domestic servant, Hazel wanted for nothing. How could a young woman making low wages afford such fine clothes and jewelry and travel as much as she did?

The known men in Hazel's life supports the call girl theory. The fact that she dated a soldier and was carrying his news clipping in her suitcase, that she had the name and address of a train conductor in New York City and possibly paid him a visit, the flirtatious relationship with the visiting "Knight of the Napp Kinn", and the fact that she was possibly seen in the company of a traveling insurance or real estate agent in the fine restaurants in Averill Park doesn't necessarily mean that Hazel was involved in prostitution. It is possible that she just happened to date men who traveled a lot or were stationed in distant locations.

Those closest to Hazel were steadfast in defending her reputation. At the time of her death, no one who was close to Hazel believed she was dating anyone. Yet interviews with other people, letters found among her personal effects, and circumstantial evidence paint a much different picture. Her strange actions the days before her death imply that she was involved with someone, although to what extent is not known. Fred Schlafflin told investigators that he met Hazel at Rensselaer Park and went home with her the same day. He did state that Hazel behaved appropriately that day and throughout their short dating experience but her actions indicate that she could be enticed to go off with men she just met. The "Knight of the Napp Kin" letter, printed in the July 22 Thrice-A-Week World supports this. Hazel apparently took a boat ride with some men she had just met. She later held this man's hands and the two stared into each other's eyes. In his letter he states,

> "I trust that your wrists are not injured for I could not forgive myself if I had caused even the slightest bruise. T'is true that I had to use force on some occasions, but I tried not to be rough or rude in my actions."

What had been going on between the two and why it was that he had to use enough force to bruise Hazel's wrists is left only to conjecture.

William Clemens claimed he interviewed a man whose statement shows a consistent pattern in Hazel's behavior. Clemens wrote about the man's knowledge of Hazel in the July 24 edition of the Auburn Semi-weekly Journal.

A young lawyer who lives in Green Island confided to me Tuesday night that he had known Hazel for several years. He said she was a respectable girl as far as he knew, although he got acquainted with her by "picking her up" in the street. He also met her and another girl by appointment at the Union depot. He said that as long as three years ago Hazel was well known to the young men about town as a flirt.

Typical of Clemens, he didn't provide the name of the Green Island lawyer and as always the reader must be careful when using William Clemens as a credible source. But Hazel's actions in Clemens' story are consistent with other known actions in her life and she seemed very confident and comfortable around men she just met.

Mrs. Cary claimed that Hazel received no male callers the entire time she was employed with the family. Carrie Weaver said she never knew Hazel to have a sweetheart the entire time she knew her. Hazel's brother, Joseph and her uncle, William both stated that Hazel was more comfortable around women than men. Yet the evidence indicates that Hazel was very flirtatious and at ease around men. Perhaps too much so.

Hazel's being a call girl could explain Minnie Taylor's reluctance to cooperate with the investigation and her insistence that Mina Jones destroy the letters that Hazel wrote to her. It could explain Hazel's statement to Mina that a man working in a dentist office, perhaps an enamored client, wanted to marry her and that another man of Italian or Armenian descent, perhaps an unhappy or sadistic client had been rough with Hazel on two separate occasions, information no one else claimed to have known. It could explain why so few people attended Hazel's funeral although she was supposed to be very popular. It could also explain Hazel's seeming distant relationship with most members of her family.

Assuming that Hazel was not the virtuous young lady that friends and family portrayed her as and if the prostitution theory is to be explored, what might the scenario have been leading up to Hazel's death? Hazel could have been at Union Station the morning of July 6, intending, as she told her Aunt Minnie, to take the train to Watervliet to visit friends. While at the station she ran into a "client" who she had been with before. Hazel had just quit her job and her funds were low. They left the station in his car and spent the rest of that day and that night together. The man may have had a home in Sand Lake, possibly on Taborton Mountain. This man may have been one of the unidentified men that Hazel and Minnie were reportedly seen with on a carriage ride on June 21. On Tuesday July 7 the two planned to go to the man's home in the country with the intention of returning to Troy later that evening. Hazel placed her suitcase in the baggage area of Union Station and the two drove out to Sand Lake. Somewhere along the line the couple had an argument and the man kicked Hazel out of his car. With no other option she was forced to go to her uncle's farm. The irate man returned before Hazel was able to get to Taylor's farm and for reasons known only to him, killed Hazel and deposited her body in Teal's pond, most likely to avoid detection.

Theory 2: Hazel was the victim of a serial killer

Could Hazel have been the victim of a serial killer? Serial killers are known to target a preferred type of victim. Hazel was extraordinarily pretty and was apparently at ease around men. A serial killer would have no problem approaching the flirtatious twenty year old and could easily entice her with his charm. Over time he could have feigned an interest in Hazel's home town and convinced her to take him out to the secluded area. Once alone on the remote mountain the psychopathic killer would have the perfect opportunity to end Hazel's life.

Hazel's murder, the death of Mamie Killian and the disappearance of Mary Lewis may all be connected. It may account for the seeming lack of motive in all three cases.

> While it is not completely accurate to say that these crimes are motiveless, the motive may all too often be understood only by the perpetrator. D.T. Lunde (1976) demonstrates this issue in terms of the victims chosen by a particular offender. As Lunde points out, although the serial murderer may not know his victims, their selection is not random. Rather, it is based on the murderer's perception of certain characteristics of his victims that are of symbolic significance to him. An analysis of the similarities and the differences among victims of a particular serial murderer provides important information concerning the "motive" in an apparently motiveless crime. This, in turn, may yield information about the perpetrator himself... (Profilers, p.15)

The three young women were all attractive with well developed figures. At least two of them, Hazel and Mary Lewis, had blond hair. All three came from working class families and were easily approachable. The Times Union provided the most comprehensive details of the Mamie Killian case as reported on July 16, 1908.

> In many ways the (Hazel Drew) case is beginning to assume the same air as the Mamie Killian case seven years ago next September. Like Mamie Killian, Hazel Drew was pretty and had admirers in different walks of life than her position as a domestic would bring her naturally in contact with. Mamie Killian was a collar girl and had many admirers. But Mamie was better known about town than the Drew girl. She was a frequenter of places that girls careful of their reputation would not care to be seen in. One Saturday morning her lifeless body was found floating in the Hudson near Bath (between Troy and Rensselaer). At first the cry was made

that it was the case of suicide. But the coroner's physician stated that the girl, like Hazel Drew, was dead before the body reached the river. Politicians of high and low degree united, apparently in an effort to suppress the news. Everything was done to destroy clues. Policemen, instead of looking into clues were detailed to watch the reporters, detectives and others who were working on the case. A newspaper man running down the story was assaulted by a policeman in front of the City building in Troy, the chief of police watching the assault. Anyone who could furnish information as to the possible end to Mamie Killian was subjected to persecution. Witnesses who had been the last to see her before her body was taken out of the river were mysteriously absent every time an inquest was held.

If what the Times Union reported was accurate, it appears that a cover-up may have been involved in the investigation of Killian's death. The only person who publicly claimed that politics was behind an inefficient investigation of Hazel's murder was William Clemens. The similarity between Mamie's and Hazel's deaths is not necessarily that a cover-up occurred but that the two girls had similar lifestyles and associated with similar type men. Both women were subsequently murdered, their bodies placed in water postmortem and their possessions arranged to give the appearance of suicide.

If Peter Cipperley is to be believed, Hazel was sitting with a man on the train from Troy, going to Averill Park. Cipperley may have been a witness to the man who lured Hazel back to Sand Lake with the intention of killing her. The man appeared to take a great interest in the woman and the woman was appreciative of his attention. He apparently had won her trust, a tactic commonly used by experienced serial killers.

Later that evening as the two walked up Taborton Mountain together, possibly under the pretense of seeing William Taylor or young Willie Drew, Hazel's suitor could have ducked into the woods when he heard wagons approaching. Hazel, thinking it was a game and not realizing that the man's real motive was to avoid detection, playfully joined him when she heard the Ryemillers and then the Hoffeys ride past. Somewhere along the way the attacker ended Hazel's life with a single blow to the head. He carried her lifeless body up the dirt farm road by Teal's pasture then down the cowpath and threw it into the pond, a post-murderous behavior similar to that involving Mamie Killian. He then placed the hat and gloves on the cowpath to either give the appearance of suicide or to simply remove them from sight.

Mamie Killian's killer was never apprehended. The media coverage of her death was not as extensive as Hazel's so not as much information is available. However, Hazel and Mamie were very similar people. Their deaths and attempts by the killer to cover them up were also very similar. Could the two murders be related? Serial killers often choose their victims based on predetermined characteristics. For example noted serial killer Ted Bundy typically targeted young, attractive, middle class women, mostly in their late teens and twenties with brown, shoulder length hair that was parted in the middle.

If Hazel and Mamie were victims of the same killer, what characteristic was he looking for? Working class girls? Troy girls? Pretty girls? Popular girls? A modern profiler would not have enough information to accurately connect the two murders but it couldn't as yet be ruled out either.

The fate of Mary Lewis is unknown, therefore she cannot be a confirmed victim of a serial killer. Likewise, only by conjecture can her disappearance be at all connected to Hazel's murder. However, the details of the two cases are similar. The Times Union reported on July 16, 1908,

> After a search since April 29 the police of Albany, Schenectady, Troy and New York city...have been unable to

locate pretty Mary A. Lewis, the fifteen-year-old daughter of Mr. and Mrs. Richard D. Lewis of 238 Elk Street. The disappearance of the girl is mysterious because no motive for her going can be imagined...No trace of her has since been seen, although she is said to have been in Schenectady during the week of the 29th.

The Troy Daily Press provides more information:

Mr. and Mrs. Lewis have not seen or heard from their daughter who left her home April 29 last with the ostensible purpose of attending School 9.

Mrs. Lewis said last night that she was never severe in her discipline with her daughter and never gave her any occasion to wish to leave home. She has no idea where her daughter went. They have no relatives where she could visit, nor did she have any acquaintances who would be likely to harbor her or prevail upon her to remain away from home.

Mrs. Lewis was informed that her daughter had purchased a ticket at the Union station Sunday May 4 (read 3) at 5 a.m. for New York. She was said to have been alone at the time.

Mary Lewis, according to her mother, had no male friends, so far is known. She was always of a happy and contented disposition and this fact makes her desire to leave home mystifying to both her parents and playmates.

The girl is about five feet in height, light hair, blue eyes, and turned-up nose. She is rather slim of build...

It may just be coincidence but at about the same time that Hazel was murdered, another young lady, popular, attractive, blond with connections to Albany, Schenectady, Union Station and New York City disappeared.

On Sunday August 16, 1908, just over two weeks after Hazel's case had drawn to a close, the body of a young woman was discovered in a pond in Palmer, Massachusetts approximately ninety miles from Averill Park. An examination of the bank of the pond revealed prints from both a man's and a woman's shoes.

Medical Examiner Schneider performed the autopsy and found there was no water in the victim's lungs. Like Hazel and Mamie, she was dead before she was put in the pond. It was estimated that she died at least four hours prior to her body being placed in the water. The autopsy further revealed that the young woman had not been sexually violated. The Medical Examiner stated that the girl was not pregnant, her character pure, she had not disgraced her family, and was a "good girl". District Attorney S.S.Taft was notified that the death was suspicious.

The victim was identified as sixteen year old Faith Davis. She lived down the road from where her body was discovered. She left a note on her kitchen table on Friday, saying she was going out for a short walk. She did not return that night. She was seen by a neighbor on Saturday evening between 4:30 and 5:30 walking along the road in the company of an unknown young man.

Faith Davis' killer, like that of Hazel Drew and Mamie Killian, was never caught. However, unlike Jarvis O'Brien, District Attorney Taft appeared to have caved to the pressure. Despite the medical and crime scene evidence, Taft ruled that Faith Davis had committed suicide.

As with Mamie Killian, there is no solid proof that the death of Faith Davis is connected in any way to Hazel's murder. However, the similarities between the cases cannot be ignored. In the same general area at around the same time three women died in very similar ways and their bodies were all placed in water after death (including Faith Davis who was somehow able to place her own body in the pond four hours after she killed herself). The deaths were all staged to give the appearance of suicide. It is not known if Mary Lewis was a fourth victim. If the disappearance of Mary Lewis and the deaths of Mamie Killian, Faith Davis, and Hazel Drew were the work of a single serial killer, the number of other victims remains unknown.

Theory 3: Hazel was simply in the wrong place at the wrong time

To know why Hazel was traveling up Taborton Mountain on the night of July 7 could be central to solving the murder. She may have been going to Taylor's farm or to the Sowalsky's to visit her brother. She could have been going to the Bly's to inquire about a place to stay or she may have been seeking the job that was posted in the Troy Record newspaper on July 6. It's possible that she had a prearranged to meet somebody at the pond. Whatever her reason, the fact that she was seen by four people leaves no doubt of her presence on the desolate road. Hazel may have encountered a homicidal maniac who had no other purpose but to attack and kill whoever he came in contact with. Hazel could simply have been unlucky when she was seen by the unknown predator.

Beverly Neustiel had been attacked in the same general area that Hazel was believed to have been murdered. The place was known to be dangerous as evidenced by the warnings Frank Richmond was given by his friends. In the July 14 Troy Record he "...remarked that when he first took up farm work on the mountain, having lived in Troy, he was told that it was a tough place near Teal's pond." Henry Rollman, after his wife pointed to the pretty blond standing by the raspberry bushes commented, "...she's a fool to be alone on this road. It's a bad place." (The Troy Daily Press, July 18, 1908)

The unknown man in the Taborton hotel who gulped down several glasses of whiskey in quick succession complaining that something regrettable had just happened, "Too bad, too bad, but it had to be done." (The Evening World, July 20, 1908) further supports the theory. The man was never located despite a massive effort by the authorities who reportedly visited nearly one hundred homes in the area. According to witnesses in the hotel, the man claimed he was returning from Troy the same night that Hazel was seen walking along Taborton Road. Witnesses said he arrived at the hotel around 8:30. The man would have had to come up the same road at approximately the same time that Hazel did.

The man's statement in and of itself does not necessarily implicate him in Hazel's death. But the fact that he arrived in a state of near shock, drank a lot of whiskey very quickly, uttered such apologetic words and left, never to be seen or heard from again under the circumstance is very peculiar and something the authorities took very seriously.

The two men seen by William and Elizabeth Hoffey at Teal's pond may have been responsible for Hazel's death. They were in the area where Hazel would have been if she continued up the road after leaving Frank Smith and Rudy Gundrum. Mrs. Hoffey saw something in the back of the wagon that she could not identify but did attract her attention. The disappearance of the two men after the murder and the fact that they could not be tracked down further supports the theory.

Theory 4: Hazel was murdered by a scorned lover

Hazel spent much of July 6 and 7 at Union Station apparently waiting for someone to either arrive or depart. Her suitcase was packed for an overnight excursion and her plans were kept secret from everyone she knew. It is difficult to imagine that Hazel was doing anything other than planning to go away for a romantic encounter, possibly even an elopement. Who she was planning to leave with, where she was planning to go, and the circumstances that led to her death remain a mystery. However, by placing all of the miscellaneous pieces together, it may be possible to narrow down a list of suspects.

The Indianapolis Sun on July 17, 1908 stated,

> (Hazel) had many admirers among the young men of her acquaintance. Not a few were willing and anxious to press their attention, but received no encouragement. She liked them collectively and was desirous of their general admiration, but during the time she lived in Troy she was not known to give any one admirer right to claim her particular attention. "Oh you need not waste your time," young women used to taunt the young men suing for Miss Drew's favor. "Hazel has someone she doesn't want anyone to know about. Her heart is already given away."

> If Hazel had such a secret she kept it so closely that no one of her many friends has been able to give the slightest clue to the identity of this mysterious admirer who is anxiously sought today.

Suspect 1: An unknown married man with a summer house on Taborton Mountain

Hazel was seen by the Rollmans and by Smith and Gundrum casually strolling up the mountain road without an apparent care in the world. At one point she was loitering by a clump of raspberry bushes. The Rollmans were under the impression that Hazel was eating the berries although the autopsy revealed there were no berries in her digestive track.

What Hazel was doing on that road on that night is central to solving the mystery. Whereas it is possible she could have been going to see her uncle or her brother, it may also be possible she had another, more ominous reason to be there. To speculate, based primarily on her last known activities, Hazel could have been seeing a married man who owned a summer home somewhere on Taborton Mountain. It would explain her deception, and her unexplained movements the last two days of her life.

The specific words Hazel used when she and her mother discussed her relationships take on a new meaning when read with the possibility that Hazel was seeing a married man.

> "Hazel to my knowledge, has not had a beau for more than a year," said Mrs. Drew. "I asked her recently, Haven't you got a fellow yet Hazel? And she replied, 'No, I don't care for one. If I got one some other girl would cut me out.'" (Troy Record, July 18, 1908)

Her relationship could have begun in the fall of 1907. Carrie Weaver met Hazel early in 1908 and claimed Hazel never dated anyone the entire time she knew her. In fact, Hazel could have been dating the entire time but due to the nature of the affair, she was forced to keep it secret.

If William Clemens was correct, this man may have gotten Hazel pregnant the previous winter which led to her "escape" to Taylor's farm. The affair continued and intensified throughout the spring. Hazel, at that time, appeared to be cutting ties with her past. She stopped writing old friends and destroyed their letters and photographs. For the first time she began to travel. Never having been far from home in her life, within a two month span, Hazel took four vacations. The many trips she took in so short a time span is more consistent with someone who is enamored and wants to be with someone than a person merely wishing to travel.

> "From what Hazel told me, she must have had an awfully good time when she went away from home. She said she had dandy dinners and not the slightest attempt was ever made anywhere to offer her an insult any more than if she had been accompanied by a brother or her father. She knew how to take care of herself, all right, but from what our little trips together cost I know she must have spent a great deal of money on pleasures of this kind, and for the life of me I don't see how she managed to save enough from her wages."
> (Troy Record, July 28, 1908)

The man would have to have been both wealthy and married. He paid for Hazel's trips, he bought her nice clothes and took her to exclusive restaurants. Hazel was smitten but because he had a wife, she could not reveal the relationship to anyone she was close to. No proof of a relationship exists. No correspondence between Hazel and the man was ever found, not because she destroyed them but because he was smart enough not to write her.

After seeing each other in New York, the two made plans to meet in Lake George for the Fourth of July. The man may have promised Hazel he was prepared to leave his wife or maybe that's just what Hazel believed but she was expecting a marriage proposal that weekend. The trip never transpired because Minnie Taylor, Hazel's traveling companion, did not want to get on a crowded train. She could not reveal to her aunt the real reason or the importance of the trip.

On Monday morning Hazel quit her job in an effort to locate the man she unwittingly left stranded in Lake George. She spent much of the day at Union Station hoping to catch him when he passed through.

At some point they met and the two went someplace to talk. The couple spent the night together supposedly discussing future plans.

Hazel was committed to a future with this man. Unbeknownst to her however, he had no intention of leaving his wife. The promises he had made were meant to mislead. Hazel was his mistress and that is how he wanted it.

Over the course of the night, the man learned that Hazel had quit her job and was committed to an elopement. He realized he could no longer keep the relationship the way it was. Hazel put him in a precarious position. The enormity of the affair became apparent. The man had to make a choice; his wife (and possibly children) or his mistress. He made his decision and Hazel was devastated. He told her the affair was over, he never loved her and he never wanted to see her again. He had to be blunt and harsh to create an emotional separation. He made it clear that there was no future between them and they would never see eachother again. Hazel was expecting marriage and a life with this man. In an instant everything she hoped for and desired came to an abrupt end. He left Hazel alone and crying.

Hazel was incensed. The reality of their relationship became clear. The pain she felt was caused entirely by his lies. She realized now that she had been nothing but his whore. She would not stand the humiliation. She had invested too much in the relationship. She sacrificed everything for him. She had been hurt by men before but this time she would not stand idly by, he would not go unpunished. She would confront his wife. She would reveal the affair, even the abortion. Because he ruined her life, she had no problem ruining his. She would do it the next day while her emotions still ran high. She assumed when he left he went back to New York. She would visit the wife at the couple's summer home in Taborton.

Tuesday afternoon Hazel went to Union Station to catch a trolley that would eventually take her to Averill Park. She had to bring her suitcase with her because she had nowhere else to keep it. She had a purpose in Averill Park but had no intention to stay after it was over. Feelings would be hurt, a wife would be devastated, a marriage would be ruined. She would go back to retrieve her suitcase when it was all over. After that she would go to her parents house and figure out what to do next.

Having only the clothes she was wearing, she checked her suitcase at the baggage room and set out for the country.

That evening, the scorned lover, walked up Taborton Mountain. Although she did not usually like confrontation, she was surprisingly at ease, but a little nervous. She stopped at a raspberry bush when a wagon came down the mountain. She ducked into the woods when the next one came up the mountain. She met Smith and Gundrum in the Hollow but was determined to keep going.

She knew where the house was, she had been there before. She was confident but slightly anxious as she walked up to the door. She knocked. When the door opened, her courage was replaced by horror. Hazel's former lover had not gone back to New York as she expected, he was standing right in front of her. Wanting to avoid the confrontation and fearing for her safety, Hazel turned to leave but it was too late. Rage overtook her former lover and grabbing the nearest object he could find, caught up with Hazel and brought it down with all his might on her head.

He picked up Hazel's lifeless body along with her hat, gloves and glasses. He brought her to Teal's pond, dumped her body in the water and left her accessories on the cowpath. He was now rid of his problem and free to resume his normal life secure in the knowledge that his secret was safe.

Suspect 2: Edward LaVoie

When Duncan Kaye examined the contents of Hazel's suitcase, he discovered the personal ad stating that Edward LaVoie was traveling to Chattanooga, Tennessee. Why would Hazel be carrying his ad in her suitcase? The clipping was dated October 23, 1907 and penciled in Hazel's handwriting on the bottom was the date October 6, 1907.

In January 1908, three months after the October dates, Hazel went to her uncle's farm ostensibly to recover from some mysterious ailment. It could have been the grip, a form of influenza. Hazel suffered such an illness when her fiancé left and married her friend the year before. Despite Mrs. Tupper's fondness for Hazel, she was forced to terminate her employment, a drastic decision if Hazel truly was ill. While Hazel was at the farm neither her brother nor her uncle checked on her and neither, by their own admission had any idea of the specifics of Hazel's illness. Eva tended to Hazel the entire time.

William Clemens revealed in the Auburn Semi-Weekly Journal on July 24 that he discovered evidence that Hazel had gone to Taylor's farm house to have an abortion. Circumstantial evidence suggests that Hazel may have had such a procedure although the reader is again warned to question the reliability of William Clemens and any evidence he claimed to have discovered. It may also be possible that Hazel went to the farm because she was having a natural miscarriage.

Could October 6, 1907, the date Hazel wrote at the bottom of LaVoie's ad be the day he impregnated her? Three months later, forced to hide her shame, Hazel went to Taylor's farm, an uncle she wasn't very close to. She wouldn't have gone to her parents due to the embarrassment and also to prevent neighbors and people she knew from finding out which would ruin her reputation as well as that of her family. Eva's tending to Hazel would make sense under the circumstance.

Joseph and William would not have been comfortable with such feminine matters and would have avoided the situation completely.

If Hazel was pregnant, being let go by the Tuppers would be the standard protocol for the time. District Attorney James Niemann in Nassau County at first believed the victim, later identified as Margaret Lynch, was terminated under what he thought was the same circumstance. "Discovery of her delicate condition possibly led to her dismissal or retirement it is believed. (The Brooklyn Daily Eagle, April 16, 1904). It was thus a common practice at the time for employers to terminate the employment of young unwed women who became pregnant.

On January 8, 1908 Hazel wrote to William Hogardt in Massachusetts stating,

> "Owing to illness, was unable to get you a New Year's card. But I wish you a very happy New Year. Thank you for your kind remembrance. I remain H.I.D.

Several weeks later, on February 3, 1908 Hazel wrote William Hogardt again saying,

> "I received your card. Am taking a few months vacation. I never hear from Gordon. I hope to see the girls soon but I have not seen any of them lately. We are having a very cold winter. I will be up to Poestenkill with Bell this summer. My address at the present time is 400 4th St. Troy, NY H.I.D.

Hazel informed William Hogardt of her illness on January 8. On February 3 Hazel revealed that she was planning to take a few months vacation. However, shortly after the February 3 letter, Hazel found employment with the Cary's and no longer needed a few months vacation. No proof exists but circumstantial evidence indicates that Hazel was planning to take time to recover and adjust to the life of motherhood. In the first week of February, however it may have happened, she was no longer pregnant and was able to resume regular employment again.

Hazel's assumed pregnancy in this scenario makes Minnie Taylor's lack of cooperation with investigators and her stated desire to protect Hazel's friends more understandable. Her letter to Mina Jones asking her to destroy Hazel's correspondence also makes more sense. William Clemens wrote in the July 24, Thrice-A-Week World that,

> On Dec. 30 last, a few days before she went into retirement at Uncle William Taylor's farm, near Teal's pond. Mina Jones wrote from Providence the letter containing this suggestive paragraph: "I am very, very sorry for you dearie. I know just how to feel for you."

If Clemens did, indeed discover such a letter and it was not artificially created to support his theory as had happened in other cases he investigated, Mina's words cast little doubt on Hazel's condition as early as December 30, 1907.

Could it be that Edward LaVoie was the father of Hazel's child and she terminated the pregnancy? He returned in July and Hazel informed him of the abortion. In a moment of rage, LaVoie killed the pretty twenty year old.

As logical as the theory may appear, there are problems with it. The personal ad in the Troy Record states,

> *Edward LaVoie has departed for Chattanooga, Tenn. where he will remain for the winter.*

The ad, however is misleading and confusing. It implies that LaVoie's visit to the south was temporary and he would be returning to

Troy in the spring. But LaVoie must have changed his plans and instead reenlisted in the army. Records indicate that Edward LaVoie reenlisted at Fort Slocum in New York City on October 25, 1907. His address at the time of his reenlistment was 105 W 52nd Street, New York City. He was not residing in Troy. It is not known why the ad was placed in the Troy paper and the reason for its inaccuracy. On November 24, 1907 LaVoie was assigned to the 12th Cavalry stationed in Fort Oglethorpe, Georgia. As far as can be learned from army records, LaVoie wasn't in Chattanooga.

LaVoie's uncle, Edward Rice stated that his nephew was stationed up in the north someplace, but he didn't know where. LaVoie's sister had no idea where her brother was. If LaVoie was assigned in the north or if he went on leave to New York, Boston or Providence it could account for Hazel's trips to those cities.

Edward LaVoie was born August 3, 1881 in Watervliet, NY. He was the oldest of three children born to Joseph and Emma LaVoie. He grew up on First Street in Troy and attended St. Jean the Baptist Church. At some point his father remarried a woman named Odella who was only two years older than Edward. Odella and Joseph would have three children together.

As a teenager, Edward worked as a baker. On February 26, 1900, at the age of 18 he enlisted in the army. He had dark brown hair, a dark complexion, and dark eyes. At the time of his enlistment he stood 5 feet 4 1/4 inches.

LaVoie served in Co. H of the Seventh Cavalry where he attained the rank of Corporal. He served in Cuba and was discharged with an excellent record on February 25, 1903.

Nothing more is known of LaVoie until October 25, 1907 when he re-enlisted in the army. He was twenty six years old, living in New

York City and working as a time clerk. He had grown since his first enlistment and now stood 5 feet 5 ½ inches. He was assigned to Co. L of the Twelfth Cavalry where he remained until he was discharged October 10, 1910 from Fort McDowell, California.

It is not known when or how Hazel and Edward met but their relationship appears to be rather ordinary. At some point they met, dated casually, and the romance ended. Like everybody else, LaVoie spoke very highly of Hazel.

No records exist to show that Edward LaVoie was in the north either at the time of Hazel's death or in April or May when she was taking her frequent trips. If he were, chances are the authorities at that time would have discovered and pursued it. Try as they may the investigators could not connect Hazel's two New York trips to LaVoie. The newspaper ad that was found in Hazel's suitcase is the only connection that LaVoie had to the case.

Suspect 3: William Knauff

Hazel confided to her friend Mina Jones that she could get married anytime she wanted. According to the July 19 Northern Budget,

> Mrs. Jones said that Hazel often made reference to a friend who worked in a dentist's office in Troy, but never mentioned his name. She said that one day she asked the girl: "Who is your fellow?" and Miss Drew replied that she could get married any time she decided, as there was a fellow in a dentist's office in Troy anxious to marry her.

It appears that the "fellow in the dentist's office" was enamored and Hazel was fully in control of the decision if and when they would marry.

Through their investigation, detectives learned that Hazel's dentist was Edmund Knauff whose office and residence was at 49 Third Street in Troy.

One evening, several weeks before her death, Hazel asked Mrs. Cary if she could go see her dentist. Mrs. Cary did not allow her to go because she felt the hour was too late. Hazel stayed in that night and never brought the subject up again. Mrs. Cary thought the matter was dropped. However, Dr. Knauff told detectives that Hazel, along with a friend, stopped by his office one evening several weeks before Hazel died. Hazel requested an evening appointment. Dr. Knauff told Hazel that he did not schedule evening appointments. Hazel and the friend left and never returned.

There is nothing unusual about either incident until the two stories are combined. Hazel did not go to Dr. Knauff's office the night she asked Mrs. Cary's permission. So at what point did she see Dr. Knauff to try to schedule the appointment? If it was after Mrs. Cary denied her permission, why did Hazel ask Dr. Knauff for an evening appointment knowing that Mrs. Cary would not allow her to see the dentist at such a late hour. Mrs. Cary said she would permit Hazel to see her dentist during normal operating hours. If she saw Dr. Knauff before she talked to Mrs. Cary, why would she ask to go out in the evening knowing that Dr. Knauff did not keep evening hours?

What was Hazel up to? If she did need her dentist why didn't she return during normal operating hours? Why didn't she ever return? Did she really need a dentist or could Hazel have other reasons to visit Dr. Knauff's office after hours? Was she just looking for an excuse to go to his office? It is possible but for reasons that are not yet apparent.

If Hazel and Dr. Knauff were having an affair it is unlikely that the dentist would have shared the evening visit story with the authorities. It is also unlikely that Hazel would have brought a friend with her, as Dr. Knauff claimed. It is further unlikely because Dr. Knauff lived with his family in the building that his office was in and where Hazel and her friend went to schedule the appointment. Her appearance there after hours would draw suspicion.

There is no doubt that Dr. Knauff knew Hazel. Although neither Mrs. Cary nor Hazel's mother could recall the name of Hazel's dentist, the fact that Hazel went to Dr. Knauff's seeking an evening appointment and the fact that he recognized her supports the idea that Dr. Dr. Knauff was her dentist. Hazel did have gold fillings in her teeth. It is not known if Dr. Knauff was the dentist who did the work but it is a reasonable assumption.

Dr. Knauff was in Kerin's store when Lawrence Eagan and Anna O'Donnell saw the pretty woman walk by. Dr. Knauff also saw the woman and claimed she was not Hazel.

It could simply be that Hazel was Dr. Knauff's patient and he knew her in that capacity. However, Mina Jones statement that Hazel told her she could marry a man who worked in a dentist office in Troy leads to the possibility that Hazel and Edward Knauff may have had more than a doctor-patient relationship.

Hazel's mother told investigators that Hazel had at one time been engaged. She could not recall the name of the man but thought it may have been Wolf. Wolf...Knauff. Could they be one and the same?

It is very unlikely that Hazel was dating Dr. Knauff. Mina said that Hazel had met the "young, good looking" man nearly two years before at Hazel's church. Hazel attended the Third and State Street Methodist Church, Dr. Knauff attended St. Paul's Episcopal Church.

The likelihood of his attending a ceremony at the Methodist Church, meeting a then eighteen year old Hazel, having a two year affair and all the while keeping it a secret from everyone is unlikely. But even if it were true, why would Hazel reveal her secret affair with a married man to Mina Jones?

If Hazel was not having an affair with the dentist could there have been another reason for her evening activity at the Knauff office on Third Street?

Edward Knauff was 49 years old at the time. When newsmen asked about his possible affair with Hazel, "Doctor Knauff smiled and said that so far as he was concerned he was a married man with a family." (New York Herald, July 19,1908).

Edward Knauff was married to Louisa (Kolbe) and the couple had a daughter, Flora and a son, William. William Knauff was born on February 9, 1889 making him eight months younger than Hazel.

Mina did not say specifically that Hazel had an engagement offer by a dentist, she said, "There was a fellow in a dentist's office in Troy anxious to marry her." If Edward Knauff was in fact Hazel's dentist, as it appears he was, and William lived in the same building that his father's office was in, this may connect Hazel not to Edward Knauff but to his son, William.

According to the Baltimore American, July 15, 1908:

> Hazel Drew was a native of Poestenkill, a village about 9 miles east of Troy, and her parents, Mr. and Mrs. Drew resided there before moving to Troy about 2 years ago. Hazel, however, had been a resident of this city about 6 years, coming into young womanhood amid all the gayeties of city life. Although the daughter of a farmer, she chafed under the seclusion of country life, and at the age of 14 she came to Troy and made her home with the former city treasurer, Thomas W. Hislop, a friend of her family. She remained with the Hislop's 2 years under Mrs. Hislop's care.

Hazel was a quiet girl, attended Sunday School regularly, and was respected and beloved by all her acquaintances.

She attended school, stood well in her classes and was grad- uated from the local high school.

No record can be found indicating when, or even if Hazel attended the local high school. William Knauff attended Troy High School and graduated in 1906. Although about the same age as William, Hazel is not listed among the 96 graduates in that class. However, it is pos- sible that she at one time was part of the class but never completed high school.

A class of approximately one hundred students is relatively small. A teenage girl possessing Hazel's charm and good looks would certainly attract the boys attention in school. Assuming that Hazel did attend the Troy public schools, being the same age as William Knauff, it is likely the two were at least acquainted.

After graduation, William attended RPI and was the manager of the hockey team. In May 1907, during his freshman year, William was struck on the head by a baseball. It was a serious although non life threatening injury. In January 1908, during his sophomore year, he was selected to be on the Calculus Cremation Committee.

During that time, students at RPI were placed in either the Civil Engineering track or the Natural Science track. There is no record of which track William was pursuing but because later in life he worked as a Senior Assistant Engineer for the Road Commission in West Virginia, it must be assumed William's background was more aligned with the Civil Engineering track. If so it is possible that William had Edward Cary, Hazel's employer, as a professor.

William appeared to be doing well at RPI, keeping active in college affairs and activities. He was listed in the 1909 yearbook as a junior with his expected graduation in 1910. However, William is not included in the 1910 yearbook. He dropped out in 1909 or 1910. His senior thesis, a requirement for graduation was never submitted. No explanation has been found to account for his early departure.

On July 6, Dr. Knauff was in Kerin's store on Congress Street when Lawrence Eagan mistakenly thought he saw Hazel stroll past. The story regarding the incident was printed in the July 18 Troy Record.

> Dr. Knauff was in the grocery store on Congress Street on Monday afternoon, July 6, when Lawrence Eagan, a young man employed in the store, was said to have seen Hazel Drew passing. The dentist said today that the girl was not Hazel Drew. "I was in the store a few minutes before 6 o'clock making some purchases when I heard one of the employees say, 'Ain't she a daisy?' referring to a girl who was passing. I glanced at the girl who was blonde, wore glasses and had on a white dress. A few minutes later the same girl boarded an Albia car on which I was going home, and I am positive she was not Hazel Drew."

Dr. Knauff lived with his family at 49 Third Street in the city of Troy. Kerin's Store was on Congress Street between Fourth and Fifth Streets, about a block from his residence. There would be no reason for him to take the train, as his home was in close walking distance and in the opposite direction from where the Albia train would be going. The Albia section of Troy is approximately three miles southeast of the city. Before arriving in Albia, the train would travel up Pawling Avenue, pass Whitman Court where the Cary's lived and later pass the Harrison residence where Minnie Taylor worked.

Dr. Knauff's statement in the Troy Record said that he was on the Albia train "on which I was going home" an unusual statement under the circumstance. If Dr. Knauff continued past the Harrison's, the trolley would eventually stop at the Albia Station and passengers would transfer to the Troy and New England Rail. This is the same station where Peter Cipperly claimed he saw Hazel and the young man board the train. The Troy and New England train continued on to Averill Park.

According to The Troy & New England Railway Co. 1895-1925 booklet written by Charles Viens & Sanford Young, there were twenty eight stops between Albia and Averill Park. Stop number 10, just after the Snyder's Lake stop at Snyder's Corners, is called "Dr. Knauff's". Could this be the same Dr. Knauff?

Edward Knauff died on June 13, 1915. His obituary appeared in The Troy Times, on June 14, 1915.

> Dr. Edward J. Knauff, one of the founders of the Pioneer Building-Loan Association and a well known dentist, died yesterday at the Samaritan Hospital, where he had been under treatment since last Tuesday. Dr. Knauff was born in Troy about 56 years ago.
>
> For the last thirty-five years he was a practicing dentist. In the city he had been twenty-four years at 49 Third Street where his family resides...Dr. Knauff is survived by his wife, who was Miss Louise Kolbe; a daughter, Flora Knauff; (and) a son, William B. (read K) Knauff.
>
> Dr. Knauff was taken ill at his summer home near Snyder's Corners...

In the summer of 1907, in addition to staying with the Bly's, Hazel spent a week with the family of John Link at Snyder's Lake. Little is known of the Link's or why Hazel stayed with them. It was while she stayed at Snyder's Lake that Hazel met her "Knight of the Napp Kinn". Snyder's Lake is within walking distance from Stop Number 10,

Knauff's Stop. It is conceivable that Hazel and William Knauff, possibly former classmates could have been dating. This may explain Hazel's evening visit to 49 Third Street, not to make an evening appointment with her dentist but to see William, and her reason for moving from the Bly's to the Link's.

Mrs. Drew, regarding Hazel's engagement, made the following statements to investigators.

> "Hazel to my knowledge has not had a beau for more than a year..." (Troy Record, July 18,1908)

> Hazel...referred to her last love affair with a man who stopped calling on her when she became ill with the grip a year ago last spring... (Troy Record, July 18,1908)

> He told Hazel that in three years he wanted her to be his wife. According to Mrs. Drew, her daughter did not care for the young man, and said she would never marry him. (Troy Daily Press, July 18, 1908)

Mrs. Drew made these statements in the summer of 1908. She said Hazel had not had a beau for more than a year, the last one ending in the spring of 1907. The man reportedly wanted to marry Hazel in three years, which would make it 1910, the year William Knauff was scheduled to graduate from RPI.

STOPS ALONG THE T.N.E.R. WITH THEIR RESPECTIVE NUMBERS

Albia Station

1. Bentley's (before first trestle and west of Wynantskill)
2. Wynantskill
   Between Wynantskill & Snyders Corners were the following stops:
3. Barringers (on flats east of Wynantskill)
4. Worthingtons (further east behind Worthington's house on Rte 150)
5. Myers (just west of trestle on flats)
6. No name given (just east of trestle)
7. No name given (west of Myer's switch and trestle)
8. Snyders Lake or Snyders
   Between Snyders Lake and Stop 13 - Reichard's Lake Road were the following stops:
9. Daniel Shea's Camp
10. Dr. Knauff's
11. 5¢ fare limit stop
12. Ellsworth's Springs (near town line of Sand Lake and North Greenbush)
13. Stop 13 Reichards Lake Road (present day Stop 13 Road)
    Between Stop 13 Reichards Lake Road and Averill Park Terminal were the following stops:
14. Power House (site of the present Jack Lawrence house)
15. Calkins (next east of Power House)
16. Milo Hastings (rock cut- behind Sno-Fun shop)
17. Brookside Park
18. West Sand Lake Station (behind 43 Shopping Mall)
19. Cedarhurst
20. Mill Yard - Cipperly's
21. Reichard's Lake Road
22. Arlington Hotel (present Journey's End Hotel)
23. Werger's (Harry Werger's house)
24. Miller's (next to trestle on east end)
25. The woods (short distance to the east and immediately after another trestle)
26. Smauders or Sunset Terrace
27. Lake Avenue (opposite St. Henry's Cemetery)
28. Averill Park

Stops along the Troy and New England trainline running between Albia Station and Averill Park. Note that Stop 10, Dr. Knauff's is two stops past Snyder's Lake. Note also Stop 11 is the 5 cent fare limit. Source: Troy and New England Railway Co. 1895-1925 by Charles Viens and Sanford Young

Stop Number 10 on the Troy and New England Railway was approximately five miles from Albia and on a direct train line to Averill Park. Stop Number 11 was referred to in Viens and Young's

Troy and New England Railway booklet as "The 5 cent fare limit stop". Remembering that a nickel was all the money Hazel had with her when she was killed, she may have taken the train to Averill Park and had the five cents left to get her back to Stop 11.

If William Knauff and Hazel were dating or even engaged it explains why Dr. Knauff was so familiar with Hazel.

Peter Cipperley claimed he saw a woman that resembled Hazel along with a man board the Albia train on July 7. He described the man as tall and slim. He had a long, thin face, long nose and a receding hairline with possibly brown hair.

Because William Knauff did not not graduate, his portrait was not included in the 1910 RPI yearbook. There is one possible picture of him taken with the hockey team for the 1908-1909 season but because the names are listed on a separate page and they do not coincide with the players in the team picture, one can only speculate which, if any of the people in the photograph is William Knauff. Therefore, there are no known pictures of William Knauff and Peter Cipperley's description can not be applied.

If Mina Jones' story was true and Hazel could get married any time she wanted to a person she knew in a dentist's office the evidence points to William Knauff.

Suppose Hazel followed through and accepted William's proposal but because she was only a servant girl and thinking his son could do better, and wanting him to finish college first, Dr. Knauff objected to the marriage. But William was smitten and despite his father's objections, convinced the beautiful and popular twenty year old to elope.

On July 6 Hazel quit her job at the Carys. She left the house carrying a suitcase packed only with items appropriate for a honeymoon night. Mary Robinson saw her at Union Station. Hazel could have been waiting for William but for some reason, maybe he was attempting one last time to get Dr. Knauff to bless the union, he arrived too late and they missed their train.

They decided to go to Knauff's residence at Snyder's Lake to spend the night. That would account for why there was no record or sighting of Hazel in any of the boarding places in the area. It is unlikely that the Knauff's had access to a carriage or automobile so the couple took the train. The next morning Hazel and William went back to Union Station to catch the train to New York like Hazel told Mary Robinson the day before.

The 1908-1909 RPI hockey team

TRANSIT, VOL. XLIV   207

Hockey Team, Season of 1908-09

KNAUFF ....Manager
JOYCES .... Assistant Manager
STEVENSON ....Captain

Centre—STEVENSON   Coverpoint—BENJIMAN
Rover—FLEEGER   Point—HAMMOND, OWEN
Right Wing—BREED   Goal—DION
Left Wing—MUELLER, HARDING   Substitutes—VAN EMAN, MENARD, REYNOLDS, STARK,
                                             SMITH

R. P. I. 6; Williams 4.
R. P. I. 3; Cornell 2.
Yale 3; R. P. I. 0.
Columbia 3; R. P. I. 2
Carnegie 4; R. P. I. 1.

The names of the 1908-9 hockey team and managers, including William Knauff. Because the names do not align with the players in the photograph, it is impossible to know which person is Knauff. Photos from 1910 Transit (RPI yearbook).

But Hazel was having second thoughts, possibly blaming herself for the dissention between William and Edward. Rather than board the train, she convinced William that they needed to talk. He begrudgingly agreed. He knew what Hazel had on her mind but also knew he had an opportunity to save the relationship. He was scared but determined. Hazel, having already decided she would be returning alone, checked her bag. It would be waiting for her when she came back.

The couple took the trolley from Union Station to Albia then boarded the 3:00 train. They took the seat in front of Peter Cipperley. Cipperly said the man was overly attentive to the woman. William was hoping it would make a difference. Cipperly got off the train at the Snyder's Lake stop. William and Hazel remained on the train and got off at Stop number 10.

The couple went to Knauff's house and began the epic conversation that neither was looking forward to but both, for different reasons, knew had to happen. The exchange was uneasy. Only one would be satisfied but neither would be happy when it was over. Hazel was confident and determined to amicably end the relationship; William was insecure but just as determined to save it anyway he could. Although better educated and of higher status than Hazel and as much as William wanted to deny it, the fate of their future was in Hazel's hands. She loved less, therefore she controlled the relationship. He did his best to convince Hazel that they had a future but he knew he was failing. He was frustrated. No matter what he said and despite his best attempts to reason with her, William couldn't get through to her. Frustration turned to anger.

After several hours, Hazel had enough. She calmly excused herself and prepared to leave. William's anger turned to rage. Hoping to glean some satisfaction, he refused to go back to Troy with her. She didn't want him so he wouldn't go with her. He watched her go to the train stop but was confused when he saw her board the train heading east to Averill Park instead of west, to Troy. Where was she going? What was she up to? His mind, already clouded by rage and despair, began to wander. He wasn't thinking clearly. Could Hazel have ended their relationship because there was another man? That had to be it. She was going to Averill Park to see another man.

Hazel had enough money to go back to Union Station but it occurred to her that she had no place to stay. If she went out to Sand Lake she could spend the night with her uncle or maybe with the Sowalsky's. She would not have enough money to get back but she was sure someone would loan her what she needed. She would pay them back when she could.

Hazel arrived in Averill Park at 6 o'clock with only a nickel, not nearly enough for a taxi. She set out on foot for Taborton Road.

William remained at the house. He was seething. It was bad enough to lose Hazel but the thought of her with another man drove him to madness. He convinced himself that if he couldn't have Hazel, nobody could have Hazel. The scorned ex-fiance caught the next available train to Averill Park. He knew the area. After getting off the train and quickly searching Averill Park, he ran towards Taborton Mountain. Moving at a much faster pace than Hazel, he began his journey up the desolate mountain road, the perfect place to do what he went there to do. He skillfully ducked into the woods when he heard people approaching. He caught up with Hazel after she passed Smith and Gundrum. There was nothing for him to say. William picked up a rock or piece of wood and violently brought it down on the head of the woman who only a few of hours ago he planned to make his wife. He felt relief. William picked up her lifeless body and carried it to Teal's pond.

The following month William returned to RPI but he was never able to get over Hazel. With difficulty he was able to finish the year but was too distraught to return for his senior year in 1909. Although William had done well academically and had a bright future and although he was a very active in athletic and extracurricular events, he couldn't bring himself to go back. The loss he suffered and the grief he felt was just too much for him to overcome.

Suspect 4: C.E.S

Clues exist to support the theory that Hazel was involved in an abusive relationship. Enough evidence is available to come close to revealing the identity of the person she was having that relationship with. The July 14 edition of the Evening World reported that six letters, written by a person with the initials C.E.S., were found in Hazel's trunk. The Evening World printed an excerpt from one of those letters. Investigators never discovered the identity of C.E.S. but what he wrote fits the psychological profile of a person who exhibits abusive tendencies as described by John Douglas and Mark Olshaker. Abusers can take on many forms but tend to have certain consistent characteristics.

As previously noted, Douglas and Olshaker stated that an abuser will frequently change moods, switching from tenderness to jealousy to rage. He does this in order to keep his partner insecure, confused, and off guard. The press did not print all six of C.E.S.'s letters. What they did print however, reveals the pattern Douglas and Olshaker described. In one instance, C.E.S. confides his total enamoration for Hazel, as printed in the July 14 Evening World.

> Your merry smile and twinkling eyes torture me. Your face haunts me. Why can't I be contented again? You have stolen my liberty.

In another letter, which wasn't printed but was eluded to in the same July 14 Evening World, C.E.S. scolds Hazel for being a flirt. C.E.S. appears to switch moods in what Douglas and Olshaker said an abuser does as a concerted effort to keep his victim off balance, in this case Hazel.

The six letters that Hazel received from C.E.S. were sent from Providence, Boston, and New York. The author appears to be well traveled, possibly some sort of businessman with a well paying job. It can be no coincidence that those are the same cities where Hazel traveled the previous spring.

However, both Mina Jones in Providence and Carrie Weaver in New York claimed that Hazel didn't meet anyone on these trips. As forthright as they appear, both women, loyal friends were likely covering for Hazel. Except for some of the conversations Hazel had with Mina, nothing has been written about those trips to Boston and Providence. It has been established that Hazel asked Mina to mail the postcard to William Hogardt in Massachusetts. If she was involved in an abusive relationship, she would not want to be caught sending a postcard to another man, even if it was an innocent correspondence. It was also about this time that Hazel suddenly and with no explanation stopped writing to Hogardt.

Jarvis O'Brien informed reporters that Hazel had received a letter, postmarked in New York City, from the mysterious C.E.S. approximately three weeks before her murder. He would not reveal the specific date but said it was not later than June 13.

Hazel and Carrie Weaver vacationed in New York City during the last weekend in May. The timing of the C.E.S. letter and Hazel's vacation in New York closely align. It is very likely she met with C.E.S. while in New York.

Carrie's employer, Mrs. Greene told investigators that she trusted the two young women and allowed Carrie to travel to New York with Hazel. Mrs. Greene said she went so far as to make arrangements for the two women to stay at the YWCA.

Carrie Weaver gave a slightly different version as printed in the July 18, 1908 Times Union.

> "Hazel and I went by way of the River on Memorial Day. We had intended to stay at the Margaret Louise home but it being full we stayed at a private boarding home recommended by the people at the home."

A closer examination of the Margaret Louise home raises some questions.

The Ladies Home Journal in November 1893 wrote:

> The Margaret Louise House in NYC was established as a temporary house for Protestant self supporting women. The liberal endowments of the Sheppards and the Vanderbilts have made it possible for the managers to furnish accommodations to business women at an almost nominal price. The home is located at 14 & 16 East 16th Street. Applications for rooms must be made by letter in advance. Children and invalids will not be admitted and guests may not remain longer than four weeks.

A description of The Margaret Louise Home, as printed in <u>The Arrow of Pi Beta Phi</u> reveals more.

> It is a women's hotel of beautiful architectural design, luxurious in its furnishings and with perfect sanitary equipments.

And the best part of all, is, that all its refinement and elegance, it is designed especially for working women and accordingly the prices are within their reach. Two references are required for admission and one can remain there but a month, for the purpose of the hotel is not to give permanent homes, but to provide a comfortable stopping place for women who come to NY to work, until they can make arrangements for a permanent home. The price of a room for women workers is 3 dollars and a half a week, to others 6 dollars a week. A large number of women students of art and medicine, women engaged in newspaper or journalistic work and representative of many of the professions in a large city, have found this hotel to be a delightful stopping place.

The hall into which one passes through the main entrance is spacious and lofty, furnished in native oak, having a floor in-laid with exquisitely colored tiles. The parlor is furnished in soft shades of gray and blue and is home like as well as artistic. There is a library, too, with shelves of choice books and a piano.

The bedrooms are as dainty as one could desire. The furnishings are simple but tasteful- white enameled bedstead, oak dresser and table, pretty lace curtains at the windows, while bathrooms of the latest sanitary designs are conveniently near.

The appointments of the dining room are as elegant of those of any first class hotel in New York. The linen is of the finest quality and daintily marked. While the service is perfect, the food is plain, but of the best quality and well cooked. The crowds that have come to the Margaret Louise home show that such a hotel is needed and appreciated by thousands of weary women workers.

The Margaret Louise home was not the type of boarding establishment that two domestic servants from upstate New York traveling to the metropolis for a brief weekend visit would ordinarily stay. The home was intended as temporary housing for professional women.

Mrs. Greene told investigators she arranged a room for the two women at the YWCA. Whereas the Margaret Louise home was associated with the YWCA, Mrs. Greene would not arrange for her servant to stay in such a luxurious and exotic establishment that would cost the girl's approximately one week's wages. She, instead would have made arrangements for the two at the YWCA, like she said she did, the one that was intended for young women of Hazel and Carrie's station in life.

The only way to get a room at the Margaret Louise Home was to request one in advance by mail. Mrs. Greene did not receive confirmation that a room was available at the Margaret Louise home because she didn't request a room there and did not know the girls had plans to stay there. Mrs. Greene did procure a room as she claimed at the YWCA but the girls had other, more mischievous plans instead. Nowhere is it printed that Mrs. Greene was aware that the girls made plans to stay at a place other than what she reserved for them.

Hazel, however would have been the one who had other ideas and had the means to stay at the more exclusive establishment. If Hazel was in fact dating C.E.S., a wealthy businessman with connections to New York, it is more likely that he would be the one to try to arrange for a room in a place like the Margaret Louise home; probably for Carrie by herself or maybe for both women. As it turned out there were no rooms available for either of them. It has never been established where Hazel and Carrie stayed that weekend.

Hazel reportedly lost her purse when she and Carrie arrived in New York but Carrie supposedly had enough money for both women to go to the theatre, ride the trains, take in the sights, spend two nights in an undisclosed private boarding place, have meals and buy return tickets on a boat back to Troy. A remarkable accomplishment for a woman of Carrie's limited means.

Carrie could never figure out how Hazel was able to buy the most stylish clothes, take so many vacations, some on First Class boats, and eat in the finest restaurants. She claimed that Hazel made only slightly more money than she did and she could not even come close to affording the things Hazel could.

On their return trip from New York, Hazel talked about plans for her next vacation. The Daily Democrat and Recorder (Amsterdam, NY) July 17, 1908 reported:

> The girls (Hazel and Carrie) made the trip to the metropolis on Friday May 29, and returned here on the following Monday morning. Hazel at that time told her friend that she intended to take a trip to Lake George on the 4th of July...

So the Fourth of July plans were made while Hazel was still on her New York vacation. Except for this trip to New York with Carrie, Hazel supposedly traveled to the other cities alone. It is very unusual that Hazel was planning and discussing her next outing, one she would supposedly go on by herself again, when she hadn't even returned from her current one. She didn't ask Carrie if she would be interested in joining her she just brought it up as if it was already established, as if it had already been discussed and decided with somebody else.

The Washington Times reported on July 16, 1908,

> Hazel Drew's unexplained trips to eastern cities were revealed by Mrs. Cary, the girl's last mistress. It is believed she went to meet a man whose initials, "C.E.S." were signed to several letters found in the girl's trunk, and there is a possibility, the police believe, that she left the Cary home expecting to meet this man in Troy.

It is possible that Hazel met C.E.S. in New York and sometime over the course of the weekend the two made arrangements to meet again on the Fourth of July in Lake George. Circumstantial evidence appears to be very strong that this is what occurred but something happened over the next few weeks to disrupt the plans.

From the time Hazel returned from her New York vacation to the weekend of the Fourth of July, very little has been written but the little that is available suggests something went terribly wrong with Hazel's plans and with her relationship. Hazel appears to have become frightened and indecisive, classic characteristics of a person who realizes events in their abusive relationship have spiraled out of control.

Approximately one week after Hazel received her last known correspondence from C.E.S. (no later than June 13), she sent the letter to the Young Women's camp in Altamont. Dated June 20, 1908, Hazel wrote, "Saw your advertisement for a summer boarding place and I enclose stamp for which to send me circular."

It appears that Hazel was looking to flee. Something scared her enough to contemplate leaving a job she was happy doing and with a family who greatly respected and admired her. She was not looking to go back to Sand Lake, a place she loved and wrote about returning to. Instead she was looking in the other direction, to the west of Schenectady where people didn't know her and where it would be more difficult to find her.

Hazel seemed to be planning her escape but something changed her mind. Perhaps it was the manipulative head games that abusers use, like the ones Douglas and Olshaker discussed in their books. Perhaps C.E.S. turned on the charm and convinced Hazel he was sorry and begged for another chance. Perhaps he convinced Hazel to go away with him to Lake George as originally planned where they could discuss and fix their problems. He may have promised to leave his wife. Perhaps he even promised marriage.

Whatever he said Hazel fell for it but didn't have much time to get ready. She was unprepared for a weekend that had so much at stake. With no money and nothing special to wear, Hazel went to her mother for a loan. The next afternoon she made an unexpected visit to Mrs. Schumaker where she waited until 11:00 to have a new shirtwaist made. This was July 3, the night before her planned trip.

Hazel must have been struggling with her emotions but she convinced herself to go to Lake George to reconnect with the man she thought she loved. The man who most likely made promises to her but had no intention of keeping. There was only one problem that Hazel hadn't counted on...Minnie Taylor.

The Evening World reported on July 22, 1908:

> Minnie Taylor, the aunt was brought to the District-Attorney's office yesterday afternoon and put through another severe examination. She steadfastly maintained that she last saw the girl on Monday morning July 6 when they returned from Schenectady together. It is the general belief of the police and the public alike that the woman is withholding information to shield herself or a friend.

> After the interview with Miss Taylor it was announced at the District-Attorney's office that there is reason to think that Hazel spent the night at Lake George.

As close as Hazel seemed to have been to Carrie Weaver, it doesn't appear that she held Hazel's confidence. Carrie, for the most part was open and honest with the investigators. She portrayed Hazel as she perceived her, not as Hazel really was. Hazel never revealed to Carrie her inner most secrets. She never told Carrie about her relatives or of her life in Averill Park. Carrie hadn't yet earned that level of trust.

Minnie Taylor, on the other hand, had won Hazel's confidence. Minnie was privy to Hazel's secrets and desires. From the very outset, Minnie refused to fully cooperate with the detectives, confounding them every day. She claimed she was protecting Hazel and her friends.

Minnie, nearly twice Hazel's age, knew about her niece's relationship with C.E.S. Minnie also knew the kind of person he was and at some point, one way or another, if she liked it or not, Minnie was going to protect Hazel. She appears to have been aware of Hazel's desperate plan to escape to the Young Women's camp in Altamont. The Troy Times on July 20, 1908 reported, "District Attorney O'Brien said this morning that he heard yesterday from the aunt, Minnie Taylor, that Hazel had been thinking about going down to the Young Women's Camp at Altamont to spend a short time this summer."

On July 4, wearing her best new clothes and carrying a suitcase packed for a romantic overnight excursion including at least one shirtwaist, Hazel intended to go to Lake George to rekindle her relationship with C.E.S.. Minnie Taylor intervened.

Maybe it was prearranged but somehow Minnie convinced Hazel to meet her on the morning of July 4. Carrie Weaver was under the impression that Hazel was traveling with some of her girlfriends. However it happened, Hazel and Minnie probably went to Union Station but Minnie would not allow Hazel to board the train for Lake George. She would later tell investigators that the trains were too crowded and they both decided to remain in Troy but his is hard to believe. Hazel had been looking forward to this trip for over a month. She bought a new waist with money she didn't have. She packed a suitcase with overnight apparel that is indicative of a woman that has made up her mind. As late as July 3, she spoke openly and enthusiastically about the trip to everyone she was close to. Under the circumstances it is not likely that a crowded train would have kept Hazel from Lake George; but Minnie Taylor could.

The wording of Minnie Taylor's explanation about the crowded trains is important.

> "Hazel was with me here and in Schenectady on the Fourth," said Miss Taylor today. "*She* had intended to take a trip to Lake George and wanted me to go with her but I didn't want to go there *on that day* because the trains are so crowded on holidays." (Italics added) (The Rome Daily Sentinel, July 17, 1908)

"She," meaning Hazel had intended to take the trip. Minnie did not say "we" had intended to take a trip. This was coming from Hazel. "I didn't want to go there *on that day*." Minnie is implying that Hazel had already made the plans to go to Lake George (which she did) but Minnie was included at the last minute. It is more likely that Minnie intervened to prevent Hazel from going.

Perhaps they did go to the parade and on to Rensselaer Park. There is only Minnie's word on that. If they did, Hazel could not have been happy spending her vacation at a parade in Troy and at an amusement park she had been to many times before. Perhaps they walked around the city talking and arguing. As reported in The Troy Times on July 17, a witness claimed she saw Hazel with another woman, probably Minnie Taylor, on Fulton Street around 4 o'clock. Minnie denied it. She claimed that she and Hazel left Rensselaer Park at 5 o'clock. At the Inquest John Drew said he thought he saw Hazel at Franklin Square, (which is near Fulton Street) in Troy. Minnie looked at him disapprovingly when he said that. Where ever they were that Saturday, Minnie successfully kept her niece away from Lake George and from C.E.S. but she still had Sunday to worry about.

Instead of letting Hazel go back to the Cary's where she would have no control, Minnie took her to Schenectady to spend the night with relatives. The two remained there the entire next day and did not return to Troy until 10:30 that night, much too late for Hazel to do anything. Minnie must have felt relieved after Hazel departed the trolley at Whitman Court that Sunday night. Little did she know Hazel's intentions the next day.

Hazel must have had a sleepless night. She had made arrangements to meet C.E.S. in Lake George but didn't show. She had already made the decision to remain in the abusive relationship, one that she thought she could change. Promises had been made but now C.E.S. had been stood up and Hazel knew she had to make amends. She had to find him.

In his June correspondence, C.E.S. wrote,

> Please don't forget a promise to write. When I reach Albany again, I will meet you at the tavern. I must see you soon or I'll die of starvation.

The two apparently had a prearranged meeting place at some tavern in Albany. Although C.E.S. possibly had access to an automobile, it is reasonable to assume he would have taken the train to Lake George. That train would have come through Union Station in Troy.

On Monday morning, July 6, Hazel stunned Mrs. Cary when she abruptly quit. Hazel didn't leave because she was unhappy, she left because she was desperate. She had to find C.E.S. and explain to him what had happened.

Wearing the same new clothes she wore for her expected trip to Lake George and her favorite society pin, Hazel left carrying a suitcase packed with most of the same clothes she planned to take to Lake George. The notable exception was a shirtwaist. She didn't know where she would end up so she needed to bring clothes sufficient for an overnight stay, nothing more. Hazel then went to the Harrison's house to return Minnie clothes. She arrived around 9:45 on a weekday morning. Minnie must have questioned why Hazel wasn't at work. She probably realized then that Hazel had made a rash decision. Hazel may have tried to smooth over the awkwardness by telling Minnie she was going to Watervliet, a lie that Minnie never would have believed. Minnie knew what Hazel was up to but could no longer stop her.

It was about 10 o'clock when Hazel boarded the trolley for Union Station. Minnie reported that when Hazel left, she was carrying her suitcase and her purse. She even included that Hazel was wearing her nose glasses but for some reason Minnie didn't mention Hazel's most obvious apparel, the black hat with the large plumes. The first thing almost every other witness who saw Hazel over the next two days mentioned was the hat. It stuck out more than a purse or glasses. Could it be that Hazel was not in possession of the hat at this point? Or did Minnie simply fail to mention it?

Hazel had promised to meet Carrie Weaver at Union Station at noon to say good-bye before her month's vacation to Ohio. Although Hazel was seen at the station around that time, she had bigger things on her mind and Carrie did not fit into her plans.

It doesn't appear that Hazel was familiar with C.E.S's specific travel plans but she knew he would have to come through Troy, possibly before going on to Albany and then maybe to New York. Her plan was to intercept him at Union Station.

Around 11:30 Mary Robinson saw Hazel in the station. She went over to say hello. No where is it printed if Hazel was in possession of the black hat. When asked, Hazel told Mary she was going down the river and maybe even to New York but she didn't complete her thought. She left her friend, literally in mid-sentence, and purchased a train ticket for the 12:00 local to Albany. Hazel was anxious and preoccupied and didn't want to be distracted by small talk or run into Carrie Weaver who was expected at that time. She decided to take a chance and go to Albany. C.E.S. would probably have to pass through there anyway. Hazel may have wanted to see if he was waiting at the tavern. If he wasn't, she could leave a message that she was looking for him if he did stop in to look for her. If she discovered that C.E.S. had already passed through, she could continue "down the river".

Hazel arrived in Albany, checked the depot and went to the tavern but C.E.S. hadn't been there. She didn't wait very long. She could have been thinking that she had a better chance to meet him passing through Troy. She may have thought that C.E.S. would be looking for her and Troy would be the logical place for him to look, not Albany. She left word at the tavern that she would be waiting for C.E.S. at Union Station and quickly returned.

Hazel went back to Troy knowing that some personal details needed to be addressed. She was committed to leaving that day but her clothes and other possessions were still at the Cary's house on Whitman Court. She went to the Westcott Express Company whose office was at the depot. At 1:15 she placed the order for her trunk to be picked up and sent to her parents house. She wasn't certain about what was going to happen but she knew she would not be welcomed back at the Cary's. Hazel then settled in and spent an undetermined amount of time waiting for C.E.S..

At some point Hazel's patience and determination paid off. She found C.E.S. and convinced him they needed to talk. Because he shows the traits of an abusive man who has little respect for women in general, C.E.S. would not have been happy about how the weekend transpired. His first inclination would have been to lash out at Hazel but being in a public place he would have had to control his rage. He would have blamed Hazel for the wasted weekend. Hazel, on the other hand would have already known that he would be angry but would have been determined to explain the situation to him. The two left Union Station together to spend a long night talking and figuring things out. Unbeknownst to Hazel however, C.E.S. had already made up his mind that the two did not have a future together.

Hazel and C.E.S. left Union Station and found a place nearby to spend the night, and it was going to be a long night. They had a lot to talk about. They had already been at Union Station. Hazel had her suitcase with her. They could have traveled anywhere together but they remained in Troy. C.E.S. was the one who made the decision to stay. He was still in control.

Despite her best efforts, the night did not go as Hazel had hoped. C.E.S. was too powerful. He controlled the conversation. He was cold and not receptive to Hazel's emotional pleas, but he underestimated Hazel's desperation. He did not know, understand, or care that Hazel had sacrificed everything for him. She quit her job and had for all intent and purposes severed ties with everybody she was close to. She had nothing to go back to and she had nothing to lose.

What Hazel could not comprehend was that C.E.S. had no interest in continuing the relationship. In his mind the affair was over but he was beginning to realize that Hazel wasn't giving up. If he was a single man he could just walk away. He didn't because he couldn't and now Hazel had become a liability.

It must have been sometime during the night of July 6 when C.E.S. realized that Hazel had to die. She was too determined to make their relationship work. Hazel probably knew that C.E.S. had a wife. She may have even threatened to expose the relationship.

C.E.S. had always been able to control Hazel but now he was the one on the defensive. Hazel had outmaneuvered him and now he was the one who was desperate. He knew what he had to do and now had to decide when and where he would do it. He couldn't kill her at that time, there was too great of a chance that he was seen. It had to be done the next day. C.E.S. was exhibiting the characteristics of an Organized killer.

C.E.S. knew how to manipulate Hazel. He would have pretended to give in to her, told her she was right all along and he was being foolish. He would probably have promised Hazel that he was going to leave his wife and whisk her away to New York or some other big city. He was expertly telling Hazel exactly what she wanted to hear and desperately wanted to believe. She was falling for his story.

By the morning of July 7, C.E.S. had figured out the details of his plan. Knowing that he needed an isolated place he would take Hazel to the seclusion of Sand Lake. He was probably from that area or he may have been a visitor. Perhaps that's where he met Hazel. One way or another he was familiar with the Town. It was the perfect place for what he was going to do but he couldn't risk being seen on a train, he would need another form of transportation. He may have had his own car or possibly had a friend or close relative nearby who had access to one. In any event he left early to arrange the transportation. When he left, he didn't tell Hazel where he was going, only to have her bag packed and to meet him at Union Station sometime in the late morning or early afternoon.

With the possible exception of Thomas Carey, there are no known sightings of Hazel until approximately 1:30 when Jeanette Marcellus saw her at Union Station. She was dressed nicely. Marcellus claimed a short time later she saw Hazel in the ladies room looking in the mirror, fixing her appearance. For the first time the hat was mentioned. It is possible that C.E.S. bought the hat that morning, all part of the deception.

C.E.S. arrived at Union Station just before Jeanette Marcellus saw Hazel. He reminded her that the move would be permanent, that they could never return to the area. He told Hazel he had a car and he would take her out to the country so she could say goodbye to her brother Willie. C.E.S. was smart. Hazel certainly would have told him in the heat of the argument the night before that she had alienated herself from Minnie Taylor and her other relatives. Everyone, C.E.S. realized, except her favorite brother Willie, who was staying with the Sowalsky's in the desolate mountains of Sand Lake. C.E.S. was smooth, he was convincing. He presented himself as a man who was genuinely thinking of Hazel. Again, Hazel wanted to believe his lies and she fell for them. She checked her suitcase at the baggage station. She wouldn't need it in Sand Lake. It would be waiting for her, she believed, when she returned. They left Union Station in the car for the one way trip to Taborton Road.

Investigators were never able to learn where Hazel was between 1:49 when her bag was checked and 7:20, the approximate time that the Rollman's saw her standing alone on the side of the road. Perhaps she and C.E.S. went for a long drive. Maybe they went to the tavern in Albany or to one of the scenic lakes where they enjoyed a private picnic. Wherever they went, C.E.S. was keeping Hazel out of sight. He was stalling, waiting until it was dark and there would be fewer people mulling about on the mountain, again showing signs of an Organized killer. When the time came, they drove over to Taborton Road.

When they reached the road, C.E.S. told Hazel that he was unwilling to drive the car up the narrow mountain lane that was built for horse traffic, not automobiles. He parked the car near Crape's hotel or possibly on the so called New Road.

C.E.S. knew that he was going to kill Hazel in the seclusion of Taborton Mountain. He couldn't drive her because he would have no way to get her out of the car to do what he was going to do before they reached the Sowalsky's, and he couldn't take her all the way to the house because he would be seen. Instead, he figured out a way to walk. If Hazel objected, C.E.S. would have reminded her of the importance of saying goodbye to her brother, that she would not see again for a very long time. He promised to accompany her up the mountain. Hazel stepped out of the car, leaving her purse on the seat.

As they walked up the mountain together C.E.S. kept a constant lookout for other travelers. In order to get away with what he was about to do it was imperative that he wasn't seen. When he heard the first wagon approach, the Rollman's, he ducked into the woods to avoid detection. Perhaps he convinced Hazel he was playing a game and as the Ryemillers approached, she too played the game and hid in the woods. When Smith and Gundrum came down the mountain, C.E.S. again slipped into the woods but Hazel was too slow and was spotted. By the time the Hoffeys passed through the Hollow, Hazel and C.E.S. may have already made the turn onto the road that the Sowalskys lived on, the road leading to Glass Lake.

Before getting to Conrad Teal's farmhouse, with the Sowalsky's further up the road, when the couple was adjacent to Teal's pond, C.E.S. somehow maneuvered Hazel onto the dirt farm road. He may have playfully told her another rig was approaching which may have been the Hoffeys or he may have said he wanted her to see something. However he was able to do it, he made sure Hazel was in front of him. He may have taken a rock from the stonewall or a branch from the ground. With her back still turned, C.E.S. forcefully slammed it down on Hazel's head. She died instantly, his problems were over.

C.E.S., possessing the characteristics of a person who lacks emotion felt justified and would have blamed Hazel for putting him in the situation he was in. Partly to destroy potential evidence and partly because he would not yet be satisfied with her punishment, C.E.S. picked up Hazel's lifeless body and carried it to the cow path that led down to the pond. From his vantage point he may have seen the man near the dam that the Hoffeys had seen. He may have watched the Hoffeys drive past the wagon parked along the side of the road. He set the body down and went back towards the road. He noticed Hazel's hat, gloves and glasses lying on the ground. He picked them up, returned to the cowpath, and placed them near the body. He may have seen that the man by the dam was finishing what he was doing or he may have waited, contemplating his next move. When the coast was clear, he carried Hazel's lifeless body to the water and dropped her in. C.E.S. then casually strolled back to the road and disappeared into obscurity.

Just like Jarvis O'Brien and the detectives working the case experienced, each of the above theories has flaws and gaps in the logic. Each scenario is based on information available both at the time and with more contemporary research.

A fire in Troy City Hall in 1938 and water damage to many of Troy's archives in the 1990's has destroyed any primary sources that had survived. Therefore information on Hazel Drew's case has come almost exclusively from various newspaper accounts and the accuracy of the newspapers was not always reliable. Therefore, the reader and researcher is limited in the scope of available information but at the same time free to concentrate on evidence that is logical. Perhaps somewhere in an old dusty trunk in someone's attic lies some piece of evidence waiting to be discovered that once and for all will answer the question that has been asked since 1908, "Who killed Hazel Drew?".

AFTERWORD

Elias Boyce

    Dr. Elias Boyce almost single handedly perpetuated the theory that Hazel was strangled with her corset string in the course of a sexual assault. The only other person associated with the case who gave any credence to the theory was William Clemens.

    Born November 5, 1837 Elias was one of Anaias and Sarah Mead Boyce's fifteen children. Elias graduated from Albany Medical School in 1858 and on February 5, 1860 he married Harriet Nichols. In 1862 they had a son, William. Four years later, Boyce caught Typhoid fever. He was temporarily forced to give up his practice but returned in 1872. In 1881 tragedy struck when his son, William died. Eight years later, on August 10, 1889 his wife, Harriet died. Boyce married Angeline "Angie" Duncan from Northville, NY on September 5, 1900. Angie was 26 years younger than her husband. Together they had one son, Elias Burton Boyce born August 1, 1901.

    Following the Drew case, in either 1909 or 1910 Boyce replaced Morris Strope as Rensselaer County Coroner. His term was short lived however. He died on September 23, 1910 at the age of 72. His wife Angie outlived him by more than forty years. She died on September 29, 1953 in Newton, Massachusetts. They are buried together in East Schodack, New York.

Edward Carry

Born in Troy on December 19, 1865 Edward Cary was educated in the Troy schools and graduated from RPI in 1888 with a degree in Civil Engineering. He immediately took a position as a professor of Geodesy at his alma mater. Professor Cary later taught Surveying and Railroad Engineering.

On June 21, 1892 he married Mary Lyman, they had one daughter, Helen who was born November 24, 1896.

Cary served as Troy City Engineer between 1900-1902, then again from 1906-1908. His wife, Mary died on October 19, 1927 at the age of 60. He retired from teaching in 1936 after 47 years in the classroom. Edward died on July 17, 1941 in Columbia, South Carolina at the age of 75.

William Clemens

William Clemens continued to investigate and publish articles as a so called expert criminologist. His later writings were just as controversial as his earlier ones. He died on November 24, 1931 in Ocean Grove, New Jersey. Services were held in Pompton Plains, New Jersey. By the time of his death, he had been married three times and had three surviving daughters.

John Drew

Following the death of his daughter, John Drew moved his family from Fourth Street in Troy to a house a few blocks away on Hill Street. John died on August 26, 1914. He is buried in the family plot in Barbersville Cemetery in Poestenkill. He was 59 years old.

Eva and Joseph Drew

When Eva Drew died in 1930 at the age of 44, she left $1750 (over $25,000 in today's currency) to be divided equally between her mother and her husband, Joseph. It is not known how Eva was able to amass so much money. Eva is buried in the Drew plot in the Barbersville Cemetery.

In 1940 Joseph was 54 years old living on 5th Avenue in Troy with a 48 year old widow named Carrie Barrow and her three children, John who was 31, Esther who was 30, and Donald who was 11 or 12. Joseph was making a living repairing train cars. He was alive in 1941 living in Lansingburgh (North Troy) when he was named as a survivor in his mother's obituary. There is no record of him after 1941. It is not known when or where Joseph died but he is not buried with Eva or the rest of the Drew family.

Julia Drew

Following the death of her husband in 1914, Hazel's mother moved to Fifth Avenue in Troy. Nearly all of Julia's adult life was filled with pain and loss. Before Hazel's death in 1908, she lost two sons. Emery was born May 17, 1900 and died February 24, 1902. Thomas was born January 4, 1903 and died December 11, 1904. Julia's daughter Carrie, married Roy Dodge and in 1918 the couple had a son, Earl. Earl Dodge died on May 28, 1919. Julia Drew died on June 13, 1941 in Pleasantdale, NY (North Troy) at the age of 79. She is buried next to her husband John, Hazel, Emery, Thomas, Earl, and Eva Drew.

Harry Fairweather

In addition to his work as a doctor including Chief Physician of the Troy Hospital, Harry Fairweather was also a fireman in Troy. In 1909, a year after the Hazel Drew affair, Fairweather was called to the scene of a fire. He climbed a ladder in his effort to battle the blaze but the ladder collapsed. He fell thirty feet to the sidewalk and died a short time later.

Professor Arthur Greene

Carrie Weaver's employer, Arthur Greene was born in Philadelphia on February 4, 1872. He received his Master's degree from the University of Pennsylvania in 1894 and his Doctor's of Science degree in 1917.

In 1895 Arthur Greene became a professor at Drexel Institute and from 1896 until 1902 he taught at the University of Pennsylvania. He went on to teach for five years at the University of Missouri. He left Missouri in 1907 to become a professor at RPI in Troy. He served with distinction on the RPI faculty until 1922 when he left to organize the School of Engineering at Princeton University. He went on to become one of the country's best known figures in the field of Mechanical Engineering, retiring in 1940. He outlived his wife and died on September 2, 1953 in Madison, Connecticut.

In 1911 the Greene's moved out of their house on Hawthorne Avenue to another part of Troy. It is not known if they still employed Carrie Weaver or if she accompanied them when they moved.

Julia Harrison

Minnie Taylor worked at the home of George Harrison on Pawling Avenue. Harrison was a wealthy banker and investor, Julia was one of his children. Julia lived in the Harrison mansion until 1919 when she moved to Whitman Court just two houses away from where the Cary's lived. In 1922 Julia moved two streets up to Hawthorne Ave., into the same house once occupied by Professor and Mrs. Greene and Carrie Weaver. She remained there until 1927.

Julia Harrison was a member of the First Baptist Church in Troy, her Pastor was George Perry. The same George Perry officiated Hazel's funeral service at the Larkin Brother's in Averill Park. Hazel did not attend the First Baptist Church and no explanation can be found explaining why Pastor Perry was involved. Hazel attended the Methodist Church on Third and State Streets in Troy. Her Minister, J.H.E. Rickard presided over Hazel's burial at the Barbersville Cemetery.

Thomas Hislop

Hazel's first employer, Thomas Hislop was an active member of the New York National Guard. Enlisting as a private in 1883 he rose to the rank of Major. He served two terms as city treasurer in Troy before losing the election to Arthur Smith in 1906. Hislop never went to prison for his involvement in Frank Carrington's embezzlement case. He outlived his wife Nellie who died in 1934. He died on April 10, 1949, leaving $15,000 to his his two children, Mabel Hislop End and Thomas Hislop jr. His son died in 1970.

Duncan Kaye

Born in England June 19, 1865. Duncan Kaye came to United States in 1871. He grew up in Troy and attended the Troy public schools. In 1888, as a Republican, he began his career in public service taking a position in the State Department of Public Buildings. In 1897 he became an officer for the District Attorney. On April 8, 1905 he was appointed County Detective, the first person to hold the position. When Jarvis O'Brien lost his re-election bid in 1908, Kaye resigned as County Detective. He took the position as confidential agent to C.V. Collins who was Superintendent of the State Prisons. Kaye resigned after Collins retired, then became clerk of the Rensselaer County Board of Elections. He remained active in Troy politics until June 11, 1935 when he retired. He died on June 19, 1943 and is buried in Oakwood Cemetery. He was survived by his wife, Louise and 3 sons Duncan, George, and Jarvis. Louise Kaye died on July 7, 1944.

Duncan's son Duncan became an attorney in Troy. On February 6, 1948 he was the driver of a car that injured Elizabeth Christoffersen, secretary to a New York State Senator. Christoffersen sued Kaye and won a settlement for $10,000. However she never received any payment and sued Kaye's insurance company. She was unsuccessful in her attempt to collect any money.

In 1956 Kaye was adjudicated insane and sent to an asylum. Upon his release in June, 1957 he stood trial for misappropriation of funds. He was in charge of $55,122.21 for the estate of Miss Alice Chapin. When she died Kaye, as executor of her estate, he was supposed to give the money to several charities named in Miss Chapin's Will but instead he kept the money. He was defended by E. Stewart Jones, son of Abbott Jones, the former city judge who defeated Jarvis O'Brien in his bid for re-election for District Attorney of Rensselaer County in 1908.

On October 26, 1957 Duncan Kaye was sentenced to 15-30 months in prison.

Dr. Edward Knauff

Hazel's dentist and the father of William Knauff, Edward was born in Troy to German immigrant parents. Dr. Knauff was active in civic affairs, founding the Pioneer Building and Loan Association and the Germania Hall Association. He attended Saint Paul's Episcopal Church, was married to Louise (Kolbe) and besides his son, William, Dr. Knauff also had a daughter, Flora. Dr. Knauff died unexpectedly at his summer house at Snyder's Lake on June 13, 1915. It is believed blood poisoning caused by an infection in his arm led to his death.

He was 56 years old. He is buried in Oakwood Cemetery in Troy. His wife Louisa died at her son, William's house in Washington D.C. on December 21, 1938. She is buried next to her husband.

William Knauff

William Knauff graduated from Troy High School in 1906. He attended RPI from the fall of 1906 until the end of his junior year in 1909. No explanation has been found why Knauff did not return for his senior year. William Knauff went on to become Senior Assistant Engineer for the State Road Commission in West Virginia. He later became a member of the Technical Advisory Board for the USDA in Washington D.C. He was married twice, divorced once. He died in Washington DC on July 15, 1969.

Edward LaVoie

In the summer of 1914, the First World War broke out in Europe. Although the United States would not officially enter the war until 1917, many Americans did not wait and traveled to Europe to offer their services. Edward LaVoie was one such American. In 1916, at the age of thirty five, he volunteered for the American Ambulance Corps. He arrived in France in 1917, one month after the United States declared war on Germany. There is no record of his experience in France. He was discharged from the army in 1918, this time for good.

Edward married Theresa Yeager from New Jersey. Together they had two children, Joan and Joseph. Little is recorded about their life but they did for a while live in Forest Hills, Long Island.

Edward worked in finance but on several occasions he was involved in shady business dealings and unethical practices that landed him in trouble with the Attorney General's office.

In 1933 LaVoie was working as a stockbroker. In December of that year he was brought in for questioning for stock manipulation by Ambrose McCall, Assistant Attorney General for the state of New York. LaVoie told reporters he had no idea what the charges were in regard to but he was subpoenaed a week later. No further news was reported on the matter.

In July 1934 Attorney General John J. Bennett issued a court order enjoining five men, including Edward LaVoie, from selling securities in New York State pending a determination of action to make the order permanent. According to the complaint the five brokers bought shares of Chicago Gulf Corp for 50 cents per share and were selling it to unsuspecting investors for as much as $230 per share.

In January 1949 LaVoie and his partner, Harold Welshon, working as a two man corporation called Maple Grove Memorial Park Inc. purchased grave plots for reduced prices at a tax exempt cemetery in Kew Gardens, Queens, NY. Using what the papers referred to as high pressure sales tactics, LaVoie and his partner sold the plots at a markup of over one hundred percent. State Attorney General Nathaniel Goldstein investigated, terminated the corporation and removed its officers.

In 1947, LaVoie's wife Theresa lived in Los Angeles, California. In January 1949, at the time of the Maple Grove scandal, Edward lived in East Orange, New Jersey but isn't clear if Theresa lived with him or if the two were separated. In June of that year when LaVoie's step mother, Odella died, he was living in Los Angeles.

LaVoie was living with his daughter, Joan Pinckney in Long Beach, California when he died on November 25, 1955. He outlived his wife and his son and is buried in Nutley, New Jersey.

John Lawrenson

John Lawrenson continued to work as a detective in Troy and was involved in many high profile cases. He retired from the force in 1935. On April 29, 1936 he was shot by drug crazed ex-convict named Michael Franco who was "out to get cops". Lawrenson survived the shooting but Franco fatally shot himself. Lawrenson died on December 11, 1941. He was survived by 4 sons, 1 daughter and 6 grandchildren.

Samuel and Rose LeRoy

Following the Hazel Drew case, Samuel sued the New York World for libel and won a $5,000 settlement. Rose and Samuel had another child, a son after the Hazel Drew affair. Rose died on February 24, 1921 in Albany. She was survived by her husband and three sons Martin, Harold, and Edward. Edward was named after Samuel's father who was killed in a train accident in 1907.

Jarvis O'Brien

In 1908 Jarvis O'Brien lost his re-election bid for a third term as District Attorney. In a very contentious campaign he was challenged by Abbott Jones who at the time was City Court Judge in Troy. Jones, a Republican was not endorsed by his party and ran as an independent. He accused O'Brien of being anti-Italian, a damaging accusation in city heavily populated by Italian immigrants and their descendants. He stated in the Nova Vita, a newspaper printed in Italian, that Jarvis O'Brien would have every Italian hanged if it were in his power.

The Democrats accused O'Brien of conflict of interest for his work with the Boston and Maine Railroad. They would not let readers forget the emotion and O'Brien's role in defending the railroad during the tragic train accident in Lincoln, Massachusetts that killed seventeen people.

The Prohibitionist Party was critical of Mayor Elias Mann and Jarvis O'Brien for their lackadaisical enforcement of the Raines Law, also known as the Sunday Saloon Law which prohibited the sale of alcoholic beverages on Sundays except in hotels and where food was served.

The Prohibitionists allied with the Democrats. The Republican Party was already split when Abbott Jones broke away and ran as an independent candidate. As a result O'Brien lost the election. There is no question that O'Brien's failure to apprehend Hazel Drew's killer and all the negative publicity associated with the case played a part in O'Brien's defeat.

From 1908 to June 1931 Jarvis O'Brien worked as an attorney for the Boston and Maine Railroad. He spent much of his time fending off law suits filed by people who sued the Boston and Maine Railroad for neglect.

In 1926 Jarvis O'Brien tried once again to enter public service. He ran for Rensselaer County Court Judge, but was defeated by James F. Brearton. He died on June 8, 1936 and is buried in Oakwood Cemetery in Troy.

William Powers

William Powers remained in law enforcement and had a long and illustrious career. He died on November 8, 1932.

Dr. Elmer E. Reichard

Elmer Reichard was born in Nassau, NY on March 12, 1866. He grew up on a farm and was educated in the Averill Park schools. He graduated from Albany Medical College in 1892 and married Charlotte Hitchcock on February 27, 1895. He practiced medicine until his retirement in 1929. He became ill in the winter of 1940 while vacationing in Sarasota, Florida with his wife. The couple returned home and Dr. Reichard underwent surgery at the Albany Hospital for an undisclosed ailment. He remained in the hospital for nearly a month. When he was discharged he returned to his home on Glass Lake. On February 19, 1941 Dr. Reichard passed away. Charlotte outlived her husband by fifteen years, passing away in Kansas while visiting her sister. Her funeral was held on March 16, 1956 at Glass Lake. She is buried next to her husband in the Sand Lake Cemetery. They were survived by one daughter.

Morris H. Strope

Morris Strope was born in West Sand Lake NY. and graduated from the Albany Medical College in 1880. He practiced medicine in West Sand Lake and Poestenkill his entire life. Strope was Rensselaer County Coroner in 1908 but in 1909 or 1910 he was replaced by Elias Boyce. Following the death of Boyce on September 23, 1910, Morris Strope was reappointed Rensselaer County Coroner by Governor White.

On the morning of January 2, 1925 Strope was found dead in his bed at his home in Poestenkill. He had never recovered from a hip injury he suffered from a fall 7 years earlier. The official cause of death was apoplexy, he was 66 years old. He was survived by his wife Tilly and is buried in Barbersville Cemetery not far from Hazel Drew.

Minnie Taylor

Following the Inquest, Minnie Taylor left for a several week vacation in Pittsfield, Massachusetts.

Minnie later married Edward J. Filieau who was active in county politics and a prominent figure in the prohibitionist movement.

He was a carpenter by trade and the assessor for the Town of North Greenbush, NY. He belonged to the Poestenkill Church of Christ.

Together Minnie and Edward had two children, a daughter, Agnes and a son, Edward jr. Her husband Edward died on June 14, 1939. He is buried in Oakwood Cemetery in Troy.

Minnie Taylor died on October 12, 1954 in Pittstown, MA. In addition to her two children, her obituary reported that she was survived by several grandchildren, nieces and nephews. Her estate was estimated to be about $5000. She willed $200 to the Poestenkill Church of Christ. The rest was divided among family and friends.

William Taylor

On May 3, 1910 Sand Lake resident Julia Miller sued for divorce from her husband, Louis Miller. The couple had married in 1883 and had five grown children.

On January 12, 1911 Julia Miller and William Taylor were wed. The Reverend Walter S. Brown officiated.

On January 24, 1932, while visiting her daughter, Mrs. Addie Rowe in Wynantskill, NY, Julia died suddenly. Following her death, William moved to Third Street in Troy to live with his sister, Julia, Hazel's mother. He died in her house on July 21, 1934. He is buried in the Sand Lake Cemetery. His obituary lists as survivors, Mrs. Julia A. Drew of Troy, Mrs. H.E. Davis of Greenfield, Mass., Mrs. E.J. Filieau of North Greenbush. Mrs. Filieau was Minnie Taylor.

Adelaide and John Tupper

Hazel's employer prior to her working for the Cary's, John Tupper was a successful coal merchant in Troy. Very active in civic affairs, Tupper was the unsuccessful Republican candidate for Mayor of Troy in 1897. He died on December 29, 1919 in New York at the age of 76.

Adelaide Tupper was born in Canada to Irish parents. Mrs. Tupper had a close relationship with Hazel until she terminated her in February 1908. Adelaide Tupper died on January 9, 1933 in Brockville, Ontario at the age of 81. She is buried with her husband in New York.

Louis Unser

Detective Louis Unser was born in Germany and came to the United States when he was 18. He served on the police force for 23 years retiring in 1923. Unser died on January 14, 1943 at the age of 71. He outlived his wife Bertha and was survived by his son Louis.

Carrie Weaver

Carrie Weaver's name does not appear in any newspaper after she returned from Ohio in August, 1908. Her life after the Hazel Drew affair is unknown.

BIBLIOGRAPHY

Books

Campbell, John H. ed. and DeNevi, Don, ed. <u>Profilers</u>. Amherst, New Jersey: Prometheus Books, 2004.

Douglas, John and Olshaker, Mark. <u>Journey into Darkness</u>. New York, New York: A Lisa Drew Book/Scribner, 1997.

Douglas, John and Olshaker, Mark. <u>Obsession</u>. New York, New York: Pocket Books, a division of Simon and Schuster Inc., 1998.

Douglas, John and Olshaker, Mark. <u>The Anatomy of Motive</u>. New York, New York: Pocket Books, a division of Simon and Schuster Inc., 1999.

French, Mary D. and Lilly, Robert. <u>Images of America: Sand Lake</u>. Charleston, SC: Arcadia Publishing, 2001.

French, Mary D. and Mace, Andrew St. J. <u>Images of America: Sand Lake Revisited</u>. Charleston, SC: Arcadia Publishing, 2007.

Moore, H. Irving, ed. <u>A Nostalgic Post Card Album of Troy, NY</u>. Troy, NY: 1971.

Moore, H. Irving, ed. <u>A Visit to Old Troy in Pictures and Prose</u>. Troy, NY: 1973.

Nielsen, Brian, and Nielsen, Becky. <u>Postcard History Series: Troy in Vintage Postcards</u>. Charleston, SC: Arcadia Publishing, 2001.

Rittner, Don. <u>Images of America: Troy</u>. Charleston, SC: Arcadia Publishing, 1998.

Srebnick, Amy Gilman. <u>The Mysterious Death of Mary Rogers: Sex and Culture in Nineteenth-Century New York</u>. New York: Oxford University Press, 1995.

Stashower, David. <u>The Beautiful Cigar Girl: Mary Rogers, Edgar Allan Poe, and the Invention of Murder</u>. New York, New York: The Penguin Group, 2006.

Viens, Charles, and Young, Sanford. <u>Troy and New England Railway Co. 1895-1925</u>. 1976.

<u>Web</u>

"The Scrap Book, Volume IX", January-June 1910, New York, The Frank A Munsey Company, Publishers, 175 Fifth Avenue, 1910 <u>https://google.books.com</u>

"The Arrow of Pi Beta Phi", 1892, Original from the New York Public Library, The Pi Beta Phi Fraternity, Digitized October 25, 2006, https://books.google.com/books?id=Ui4UAAAAIAAJ.

Magazines

The Boston Cooking School Magazine, March 1905.

The Ladies Home Journal, November 1893.

Newspapers

The Albuquerque Citizen (Albuquerque, NM)
> July 18, 1908

The Auburn Democrat-Argus (Auburn, NY)
> July 17, 1908

The Auburn Semi-Weekly Journal (Auburn, NY)
> July 24, 1908

The Brooklyn Daily eagle (Brooklyn, New York)
> April 16, 1904

The Evening Telegram (New York, New York)
> July 16, 1908, July 27, 1908

The Evening World (New York, New York)
> July 14, 1908, July 15, 1908, July 16, 1908, July 17, 1908, July 18, 1908, July 20, 1908, July 23, 1908, July 24, 1908, July 21, 1908, July 28, 1908, July 29, 1908

The Greenwood Times (Greenwood, NY)
> July 24, 1908

The Jamestown Evening Journal (Jamestown, NY)
> July 15, 1908

The Lock-Haven Express, (Lock Haven, PA)
    July 16, 1908

The Morning Call (Paterson, NJ)
    July 15, 1908

The New York Sun (New York, New York)
    May 28, 1908

The New York Times (New York, New York)
    July 18, 1908, July 21, 1908, July 22, 1908

The New York Tribune (New York, New York)
    July 19, 1908

The New York World (New York, New York)
    July 22, 1908

The Northern Budget (Troy, NY)
    July 12, 1908, July 19, 1908, July 26, 1908

The Oswego Daily Times (Oswego, NY)
    July 16, 1908

The Rome Daily Sentinel (Rome, NY)
    July 17, 1908

The Seattle Daily Times (Seattle, Washington)
    October 1, 1904

The Thrice-A-Week World (New York, New York)
    July 17, 1908, July 20, 1908, July 22, 1908, July 24, 1908, July
    29, 1908

The Times Union (Albany NY)

> July 15, 1908, July 17, 1908, July 18, 1908, July 22, 1908, July 23, 1908, July 28, 1908

The Troy (Daily) Press (Troy, NY)

> July 13, 1908, July 14, 1908, July 17, 1908, July 18, 1908, July 20, 1908, July 21, 1908, July 22, 1908, July 24, 1908, July 25, 1908, July 27, 1908, July 28, 1908, July 30, 1908

The Troy Record (Troy, NY)

> July 6, 1908, July 13, 1908, July 14, 1908, July 16, 1908, July 17, 1908, July 18, 1908, July 20, 1908, July 21, 1908, July 23, 1908, July 24, 1908, July 25, 1908, July 27, 1908, July 28, 1908, July 31, 1908

The Troy Times (Troy, NY)

> July 14, 1908, July 15, 1908, July 17, 1908, July 21, 1908, July 22, 1908, July 23, 1908, July 24, 1908, July 25, 1908, July 27, 1908, July 28, 1908, July 29, 1908

The Washington Herald (Washington D.C.)

> July 19, 1908

The Watertown Review (Watertown, NY)

> July 18, 1908